C4

FILM REVIEW 1970-71

FILM REVIEW
1970-71

edited by F. Maurice Speed

W. H. Allen
London
1970

*Printed in Great Britain by
Fletcher & Son Ltd, Norwich
for the publishers
W. H. Allen & Co. Ltd.,
Essex Street, London WC2.
Bound by Richard Clay
(The Chaucer Press) Ltd,
Bungay, Suffolk*

SBN 491 00253 X

Book design by Ken Reilly and Associates Ltd.

CONTENTS

INTRODUCTION

I would be less than honest if I did not admit that it pleased me a great deal that last year's volume of *Film Review* brought far more critical and – with some notable exceptions – appreciative attention than any of the twenty-five volumes which preceded it! It was also rewarding in reading these comments to note that again and again the writer's point of departure was my shocked and worried sentences on the cinema's current depressing drift towards lower moral standards.

The year then under review was the first in what I persist in calling the cinema's Permissive Period. For the first time we had been shown full and hairy nudity, we had watched the actual sex act at least simulated on the screen, we had been offered various sexual deviations as not only an ingredient of a film but an integral part of its motivation! And we had seen the beginning of a steady output of cheaply made, really nasty little movies cashing in on the new liberality of the censorship climate.

I said then, a year ago, that I thought we might have reached the limit, that 1970 might see a return to a more balanced and healthy situation. It now seems I may have been over-optimistic. These past twelve months we have been offered a number of movies in – to put it mildly! – appalling bad taste; we have seen even more avid interest on the part of the moviemakers in sexual deviations of all kinds, even more explicit normal sex, more daring descents into the "sick" and the "black" and, as a new titillation, and increasing experimentation with the exploitation of male, frontal nudity. And the steady little stream of cheap and nasty

pornographic pictures has continued unchecked.

Of course the moviemakers have tried to justify themselves. This or that outrageous incident or scene was a necessary part of the story and therefore not only artistically permissible but wholly necessary, they have claimed: and then, every so often, a film has come along which gave the lie to this claim: a film which presented true human-carnal if you like – passion without resource to *actually showing it*. There is, after all, to the healthy-minded nothing particularly artistically or aesthetically pleasing in the visual part of copulation – and it is *very* easy to show it in more or less complete detail. What is artistic, is to *suggest without* actually showing it in detail. I have been going, professionally, to the movies now for some forty years; I am not narrow-minded; I think sex one of the most happily satisfying experiences one can have; I adore woman; and, by and large, I am on principal against censorship. But these past two years I have many times been so disgusted and even sickened in the cinema by both subject and treatment that I have been most unwillingly driven, in view of what we can expect in the even more permissive future from all reports, to thinking that the industry must in some way start censoring itself, and pretty quickly at that unless at some point we are to get the sort of reaction which will drive it back into the rather stupid rigidity within which it formerly had to work. John Trevelyan, the British censor, certainly the most loquacious and publicity-conscious one that we've ever had, has constantly gone on record through the year about his work, the cinematic trends

and his own reactions to them. In a lecture to a group of cinema exhibitors last June he said – after shocking them with the exhibition of a Swedish "trailer" illustrating a sexual orgy – "As far as sex is concerned I think parts of the world have gone mad . . . we are facing a tidal wave of sex-obsession. But we can't all be King Canutes. All we can hope for is to stem the tide, and I don't think we have been too off-course in recent years." He added that in the past eight months sex has become a "real censorship problem". In many countries on-screen sex was obsessive. Would there be a protest, a reaction? If so, what form would it take?

"I think the present situation will get worse; but we are watching the situation very carefully," he assured delegates. Some months later, in an article which he wrote for *Today's Cinema* he said: "I really believe that there is a social problem. I do not know whether pornography is harmful to people or not, although I think it is probably harmful to some people; but I think that a flood of pornography in all forms must have the effect of conditioning attitudes to sex that reflect a dehumanising of human beings. Sex with love is radiant and heart-warming; sex without love and with nothing but crudity is cold and cruel, and debases the coinage of human relations.

"Freedom demands responsibility, not only from the individual but also from society, and I believe that to let cheap porno-graphy loose would be irresponsible. It could easily come here. At the moment the Customs are keeping a reasonable control, but, however conscientious they are, they are unlikely to be able to keep it all out.

8 "Just as the strip-clubs were started by people who had no connection with the theatre, so the pornographic cinema market could be built up by people who have no connection with the cinema; indeed, there is already some evidence that confirms this. Again, as with the strip-clubs, these people would be prepared to take risks of police action, putting up front-men and keeping themselves in the background.

"I do not think that society – and the film industry – can afford to let this happen. It would be difficult to predict the results, but I believe that it could help to destroy the film industry as we know it, even if the profits on pornography were short-term. It could easily produce a swing-back in public attitudes, even to the point of producing a government-controlled, and more restrictive censorship."

A similarly sane sort of outlook, too, was expressed last autumn by Jack Valenti, President of the Motion Picture Association of America, who writing in the same trade paper said: "If I have one point to make it is this: no matter what the age or the era, the society that endures is the society that bewares of extremes. Total freedom is as awful as total repression.

"The answer, if there is one, lies with the community and not with the creators. The community will always determine what it wants and it will usually get what it deserves. Therefore, the community, the audience must be the judge of what shall be accepted and what shall be applauded and what shall be disapproved.

"But in a large sense, that is the anxious, towering problem of our time. How can we preserve what is valuable, change what is needed and enlarge what is durable?

"I don't believe our problems are greater than any other era in history. But because we have instant communications we just know about our ills sooner than did our ancestors.

"Each generation carries its own ego and likes to believe that its suffering and its hopes are wider and larger than those who lived earlier. Generations, you see, can be as arrogant as individuals, and just as wrong.

"But the answers that we seek will be given by men of cool and steady temper; men who do not panic when the clanging grows loud, who do not become frightened when the mobs grow restless, and who do not acquiesce because others think it fashionable to do so."

And there are other voices raised against the current trend towards what I personally consider the dubious taste revealed in the making of films like the *Entertaining of Mr. Sloane*, *The Killing of Sister George*, and *The Staircases* and the openly pornographic cinematic imports which we get from abroad. They may at the moment be few, but I feel they will be more as the standards drift lower, until there will be the healthy reaction, rejection and demand for higher standards which I think will eventually be called for and will bring the screen back to some sort of healthy sexual balance and normality.

Of course, cinemas and films generally are at the moment very much in a state of flux. For instance, we are being constantly told that the Big film, like the Big cinema, is doomed – and then along comes some super production to prove the claim, in the case of the films, wrong! But almost certainly it *is* true of the cinemas; they *will* get smaller, as new ones are built and the old are converted by twinning or even tripling.

The old Hollywood star system is dying, too, "they" will tell you. And by and large this also is correct; rightly so. No star, however big, can these days convert a flop into a success, though they can make success more successful. The *Easy Riders* which come along – as they always have done (well look back into celluloid history, a so-called "sleeper" is nothing new) – made without stars and on tiny budgets are very few and far between and must be seen against a background which includes *Airport* or *Marooned*, or *The Battle of Britain* and other major-budgeted productions. A couple of big, ambitious musicals flop, so we're told that the big musical is a thing of the past: and then somebody comes up with an *Oliver!* or *Hello, Dolly!* or *Paint Your Wagon* and, hey-ho, all the big producers start looking for material for a similar fortune-making blockbuster.

The cinema is and always has been – and always will one imagines – constantly contradicting itself. Because of the time it takes to make a movie it is always struggling along behind public taste rather than leading it. In the past some of its greatest curses have been its great successes, for immediately a film strikes the jackpot (a film like *Bonnie and Clyde* as an instance) all the other moviemakers try to jump on the same bandwagon, often with increasingly dire results. The plain truth applicable to a film tomorrow, as today and yesterday, is that it doesn't matter a jot what it is about, what period it is set in or who plays in it; what does matter is that it is *good*, it is *entertaining*: and the fact that it catches the fickle public's fancy just makes all the difference between a reasonable and an outstanding success.

Now let's look at some of the events and trends of the period. Hollywood, like the theatre, may be dead but it won't lie down. Certainly with films increasingly being made on location all over the world, Hollywood has thinned out a little on top, but it is still pretty virile, as was pointed out last summer when it was revealed that 27 Hollywood-based movies were then in production compared with 32 the previous year. What does appear an eventually logical move is a rationalisation of studio space, with the companies getting together in closer co-operation, probably finally resulting in one or two large studio complexes which will be rented by the various companies as and how they want it, rather than carry the vast overheads of their increasingly far less than fully employed own studios.

Last year, December in fact, saw the bowing out of the industry of the last of the old movie tycoons, when Jack L. Warner abdicated his kingdom (now a part of the giant Kinney National Service Inc.) after 41, more or less, glorious, certainly history-making years. With the American film companies increasingly becoming mere offshoots of large giant commercial complexes, 20th Century-Fox, under Darryl and son Richard Zanuck, remain one of the exceptions, and intend to continue to do so if one can believe the announcements which periodically emerge from the Zanucks.

As film production goes down, so, too, do audiences, which are still falling though always, the long term figure suggests, levelling off! One interesting sidelight on this situation was given by a survey, carried out by the Institute of Practitioners in Advertising quite recently, which suggested that while more people were actually going to the cinema now than before they were going *less often*! This seems to confirm a general feeling that the old-style regular moviegoer, one who went to a cinema rather than a film, is becoming a rare animal: these days people go to see *a film*.

Cinema admissions declined by nearly 17,500,000 in the first nine months of 1969. But there was not a lot of difference in the gross box-office takings, which dropped about £40,000.

The figures are compared with those for January to September, 1968, and are assessed from the monthly statistics issued by the Board of Trade.

Confirming the downward trend in production, by the way, were the figures issued by NATKE last March, these showing that 1,000 of the total British labour force of around 4,000 were then out of employment! At least some of this was explained by the fact that whereas in March, 1970 only 13 British films were in production, in March, 1969 the figure was 19.

At least 100 were affected by the February closing down of Pathé News, one of the last newsreels to be made regularly in the West. At the same time AB–Pathé, the makers, announced the cessation of documentaries, sponsored shorts and other allied non-fictional films.

The big shake-ups that have been going on within M-G-M in America led to the possibility this last winter of a complete closing by the new bosses of their British studios at Elstree, which had employed a regular 700 employees. This decision was later changed and it was announced that the studios would stay open but with severe spending cuts including, it was suggested, about half the employees.

But then came a subsequent story last April that the final reluctant decision was that the studios *would* be closed.

While the Americans were still arguing over their new – to them – "ratings" of films, we altered ours and by this summer (July 1 is the date fixed as I write) it is intended to switch the old X, A and U classifications to X, AA, A and U, the additional AA label being reserved for films which children above 14 can see, alone or accompanied, but which anyone below that age is strictly forbidden. With this comes a change in the X category; now allowed to be seen only by 18-year-olds and over, while the A category film will be available for any child *above five* (!) alone or accompanied – the difference between the A and the U film being that the former is thought to contain material which some parents might not like their children to see.

10 Technically there have been few events of any excitement. In this field most of the argument has been concentrated on the pros and cons of the Cassettes. Frankly, I don't understand this "revolution" as it has been called, but it appears to mean that one can see films at home, recorded on tape and played through a sort of video projector (which will cost, it is estimated, below £400). As far as I can judge from everything I've read so far (and please note the reservation implied there!) what Cassette really means is a TV instead of a mechanical projector through which tape rather than 8 mm film is run. In effect it will allow you to see the films of your choice by television-style projection in your own homes. (And I hope I'm right.) The controversy which roared through the columns of the film industry's trade papers was very similar in some respects to that which occurred with the advent of TV itself. The problem seems to be whether the film industry should ignore it (hoping it will go away?) or try to take more or less complete control of it, or just wait and see what happens next! No record of the year would be complete without a mention of the fact that for the eighth year running the vast Rank empire chalked up a new record profit (some £11¼ million in this instance), or that ABC, the other giant, announced last summer its intention to spend some £30 million on the development and modernisation of its great chain of cinemas; shortly after which, ABPC said they were going to spend more than £7 million on production.
With all these figures, have you ever wondered how your money, which you pay to go to the cinema, is used?

Apparently out of every £100 you toss into the box-office, £7 goes to the Eady (Production) levy, £60 goes to the exhibitor, £16 10s. to the distributor and the same amount finds itself returned to film production. Well, it may make you think! So that's it. A typical film year. And a neat finish to it might be a quotation of what I like to think is the movie news headline of the year, carried by *Today's Cinema*. Without a single exclamation mark it said: "*Wild Duck* To Be Shot In Norway".

Andy Warhol has been making American "Underground" films for years but it took the new climate of Permissiveness for them to be shown in Britain. Even so his *Flesh* (judged by many his best film), when shown here by one of the many new "specialist" and club cinemas which have been springing up this year, ran into trouble, being confiscated by the police. Later it continued its run and the resultant publicity brought showings of some of the other Warhol films.

The Permissive Period! Complete nudity, male and female, and completely explicit lovemaking has spread from the smaller sexploitation movies (such as was to be found in *Love is a Splendid Illusion*) to the major, big-budget productions like Paramount's *The Adventurers*.

II

On the other side of a not very clean cinematic ledger is the renewed popularity of some of the old comics, now more fully realised as unique and never to be replaced. For the past few years Laurel and Hardy have been in the revival spotlight, now it appears to be the turn of Buster Keaton, whose films, shown in snippets on the small screen in the "Golden Silents" series, helped to make the Buster Keaton Festival at the Academy cinema a tremendous sold-out success.

On a later page you will see a list of names of players who have been voted by the exhibitors of America and Canada as being the most likely youngsters to reach top stardom tomorrow, or the day after! After a year's moviegoing I'd like to illustrate my personal, and conflicting, list of entries for these stakes: players who impressed me very much as real Stars of Tomorrow (if not Today!).

First of these is LIZA MINNELLI, the late Judy Garland's daughter (who looks remarkably like her mother when she was the same age), who turned in one of the most delightful performances of the whole year as the odd, charming little off-beat character in Paramount's *Pookie*.

Then, an obvious nomination in the light of events, GOLDIE HAWN, the unconventionally attractive, obviously talented comedienne who after her big small-screen success made a most impressive cinematic debut in *Cactus Flower*.

12 BARRY NEWMAN in the title role in Paramount's *The Lawyer* was a newcomer whose distinctive features are of the kind that always register well with audiences, and his performance in this film was also brilliant enough to make it impossible to leave him out.

Ditto the statuesque-figured HELEN MIRREN, who had even some of the hardened film critics more or less drooling over her shapeliness in *Age of Consent*, in which she made her début – playing a girl who models for artist James Mason and gives him back his reason for existence.

Lloyd Bridges' son BEAU BRIDGES, making his début in U.A.'s *Chicago, Chicago* as the naïve young man from out of town who learns about life, love and corruption in double-quick time, gave a most sympathetic and smoothly competent performance and will obviously be seen again.

Worth watching, too, in every sense of the word, British newcomer JUDY CORNWELL, whose debut in British Lion's *Every Home Should Have One* revealed a most attractive little comedienne with an invigorating sense of fun.

HAVE YOU AN IDEA FOR A FILM?

by Oswell Blakeston

If you're a regular filmgoer you're bound one day to feel inspired, to tell yourself you too have a wonderful story-notion for a movie. Are you kidding? I mean I'm taking it that you have no special connection with the film industry. So . . . can you do anything about it if you feel convinced that Big Brother Luck has given you a splendid idea?

I put the question to a man who works for one of the most important agencies dealing with film matters and he assured me there are no commissionaires resolutely refusing all access between the inspired and the film makers.

You even stand a better chance to sell something to films than to TV, he told me. There is a corps of professional writers competing for space on the box; but somehow motion pictures are wilder and there is still a chance for flukey magic.

Of course it isn't as easy as that. With a famous novel, the promoter of a film has the author's name to help him raise money. It's harder for him if he's trying to promote an original idea. But it does happen.

Bear in mind that as an outsider you wouldn't be expecting to sell your notion as a complete shooting script. For one thing it takes as much time to write a complete script as to write a novel. If you have the gift to write a fully documented script, you could probably just as easily write the story as a novel: and as a book it would stand that much better chance of attracting attention in the film world.

No, I'm taking it that you have no special expertise but just a fabulous idea. Well they used to say that it was possible to sell such an idea-flash by writing it on a postcard. But the man I consulted, the man who knows, made a correction for contemporary possibilities.

"While many good film ideas start off as postcard size," he told me, "and some perhaps postage-stamp size, the vendor of an 'idea' must invest it with clothes which make it a copyright article. Otherwise someone may say, 'Thank you very much for the tip. I'll send you tickets for the première, if I remember.'"

The copyright is in the words: and you need to expand the idea to about four or five pages of manuscript to establish copyright.

"You might," my informant suggested, "have an idea about a queen stealing her own royal jewels, and it might be all a producer wanted from you. But you couldn't write a little on a P.C. and despatch it. You must expand it to establish a saleable claim, even if the producer will develop your notion in quite a different way."

I remember years ago asking a then famous director why certain stories were always being refilmed. He said: "Oh, it's because producers can't read. Tell them over lunch that you'd like to remake one of the old stalwarts, and they know what you're talking about."

But times have changed, and most producers now have a lively literary awareness and are quite prepared to read a potential. It's only fair, then, that the submitter of ideas should also be expected to have advanced from the postcard to four or five pages of distillation.

O.K. You've mastered your four or five pages. What do you do with them? You must, in the opinion of a man who knows,

14 submit them to an agent. No, he was not pressing his own firm. To prove that, he asked me to keep his name out of it. He suggested that you choose an agent from Peter Noble's *Film and Television Year Book* which you can consult at your public library. Any agent listed there will be a reputable one, one to whom a producer will listen if he says that you have sent him a blockbuster.

If you want to get a producer's ear, you must work through an agent. Also an agent will protect your interests. I'm sure, for instance, you want to see that credit title on the screen: Story Based On An Original Idea By You.

The producer has to be won over to your side, but the agent begins by being on your side. He's as anxious as you are to sell anything which, in the jargon of the profession, can be regarded as "a property". So just send him your four or five pages with a simple covering letter saying that you think you have a good idea for a film and here it is.

But don't expect an agent to write you a long explanation of why your idea is not viable if it isn't. The agent must protect his time, and he can't write your idea for you.

So it's up to you, gloriously up to you. Incredible, isn't it, that with all the wonderful organisation of the film industry you can still break through, that it's being done all the time by those who have enterprise and a good idea. It's amazing, I think, that it can still be done in a world of increasing specialisation; but aren't you glad to know that it can?

The last advice my high-powered friend gave me to pass on to aspirants was not to relax in filmgoing. If you're going to sell an idea – and everyone, it seems, hopes that you will – you must know what's been done already. It's no help to send an agent a lovely idea for making a film which is already blazing the circuits.

IN MEMORIAM

Another link with the old silent cinema was snapped in the October of 1969 with the death, at the age of 73, in Hollywood, of ROD LA ROCQUE. Born in Chicago – his parents had no connection with show-business – La Rocque made his screen début at the age of 8 in a movie called *Salomy Jane*. He was to follow this with some thirty films, including De Mille's *Ten Commandments, Our Dancing Daughters, One Romantic Night, Resurrection, Meet John Doe*, and *Hunchback of Notre Dame*. Unlike many of his fellow stars of the silent screen, he switched to the talkies without a tremor when they came in. La Rocque was married to the famous vamp star Vilma Banky (in 1927) and though their marriage was a highly publicised affair they never appeared together on the screen.

Looking much younger than his actual age of 56, PETER VAN EYCK died on July 15, 1969, in a hospital in Switzerland, following a long illness. Born in Pomerania (now part of Poland), Van Eyck fled to America when Hitler came to power in Germany, soon establishing himself in Hollywood – mostly in villainous German roles in films like *Five Graves to Cairo, Rommel, Desert Fox* and *Foxhole in Cairo*. More recently he was seen in the spy thriller *The Spy Who Came In From The Cold*.

James Mason rose to stardom via playing really unpleasant characters and in the same way it was the part of the dedicated Nazi U-boat Captain in *49th Parallel* which established ERIC PORTMAN as a major star of the screen (he was so good, indeed, that he stole public sympathy away from the hero – something not originally intended). Born among the mills of Bradford, he was never persuaded to hide his background, and it was amusing to hear him, for his friends, slide easily back into the rich language and accent of the North. Polished, wholly

16 professional, infinitely painstaking with his roles, Portman never gave a single bad or careless performance. But he never became a hero – his were always character parts. Some of Portman's best-known performances were in *Separate Tables, One of Our Aircraft is Missing, The Colditz Story, We Dive at Dawn, The Deep Blue Sea,* etc. Portman died, on December 7, 1969, in the little Cornish cottage he loved so well and escaped to on every possible occasion. The heart illness which killed him had caused him to take it easier of late, and he had been more or less in semi-retirement for some time.

It was as a man of the theatre that HUGH WILLIAMS – who was 65 when he died suddenly on December 7, 1969 – is best known, but he made many films in his time, including such great successes as *One of Our Aircraft is Missing, Charley's Aunt,* etc. It was in 1956 that Hugh's actress wife Margaret Vyner turned successful playwright and after that his work was mostly in the theatre, in his wife's plays. Williams made his stage début in 1922.

JOSEPH VON STERNBERG, who died on December 22, 1969 in Hollywood, aged 75, after a heart attack, was Viennese born but entered the United States at the age of 7 – ten years later beginning his film career as a technician. In 1924 he became an assistant director and the following year directed, wrote, produced (and even photographed) his first solo effort, a film called *The Salvation Hunters* which cost something like £2,000 to make. But it was in 1930, when he went to Germany to direct UFA's *The Blue Angel* that he established himself as a classical director. It was this film, too, which began the long association between him (as director) and Marlene Dietrich (as star) which resulted in such memorable movies as *Morocco, Shanghai Express, Blonde Venus* and *The Scarlet Empress.* In later years he made fewer films, and generally they were also less successful, ending with one in Japan called *The Saga of Anatahan* made with his own finances which, with only a few showings in America has not, so far as I know, ever been shown in this country. In 1956 Sternberg published his autobiography, *Fun in a Chinese Laundry,* in which he knocked at the industry. But his place in cinematic history is assured for all time: his lovely film *The Devil is a Woman* achieved it.

HOWARD MARION CRAWFORD, who died at the end of last year at the age of 55, was known best as a stage and radio actor, but he did have quite a number of film performances to his credit, including *Reach for the Sky, Lawrence of Arabia* and *The Charge of the Light Brigade.*

MITZI GREEN was only 48 when she died in May, 1969, in California from cancer. Bronx-born, Miss Green started her show-business career in vaudeville, specialising in mimicry. She appeared in something like a score of films, in between stage and night-club appearances, including *Tom Sawyer, Huckleberry Finn, Skippy,* etc.

ROBERT TAYLOR, mentioned briefly in this section of last year's annual, died of lung cancer in Hollywood on June 8, 1969. Originally selected for his looks – he was without doubt one of the most handsome of all screen heroes – he was not satisfied with this reputation and worked extremely hard at the craft of acting, snapping up any role which gave him opportunity to prove himself: easily recalled are his highly divergent roles in *The Crowd Roars, Camille, A Yank at Oxford, Broadway Melody* and *Waterloo Bridge.* His screen career spanned thirty years, from the time he made his screen début in the original Andy Hardy film in 1934. His leading ladies included most of the screen's "greats" of his period, including, of course, Garbo. After twenty-four years with M-G-M he left the company in 1958 and though he continued to make films until his death, his parts recently had become less important.

Another of the great Hollywood moguls, WILLIAM GOETZ, died in Hollywood in August, 1969 at the age of 66. At one time an assistant director, he rose progressively until he became head-man at one of Hollywood's largest and oldest studios, Universal – also, incidentally, becoming a multi-millionaire in the process. He was first and foremost a good and shrewd business man. It was he, it is said, who set a precedent when he offered the star, Jimmy Stewart, a percentage of the profits of his film *Winchester 73.* Some of his best-known Universal pictures included *The Egg and I, The Glenn Miller Story, All My Sons* and *The Bend of the River.* In 1954 Goetz started out as an independent producer and in this period he produced *Man from Laramie* and *They Came to Cordura,* both released by Columbia. His last film, made in 1964, was *Assault on the Queen* (the liner not the monarch!).

Rank in 1956–57, she starred in *House of Secrets* and *Town on Trial*. She is best remembered for her brief role in *All About Eve*. Her husband, United Artists' publicity man Cecil Coan, died in 1967. Surviving are her mother and two sisters.

MARTITA HUNT died, at the age of 69, in her London home on June 13, 1969; the bronchial asthma which had plagued her for years being finally responsible for her demise. Notable mostly as a stage actress, Miss Hunt began her career in Liverpool in 1921 and it was in the recently filmed play *The Madwoman of Chaillot* that she made her great success, both in London and New York. In 1933, Miss Hunt was lured to the screen, in a film called *I Was A Spy*. Subsequently she made a considerable number of screen appearances, including those in *Bunny Lake is Missing*, *Lady Windermere's Fan* and *Becket*. And was a magnificent Miss Havisham in *Great Expectations*. Her imperious air led her to latterly specialise in eccentric or grande dame roles.

Robert Taylor

BARBARA BATES, screen and television actress, was found dead in her Colorado home, March 18, 1969, at the age of 43. Born in Denver, she was a teen-age model before coming to Hollywood in 1954. She made her film début in *Salome, Where She Danced*. Among her many film credits were *Quicksand*, *Cheaper by the Dozen*, *I'll Climb the Highest Mountain*, *The Secret of Convict Lake*, *Let's Make it Legal* and *Rhapsody*. While under contract to J. Arthur

If LEO McCAREY had never done another picture after *Going My Way* in 1944 (he both wrote and directed it) his place in the cinema's hall of fame would have been assured. But in fact this versatile writer-director, and plural Oscar winner, deserves better of film history, for his credits include *The Awful Truth* (one of his Oscar-winners), *Make Way for Tomorrow* and *Ruggles of Red Gap*. A fine director of comedy, his work ranged from Laurel and Hardy comedies to the Marx Brothers (*Duck Soup*): while he was employed by Hal Roach studios he turned out

18

some 300 shorts and it is to him that many credit the idea of pairing Laurel and Hardy. The son of a Los Angeles boxing promoter, McCarey trained as a lawyer. Unsuccessful at that, he was equally a failure as a songwriter. It was under Tod Browning at Universal in 1918 that he received his first chance to direct a film. McCarey, who died in California on July 5, 1969, at the age of 71, is reported to have said that every film should be something of a fairy story and he certainly put that idea into action during his long career.

JEFFREY HUNTER, who died in Los Angeles on May 27, 1969 (he was only 42), was the stage/screen name of Henry H. McKinnies Junior; who from college was signed up by Fox (in 1950) who kept him on their rolls until 1958. His first film was *Fourteen Hours*. Other films for Fox and other companies included *The Last Hurrah*, *Red Skies of Montana*, *The True Story of Jesse James* and *Hell to Eternity*. But the most outstanding performance he ever achieved was as Jesus Christ in *King of Kings* (1961).

It was the role of the villain in *Winterset* which established EDUARDO CIANNELLI. Born in Italy, he had studied medicine and toured in opera before making his Broadway début in 1925 in *Rose Marie*. His screen career was a long one and included impressive performances in *For Whom the Bell Tolls*, *Foreign Correspondent* and *The Brotherhood*. More recently he had been appearing mainly in Italian films and his last one, *Boot Hill*, a Western, he completed only a week before his death at the age of 82, in Rome, on October 8, 1969, from a cancer. Ciannelli varied his film acting career with a

number of stage performances. He also directed on a number of occasions and once tried his hand at writing, sharing credit with Gennaro Curci for *Foolscap* in 1933.

SONJA HENIE, who died on October 12, 1969, (aged 57) from leukemia while on her way from Paris, where she had been for some months, back to her native Norway, was the only ice-skater to become a major star of the cinema. Thrice Olympic figure-skating champion, Miss Henie turned professional in 1936, when she was made star of a large-scale touring ice-show: in the same year appearing in Fox's *One in a Million*. The daughter of a prosperous Norwegian business man, she at one time studied ballet dancing under the great Pavlova. Winning the figure-skating championship of her native country in 1923, she took part in the following year's Olympics, gaining third place. It was in 1928 that she gained her first gold medal. Her film career extended over 25 years. Blonde, petite, and happy-looking, she married three times, being survived by her third husband.

Stormy petrel JUDY GARLAND was only 47 when she was found dead in her London hotel room on June 22, 1969. Real name Frances Gumm, she was almost literally born in a trunk, for her parents were vaudeville troupers and Judy, born in Grand Rapids, Minnesota, in 1922, from her earliest days started to take part in the family act. In 1935 Louis B. Mayer happened to see the Gumms and was immediately captivated by the chubby little 11-year-old Judy. He signed her up, planning to use her in his family series of films in which another youngster called Mickey Rooney was already making a considerable impact. Mayer initially teamed Judy with another young discovery, Deanna Durbin, in a short film called *Every Sunday*. It was a nice little film and revealed the promise of the two little girls, but Deanna Durbin was lost to another company and Mayer lost interest in Judy until at a party for Clark Gable she sang *Dear Mr Gable*. It stunned everyone there and Judy was rushed into the company's current production of *Broadway Melody* of 1938. Subsequently she was teamed with Mickey Rooney in one of the Andy Hardy series and then came *The Wizard of Oz* and the number which was to haunt her all her life, *Over the Rainbow*. After that, film followed film in endless succession; *Ziegfeld Follies*, *Easter Parade* among them.

FRED KOHLMAR, who died in Hollywood on October 13, 1969, (aged 64), from lung cancer, was a real veteran who started his career in show-business as an office boy. After serving Samuel Goldwyn as executive producer for several years, Kohlmar turned to producing his own films in 1939 and his "credits" list is both long and formidable, including as it does *Call Me Madam*, *The Solid Gold Cadillac*, *Picnic*, *Les Miserables* and *The Only Game in Town*.

JIMMY HANLEY, who died at the age of 51 on January 13, 1970, enjoyed a remarkably busy and successful life. *The Times* of the following day listed him as "Circus artist, film star, Commando, TV host, disc jockey, pub landlord, boat builder, children's writer: and champion fisherman" and concluded "he was all these". Born in Norwich less than a month before the Armistice of 1918 (Oct 22), Hanley attended the famous Italia Conti Stage School and actually made his stage début at the age of 12 in *Peter Pan* at the Palladium. At 14 he was bare-back riding in the circus and two years later he was making a film, the first of more than 60 in which he appeared. Some of his biggest screen successes were

made his first movie in 1919 (it was called *Little Women*) after serving in the U.S. Navy during the war. Thereafter he divided his working time between stage and screen and, more recently, radio and television. He made the transition from silent to talking films with consummate ease, thanks to his voice training.

RAYMOND WALBURN, who died on July 26, 1969, appeared in a great many films (87 according to one source!) during his life, following his screen début in the early Thirties. A great character actor, he overlaid every role with his own special personality. Born on September 9, 1887, at Plymouth, Indiana, he was educated at local schools there, entering the acting profession in 1907, when he joined a Californian touring company. He made his Broadway début in 1912. Walburn had the distinction of being one of the first of the American *Doughboys* to reach France in the First World War, subsequently twice suffering wounds while in action.

scored in *The Way Ahead*, *The Blue Lamp* and the *Huggetts* series. He was married twice, first to actress Dinah Sheridan, then to Margaret Avery, who survives him with their three children.

Another film-star old-timer, CONRAD NAGEL, died at his New York home on February 24, 1970. A founder member of the Oscar-awarding Academy of Motion Picture Arts and Sciences, he served as President of that body in 1932. Nagel, who started his acting career on the stage in 1914,

ALAN MOWBRAY, a character and comedy actor of tremendous presence and one of the screen and stage's most perfect butlers, died March 25, 1969, was London-born (August 18, 1896) and through his long years in Hollywood remained impeccably, indubitably British! After stage experience in this country he toured America with the Theatre Guild and took up residence on the other side of the Atlantic in 1923. It was not until 1931 that he made his screen début, in a picture called *Alexander Hamilton*. He appeared in a very

large number of movies, some of his later ones including *The King and I* and *Around the World in 80 Days*.

By far the most sensational and tragic death of the period was that on August 9, 1969, of SHARON TATE, who was 27 when she became the victim of a particularly brutal murder at her home in Hollywood, killed ritualistically and horribly, though pregnant at the time, together with another woman and three men, by a group of hippies. Born in Dallas, Texas, the daughter of an American

Army Intelligence Major, Sharon made her screen début in a film called *13*. Seen in this by writer-director-actor Roman Polanski, he signed her for a star role in his *The Fearless Vampire Killers*; also signing her up for another role, that of his wife.

REX INGRAM, the famous Negro actor who died September 19, 1969, had the odd distinction of actually having been born on that internationally familiar Mississippi river-boat, *The Robert E. Lee* – that was on October 20, 1895. With considerable athletic prowess, Ingram won a degree in Medicine at the North Western University. His first taste of screen acting was as an extra in *Tarzan and the Apes*, but in 1936 he made a tremendous impression in one of the leading roles in that delightful film *Green Pastures*. Other films, and there were many

22 in which he appeared, included *The Adventures of Huckleberry Finn* in 1938, *The Thief of Baghdad* in 1940 and *Watusi* in 1959.

HY HAZELL, who choked to death at a friend's dinner table in May, 1970, was only 47. London-born, she started her stage career when she was seven, and it was rather more as a stage actress that she was subsequently known. A photographic model and a mannequin, she was first in musical comedy and later became a popular pantomime principal boy. Her films included *The Body Said No, The Franchise Affair* and *The Yellow Balloon*.

BILLIE BURKE, who died on May 13, 1970, in Hollywood at the age of 85, was for many years one of the most popular character players in Hollywood, delighting audiences with her portrait of a bright, bird-like scatter-brained woman always in a state of amusing confusion. Formerly the wife of Flo Ziegfeld and star of his great *Follies*, Miss Burke's career and photograph will appear in next year's feature.

LEONARD CASTLETON KNIGHT, who died this spring, at his Sussex home, was one of the old newsreel pioneers. A former exhibitor, who really believed in the value of publicity, any publicity. He was in at the start of the Gaumont British News, becoming its editor-in-chief in 1933 and bringing it right to the forefront by his high standard and his smart scoops. But it was with the more ambitious documentaries such as *Theirs is the Glory* and *A Queen is Crowned* that he found his greatest achievement.

BYRON FOULGER, who died on April 4, 1970, after a heart attack in Hollywood, came of mixed English and Norwegian stock. He was born in Ogden, Utah, in 1899 and after leaving university joined stock companies, making his Broadway stage début in the early 20s. Subsequently he was for some eight years with a repertory company which he partly owned. Marrying Dorothy Adams in the 20s, he went on to become a play director and it was not until the 30s that he began his crowded film career. Some of his pictures were *Prisoner of Zenda, Tarnished Angel, Edison the Man, Brewster's Millions* and *The Long Hot Summer*.

On April 30, 1970, INGER STEVENS, 35-year-old Swedish actress (real name Inger Stensland) was found dead in her Hollywood flat. In America since her childhood, she had stage experience before making her screen début in 1957 in *Man on Fire*. Later films included *The Buccaneer, The New Interns, Madigan* and *Hang 'Em High*. She also appeared on TV. The cause of death was not immediately ascertained.

WILLIAM BEAUDINE, who died on March 18, 1970 (in a Californian hospital) at the age of 78, was a prolific director whose movies spanned a period of over 40 years and included pictures which starred Mary Pickford, W. C. Fields, Valentino, Theda Bara and Gloria Swanson. Latterly he had been busy with TV films.

THE FILM ARCHIVES

As these notes are written, two late silents by the great F. W. Murnau – his German *The Last Laugh* and his American classic *Sunrise* – are both playing in commercial New York theatres. Quite apart from the sheer pleasure of seeing Murnau's name up on theatre marquees forty years after his death, cheek-by-jowl with the names of currently fashionable "now" directors who probably won't even be remembered ten years hence, let alone forty, the two bookings help to dramatise in the most effective way possible the inestimable value of the film archive. For these are commercial bookings; the films are attracting crowds – and making money. Not that the film archive exists as an adjunct to the production and exhibition arms of the industry, or will see a penny from these current exhibitions. But the point is, that were it not for the film archives of the world these films – unprotected and unpreserved by the studios – just would not exist today, and thus would not be available for the aesthetic purposes of film study or the commercial ones of theatrical exhibition.

What is the purpose of a film archive? Very simply stated, it is the acquisition and preservation of film; "preservation" meaning not just its storage, but the copying of it from the old combustible nitrate stock – prone to decay and decomposition – to a long-life safety stock, a very expensive process. These two things must come first before the third basic function can come into play – making the films available for study and research purposes. How well or extensively these activities are carried out depends on the structure of the individual archive; whether, for example, it has sufficient funds to implement research projects and exhibitions, or sufficient freedom to plot its own course. For many archives are government sponsored, and their activities may thus be partially or wholly dictated by nationalistic or political considerations. The Soviet archive, for example, should be the envy of every other country. It has spacious grounds, and a huge staff at least four times as big as that of its closest competitor. But its reputation for co-operation rather matches that of the Soviet generally! It is somewhat inaccessible, some sixty miles outside of Moscow – and once the weary film student arrives there he may well find that the pursuit of film study has been abandoned temporarily, with the entire resources of space and staff devoted to some propagandist or cultural activity quite divorced from film!

For years, the film archive was considered just an expensive luxury. Nobody ever questioned the wisdom and importance of preserving books in a public library, yet the same considerations, applied to film, were suspect. Why, it was argued, should a tax-supported government body, or a private institution, underwrite the enormous expense of maintaining a film collection; surely that was the function of the studios that produced the films? Ideally, of course, it should have been; practically, however, it didn't always work that way. Many fine films were independently produced, or were possibly foreign films. Taking America as the guide-line (though with variations the same situation existed everywhere) once such a film had run its allotted seven- or ten-year distribution span, its rights expired and ownership

by William K. Everson

24 reverted to the original producers – who might by now no longer be in existence as a business entity. With nobody physically owning the property, there was naturally little incentive to spend money saving a film that one no longer owned and probably couldn't use again. When sound came in, the great libraries of silent films appeared automatically obsolete. Their commercial value seemed nil. Some studios junked huge deposits of film there and then – "junking" usually means melting the films down so that the quite valuable silver ingredients can be reclaimed. When studios did decide to keep prints of their old films, it was usually only a business consideration – some tangible item to which a value could be attached should the property later be sold for a remake. Storage problems were many and expensive: the highly combustible film had to be kept at a well regulated temperature, it had to be inspected periodically, and it had to be handled with extreme care. Because of the potentially dangerous nature of the film, ever-more-stringent union regulations through the years added to its costs. Projectionists screening the old nitrate stock got a higher rate, and there always had to be *two* of them. Most laboratories now will even refuse to handle the old material, while Los Angeles has passed laws making it a criminal offence to even *transport* such film, except under very special circumstances. Violation can mean Los Angeles' Fire Department pouncing on a shipment of film, taking it out to sea, and dumping it – not just a vague threat, but an act of modern piracy that has actually taken place more than once. Once a film starts to

decompose, its fire-hazard dangers increase tenfold; one rotting film exposed to prolonged heat – the sun beating down on a vault roof for example – can (and on too many occasions, *has*) set off a vault fire that will destroy thousands of films. Once a film starts to decompose, there is nothing that can be done to arrest it. Either the offending section has to be removed right away, or, ideally, the whole reel should be copied before the deterioration is complete. At least one major company through the years took the short-sighted policy of immediately junking the *whole* film once a single reel started to go bad. Their reasoning: it wasn't worth spending money to preserve the film; and with a ten-minute chunk missing it was useless anyway, so it might as well all be destroyed. It was to combat this form of destruction – this senseless wiping out of art, entertainment and invaluable records of our time – that the archives of the world were formed. One would suppose that the major studios would have been delighted to have outside bodies doing all their work for them: putting up the manpower, money, technical knowledge and storage space to save film, and at the same time fully acknowledging the producing companies' legal rights to them, and agreeing to give them free access to the material at any time. But such was not the case: Hollywood was suspicious of the motives, and, except in a minimal way, refused to co-operate. The archives had to start from scratch, scrounging what they could from veteran stars, directors, exhibitors. Only a few had the advantages of, for example, the Czech Film Archive. In Czechoslovakia, a marvellous law stated that a print of every film released in that

country had to be deposited for permanent reference with the archive. Whether the law added a ruling that the said prints had to be copied and preserved, or merely saved for the duration of their natural life, I don't know. But the Czechs happily liked a lot of American films in their movie diet, and thanks to that archive many of the Hollywood classics of the 20s – long lost in this country – do survive, among them the Karl Brown masterpiece *Stark Love*, and John Ford's very first feature, 1917's *Straight Shooting*.

Through the years, the archives grew slowly but steadily, rather like tough weeds. They were watered (with funds) all too rarely, they usually had to plant their roots in unprepossessing soil, and they owed their existence to the tenacity of the curators at their helm: men who knew where to find prints, what to do with them, how to fight their superiors for a meagre increase in budget and – most important of all – how to exist with twice as much work, half as much sleep, and about a third of the salary that any normal person would expect. Of course, most curators *aren't* altogether normal: they have their vanities and their ego, and a fierce protective feeling for "their" prints rather like that of a mother vulture for her young. But without these qualities, their archives wouldn't have survived, so one can hardly carp at their occasionally bizarre behaviour. Although many archives – like the Czech one – have their basic roots well into the silent era, the movement as such really only caught hold in the 30s, and was spearheaded by the work of the Cinémathèque Française in Paris, the Museum of Modern Art in New York and the British Film Institute's National Film Archive in London. The N.F.A., though, like all government-sponsored archives, constantly harassed by money problems and occasionally by an ultra-conservative *modus operandi*, is one of the most fortunate of all such institutions in that it is staffed almost exclusively by people who *love* their association with film, do all that they can to share and spread that love and would probably work for nothing if they had to. Far more amply-endowed archives do far *less* merely because their personnel is bureaucratic and only remotely rather than passionately interested in film.

Another archive extremely fortunate in the energy and loyalty of its personnel is the Royal Film Archive of Belgium, presided over by the benign Jacques Ledoux, one of the very few curators who manages to remain quite aloof from all the paranoia and espionage and intrigues that wreath themselves around the higher echelons of most of the other archives. Mr. Ledoux's one and only aim in life is to collect film, and serve his fellow men by showing it as widely as possible. Moreover, a far-sighted historian, he realises that today's first-run may be tomorrow's lost film, and has given himself the far from enviable task of seeing all the new films that he can – a case of genuine self-service when one realises how many great old films still lie in his vaults, unseen for lack of time. One of the key functions of his secretary is to check on the local theatres, and ensure that her boss gets his paperwork done every night by nine so that he can catch the last performance of a new film on its last day – – an evening existence that is a permanent combination of wake and last-reel chase! The problem of a curator seeing and knowing all of the film in his collection is a very real one. The Eastman House archive in Rochester, New York, certainly the finest archive in the United States, has made a point of trying to collect everything – an impossible goal of course, but a laudatory one when reduced to more practical proportions. James Card, the curator, reasons that film history has already shown us that values fluctuate tremendously, that the classic of one decade may be considered worthless in another era, and that conversely, the films of seemingly minimal importance often turn out to be of great sociological if not artistic value to later generations. If such discrepancies exist within the brief seventy-year span of movie history, then who are to decide what may be valuable or interesting to generations 400 years hence? Accordingly, Eastman House has collected films from every period and every country, the artistic triumphs, the box-office blockbusters, the early work of potentially great directors, the depressingly bad final films of once-great directors, the "B" pictures and the bread-and-butter programmers, negatives, prints, titled, untitled. Recent donations of epic proportions by at least two major companies have so swelled the Eastman archives that Card estimates that even if he were to devote every hour to screening, eschewing lectures and administration work, and presumably taking the very modicum of time for sleeping and eating, he could devote the rest of his life to the project and still get nowhere near to seeing all of the films that currently exist in the collection, let alone those that will doubtless continue to pour in.

Perhaps only in the past dozen years has the industry at large come to recognise the value of the film archive from a practical point of view as well as a purely aesthetical one. More and more, writers and directors have been forced to resort to them to find rare prints of films that they are about to remake. Study of the originals not only shows in a very graphic way some of the pitfalls to be avoided, but often provides genuine inspiration too. More than one film-maker, dutifully looking at a film he expected to be no more than a museum piece, has been excited by its sophistry, skilled direction or visual beauty and been moved to aim at similar qualities in his own version. And scores of the younger film-makers all over the world have openly admitted their debts to the old film masters, whose work could have taught them nothing had the archives not preserved it and made it available to them. Many of the long obsolete film history books – most of them written in the 30s, full of clichés and old canards, undisputed then since the films themselves were largely unavailable for reappraisal – have now been superseded by far superior and more specialised histories, many of them built on knowledge gained through the facilities of the archives. Undoubtedly what has impressed the industry most of all is that the old films in which they once had no faith are suddenly valuable again: for theatrical reissue, for television, for special film shows. Many of the films that the studios still own they had not bothered to protect – and if it weren't for the archives having saved them, those unexpected profits

26 just wouldn't be forthcoming. Relying on the goodwill of the industry – for a lack of harassment if not for the dispensing of largesse – the archives have always been very rigid in their rules of procedure. Films that they show publicly they first clear with the legal departments of the companies concerned; while they exchange and loan films freely within the international archive set-up, they otherwise do not as a rule loan or rent films, unless a film distribution library, such as exists at the Museum of Modern Art and the British Film Institute, is set up with film industry approval. Producers wanting access to the vaults to use film clips for documentary or other commercial purposes have to produce air-tight evidence, usually from the current copyright-holder, that they have the legal right to use such material. Archives remain vulnerable institutions: companies, planning theatrical reissues of certain films, or television specials, have been known to withdraw all of their prints from an archive lest its one or two local showings of a given film harm the international gross! And a small but malignantly fast-growing breed of modern film pirates have been an especial thorn in the side to the modern archive. A small, fast-buck operator, with no love or knowledge of film history or art, but a great familiarity with the ways in which copyright laws can be made to serve him, can buy up minor rights to a film or a group of films, and, clutching his piece of paper (which may have cost him only a pittance) try to force the archives to turn over to him for his commercial gain films that they have saved, restored and poured a small fortune into. Small wonder that many of the archives are

increasingly wary of announcing some of their most prized treasures!

After years of struggling for recognition and support, the film archives are now so fashionably "in" that many of the bigger colleges and universities are starting their own collections – which of course they term "archives", and which invariably represent a certain amount of wasted effort and duplication. Distributors aiming at the 16mm market of film societies and universities have begun to offer proudly vintage films that ten years ago they would have sneered at and refused to consider. Now the films that have been kept alive through the years only by the archives, or by enterprising little film societies that have unearthed battered old prints, are being offered to those archives and film societies at rental rates (including regular commercial sliding-scale percentages!) that are keeping them out of the hands of the very groups that most deserve and need them, but that certainly can't afford to pay more for a single one-night showing than a regular commercial theatre would be asked to pay for a one-week run! A plethora of greed and a dearth of foresight have ever been industry characteristics, and never more than in the current scramble to cash in on the old films while the fashionable vogue is at its height!

1969 certainly has been (in America at least) the greatest of all years in terms of film preservation. Apart from the work of Eastman House and the Museum of Modern Art, the American Film Institute, working with the Library of Congress, launched a massive film preservation programme which took even them by

surprise with its fantastic results. Systematic search among private collectors, old exhibitors, cameramen, etc., produced a wealth of invaluable film. And the major studios, suddenly aware of the real and permanent monetary value in their old classics – but hard hit by a business depression which didn't allow them to do much preservation work themselves – suddenly broke down and turned over whole inventories of silent prints and negatives to the A.F.I. Twentieth Century-Fox, for example, which has always stead-fastly insisted that all of its old pictures were destroyed in mysterious studio fires, suddenly produced many of the lost masterworks of F. W. Murnau, Erich von Stroheim, Frank Borzage and other great directors. Practically the entire run of John Ford films, from 1922 on, was found to be intact – and this find alone is going to cause the rewriting of a great many film histories. Grateful though we must be that all of these Fords have been found and saved, how irksome it is to think that a whole fifteen-year stretch of films from America's finest living director has for so long been withheld, its very existence denied.

Just as there has never been justification for the oft-expressed and overly-optimistic remark that somewhere in the world there must be at least one print of every film, so now it seems we can have no time for the pessimist who states irrevocably that there is no hope of finding a given film, and that it is permanently lost. The number of "permanently lost" films that have been turned up by the A.F.I. in just the first few months of their operations is staggering. So, it must be added, are the costs involved in copying and protecting them. But the A.F.I. is off to a formidable start, not only finding and saving the films, but also in getting them shown at key showcases throughout the nation – and ultimately, no doubt, throughout the world. However, in the pleasure of such a glorious moment, one can't help but wonder what treasures might have been unearthed if this massive crusade had begun a decade – or two decades – earlier. For much, undoubtedly, *is* gone forever. And this is the Last Round-up. Once the current exhaustive search is completed, the chances of further major finds are unlikely. And again the short-sightedness is well in evidence. M-G-M, for example, its financial position grim, its future uncertain, having ascertained that either it or the A.F.I. has copied all of its major old films, has been systematically destroying all its surviving prints by dumping them in barrels of water! These may well turn out to be flawless prints of subjects that have been inadequately copied. Lab work on old film is extremely tricky, and many mistakes are made. When they are finally discovered, it may well be too late – if the only original print has been sent to a watery grave. In any case, the next technical breakthrough may well be a means of discovering how to arrest decomposition in these old prints, and that would not only be an incredible saving in terms of money and labour, but it would also enable these old masters to be shown *exactly* as they were intended to be. No matter how well a dupe copy is made, it remains that – a black-and-white copy devoid of all the beauty, clarity, and subtlety of colouring and toning that made

the silent film such a rich, visual art. Many directors are totally unappreciated and misunderstood solely through their work having been seen *only* via flat black-and-white copies. Rex Ingram, for example. was a dull director dramatically; there was no dynamism in his editing, no excitement in his handling of spectacle. Basically he was a painter with the camera: seeing one of his silents (*Scaramouche*, for example) in an original tinted and toned print, with all the subtleties of lighting, details of shading and composition, is a truly memorable experience. Seeing that same film in a black-and-white dupe is literally akin to seeing a Renoir canvas reproduced in pencil, or watching a Shakespearean play with the dialogue suddenly obliterated. For the moment at least, the archives of the world are the last depository for these grand and beautiful old original prints; they realise their obligation to show them as often as they can – while they last – before the great visual beauty of the silent film is but a memory. Perhaps among today's film students is one who will one day discover a scientific formula for halting the decay of these precious nitrate films, perhaps by evolving some form of coating to keep out the oxygen, or whatever other forces cause film to decay into dust. If he exists, he'll earn the undying gratitude of archivists everywhere, and the kind of reverence and respect that the medical profession will one day heap on the man who discovers a cure for cancer. And that is exactly what he will be doing – curing the cancer of film. But he must hurry. Time is running out. The heat of the Summer is when most films die, and a few more summers will see the end – unless

there are unlikely caches of film in Alaska or Antarctica. There'll be no point in perfecting this miraculous cure if all the patients are dead.

THE ART CINEMA— DOES IT EXIST?

To discuss the nature of art cinemas it is necessary to look back to the early years of film history. The term originated in the two most aware film countries – France and America. In France after the First World War there arose the movement, *Cinéma d'Art et d'Essai* (Art and Experimental Cinema), a movement which though it spread rather thinly among French intellectuals and never had much popular influence, nevertheless linked the cinema with *avant-garde* opinion in the arts generally, and gave it an intellectual prestige which persisted for many years, so that the cinema in France had a status and a cachet possessed in England only by the live theatre and the concert-hall.

It was in France also that the first art cinema was established, the Ursulines in Paris. It opened in 1925 under the direction of Armand Tellier and his formulation of aims is as valid today as it was then. "Our taste," he wrote, "is for bold, original work, but we do not advocate any special aesthetic theory, nor preach any creed nor belong to any school, religion, or political party. All we want is to promote the best in cinema, freely and without discrimination." Tellier's words have been taken as an expression of their policy by the International Federation of Art Cinemas (CICAE), a body founded in the 50s by a group of European critics and writers on the cinema. The Federation holds an annual conference and gives a prize for the best art film of the year. Recent awards have gone to Glauber Rocha's *Antonio das Mortes* (1969), Walerian Borowczyk's *Goto, L'Ile d'Amour* (1968), and Antonioni's *Blow-Up* (1969). The Federation also constitutes a forum where matters of general interest to serious cinema directors can be discussed.

The American art cinema developed gradually in the mid-20s and 30s, when an interest was growing in foreign films. First came the tense drama of the German Expressionist School – Lang's *Siegfried* and *Metropolis*, Dupont's *Variety*, Murnaut's *Last Laugh* and Von Sternberg's *Blue Angel*. Then there were the great Russian directors: Eisenstein, Pudovkin and Dovzhenko. And later came the sophisticated, romantic French directors of the 30s, with their misty photography, their elegant artificial style of acting and décor – René Clair's *Sous les Toits de Paris* and *Le Million*, Marcel Pagnol's *Fanny*, Marcel Carné's *Quai des Brumes*, Sacha Guitry's *Roman d'un Tricheur* and *En Remontant les Champs d'Elysée*, Jean Renoir's *Une Partie de Campagne*, Duvivier's *Un Carnet de Bal*, and so on. All these schools of cinema were successful in America, and in England too, because they provided strongly individual styles different from the prevailing Hollywood idiom, and films that were more impressive and more stimulating than the average, popular screen entertainment. Thus they found an enthusiastic audience among those who were ready to try something different. The term "Art Cinema" in America, like the term "egg-head", was a mild jibe at the pretensions of intellectuals who affected to despise the good, honest fare provided by the West Coast studios, and in fact it is true that then, as now, a grain of snobbery does encourage people to go to foreign films, as in other fields it has helped the foreign musician, painter or playwright.

In London the term "Art Cinema" never really came into use. A lot of foreign films (partly because of censorship in the case of the Russians) were shown by film societies

by Nicolas Owen

30 which grew in size and number. The London Film Society, the best known and largest, gave its first performance in October 1925 and was the first to show many of the foreign films which came to the U.K. However, public cinemas in London soon followed. The Avenue in Shaftesbury Avenue showed foreign films in the mid-20s, and larger cinemas (the Marble Arch Pavilion, for example, with Lang's *Metropolis* in 1926) sometimes ran seasons of foreign films. The Academy opened in 1929, and the Everyman in 1933 was converted from a live theatre to a cinema, to carry on the work of the London Film Society and present varied and interesting repertory programmes. The Curzon, noted for its luxurious seating, opened in 1934 and has shown many excellent foreign films, principally from France. It was not until the 30s that many of the Russian films were shown publicly at the Forum under Charing Cross viaduct, where under the title of *Late Joys* there is a continuous programme of Victorian Music Hall. Though it has since turned to more popular fare, Studio One started by showing foreign films. A nostalgic occasion was the last performance of Marcel Carné's *Le Jour se Lève* before it was bought up by an American Company to be re-thought and remade in the Hollywood idiom. The Cameo-Poly opened in 1941 and has shown many outstanding films including, for instance, Antonioni's *L'Avventura* and Resnais' *L'Année Dernière à Marienbad*, both of which ran for many weeks. The Paris Pullman has had a chequered career. It had been a cinema (one of the electric cinemas) since 1911, but with no especial distinction about its programmes. After the war it became a live theatre, the Boltons, following a period

when the "little" theatre had an extraordinary vogue – the Mercury, the Little Theatre, the Embassy, etc. – but by the early 50s had to close, and was re-opened as an art cinema. Its reputation for showing the unusual foreign and off-beat British or American films dates from this period. Although the English never used the term "Art Cinema" the cinemas themselves flourished and were usually called *specialized* cinemas or *repertory* cinemas.

There existed also, as there did in most countries, the tendency to exploit the foreign film for all it was worth purely for its sensational value as a vehicle for violence and sex – straight or kinky. As in the book world, works were sometimes allowed in a foreign language which would not have been passed in English, and often also, foreign films, even if they were no more daring than their English counterparts, could be made to appear so. There has never been in England a sex-circuit on the scale that exists in the States, possibly because the English have been able to see films on the Continent itself if they felt so inclined, and the cinemas exploiting sex films have often included in their programmes some of the finest works of art. Among the right films shown for the wrong reasons, as it were, one may instance *Mädchen in Uniform*, Bergman's *The Silence*, Kon Ichikawa's *Odd Obsessions* and *Fires on the Plain*, and Abel Gance's *Tour de Nesle*. One can only report that the sex cinema goes merrily on, no doubt pays more consistently and more handsomely than other *genres*, and it is no easier now to separate the sheep from the goats than it ever was. Perhaps the only way to kill it would be to flood the market, as perhaps is the policy in Denmark, with the abolition of all

censorship.

Running an art cinema is not very different from running any other kind of cinema though, alas, the more serious-minded the policy the more rarefied the air, the more intellectual the patrons, then the less the money comes rattling over the counter, and staff may be expected to work for love of art rather than high wages – an expectation which is often fulfilled in the short term, but more seldom in the long term. Directors of art cinemas having put up the money may be faced with deciding whether to settle for a prestigious reputation and a small return, or by watering down their programmes or concentrating on sex, less prestige and more cash.

The art cinema manager, like cinema managers in general, has to be a devotee – working on Saturdays, Sundays and week-days alike, putting in the best part of the day and the evening as well, from 11 a.m. to 11 p.m. He has to turn his hand to anything – mending fuses, cleaning out the lavatories, making last-minute film collections, putting up notices, placating local government officials, tax-collectors, creditors, difficult patrons and disgruntled staff, or fill in when necessary in the role of cashier, projectionist, usherette, doorman and ice-cream sales-lady. This, of course, besides doing his "own" work of making up endless accounts and returns, safeguarding and banking the takings, appearing resplendent at the front of the house when house-breaks occur, supervising the cleaners first thing in the morning, and locking up the cinema last thing at night. The rest of the staff regard the manager as a slave-driver and a tool of the director; the director thinks he has a cushy job and wonders how he fills in his time.

It begins to look as though an art cinema is just like any other cinema, and one wonders what it is that distinguishes it from the rest. Of course, there is the fact that it shows art films, but if one looks closely at art films it emerges more and more that they are simply ordinary films or popular films which are remote in place or time. Satyajit Ray, Yasujiro Ozu, Akira Kurosawa, Ingmar Bergman, René Clair, Jean Renoir, Luchino Visconti and Glauber Rocha – in England and America they are art directors, every one. Yet in their own countries of India, Japan, Sweden, France, Italy, Germany and Brazil, their films were intended for and appealed to popular audiences. In the same way one frequently finds that the films of Alfred Hitchcock, Carol Reed, John Frankenheimer, Lindsay Anderson and John Ford are showing in art cinemas in Paris, Brussels or Mannheim. As for remoteness in time . . . Griffith, Eisenstein, Chaplin and Lang are silent directors who made films for popular audiences in their own day. We now find their work included in revival programmes by art cinemas all over the world.

Distinctions are breaking down in other ways as well. At one time the larger film companies were content to leave foreign films to the smaller distributor and the exclusive cinema. Now they very often invade this field, and occasionally a foreign film gets a circuit release. The other way round, art cinemas in London – partly to fulfil quota requirements but partly also because the intelligentsia is beginning to take more interest in out-of-the-way pictures made in England and the States – frequently show low-budget or not-so-low-budget British or American films. The Paris Pullman premièred Lindsay Anderson's *The White Bus* and Maurice Hatton's *Praise Marx and Pass the Ammunition*, the Academy launched John Cassavetes' *Faces* and Joseph Strick's *Ulysses*. Cinecenta and some Classic cinemas (though perhaps they always were too middle-of-the-road to be classified as out-and-out art cinemas) seem to have gone completely over to the more popular English or American films. And this spring *Alice's Restaurant*, the film with most stars in *Sight and Sound*'s film-guide, which one might have expected to find at some austere Temple of the Seventh Art, was showing at the Windmill.

But the conclusion to be drawn from all this is a good one. The old days when there were two kinds of art, a superior kind for educated people and another inferior kind for the ordinary *hoi-polloi*, these days are passing away. The popular cinema, in particular, has ceased to churn out weekly saccharine love-stories and action-packed thrillers for teenagers and, as much as the book trade or the theatre, provides a varied, serious, adult entertainment, often also decidedly purposeful, and with strong points of view on current issues. It is appropriate that as film production has grown richer and more varied, so too the pattern of exhibition should change, and the system of one type of cinema for the candy-and-ice-cream-brigade and another for the intelligent film enthusiast, should be brought to an end. The art cinema, as such, has fulfilled a useful purpose, and it would be an honourable end if it were to be absorbed into a wider pattern.

THE FILM AND TELEVISION

by David Francis

The relationship between the film industry and television has changed radically since the Film Industry Defence Organisation was set up twelve years ago to prevent feature films being shown on the small screen. Today, producers who rushed to sell their wares to FIDO are anxiously waiting for the agreements to end or even considering the economics of buying back their films at the full sale price so that they can offer them to television while the demand for black-and-white British films is still strong.

Now even the mighty M-G-M lion has entered our homes. Except for their beloved Garbo's, the eternal *Gone With the Wind* and a few other titles with re-release potential, the company's whole library is available to television programmers. In fact, Walt Disney, Chaplin and Jacques Tati are the only major producers who are still withholding their films altogether.

Some features like Brian Desmond-Hurst's *Playboy of the Western World*, Michael Powell's *Honeymoon* and Anthony Asquith's Swedish-made thriller *Two Living, One Dead*, all films which British Lion failed to release in the early 60s, actually had their first presentation on television and the producers of the recent 'Première' series seen on BBC-2 hoped that the individual films would receive commercial distribution after their television transmission.

Of course the union between the two media is by no means complete. The Cinematograph Exhibitors Association still protects its members by threatening to blacklist producers and distributors who allow films to be sold to television before five years have elapsed from the date of their original release, but even this edict was recently relaxed to allow foreign language features on the small screen after only three years.

This gradual change of attitude is not as surprising as it might seem at first sight. Although cinema attendances have been declining steadily for many years, certain films still attract the public away from the comfort of their sitting rooms despite competition from three television channels. Sales of their older films to television provide companies with much-needed capital for new ventures without, as was feared in the '50s, jeopardising the success of the new films themselves, and the recent practice of selling films immediately they are released for transmission in five years time generates confidence among the industrial giants who are now responsible for most film financing.

Although the big film companies have learnt to live with television and benefit from the association, producers and distributors of specialised films and re-issues still complain that it is affecting their business. In fact their anger should be directed towards the two companies who have a stranglehold on the commercial outlets. Both Rank and the Associated British Picture Corporation have not allowed the cinema-going public to see the best foreign language films in their local circuit cinema. In fact until the British Film Institute established its chain of regional film theatres, the average foreign language feature was only likely to get half a dozen commercial bookings outside London.

Even taking this unsatisfactory situation

34 into account, the attitudes of this specialised group are still tinged with a little prejudice. Both the Academy Cinema in Oxford Street and the Cosmo in Glasgow have proved, albeit unintentionally, that films of the calibre of *Knife in the Water* and *The Hopeless Ones* actually fare better after an airing on television. Likewise the British Film Institute's Central Booking Agency confirms that film society bookings often increase spectacularly after a television transmission, particularly if the film concerned has been out of circulation for some time or has never received a commercial release in Britain. A careful examination of the Classic Circuit's programming also reveals that the management often think it commercially viable to book films soon after they have been transmitted.

It is however in the field of journalism that the breach between film and television is widest. Except for Alexander Walker's succinct comments in the *Evening Standard* and the brief remarks in the *Observer*'s, and more recently the *Sunday Times's*, weekly round-up of entertainments, most national newspapers and magazines totally ignore feature films shown on television. The television critics will not consider them because they were not produced specially for the medium and the film critics because they are not presented in the manner originally intended. The cinemagoer therefore has to rely on *Films and Filming*, the *Radio* or *TV Times* or an American paperback called *Movies on TV* which was recently launched on the British market without as much as a new introduction or a cross-reference to title changes, for information and appraisals.

Of these *Films and Filming*'s efforts are the most worthy although they are continually hampered by an early press date and the inevitable last-minute programme changes.

For the television companies themselves, the feature film represents one of the most economic and consistently successful forms of programme material and at the BBC every effort is made to dispel the prejudices which still exist against films on television by presenting them in the most satisfactory manner possible. In nearly all cases new 35mm prints are drawn from the original negatives and any known cuts which the distributors made in Britain or in the country of origin are restored. Each film is considered in relation to current attitudes and its time of transmission and potential audience and in some cases censor cuts, often made many years ago, are also re-instated. For instance, Otto Preminger's *Anatomy of a Murder* was transmitted in the full version seen only at the Columbia Theatre, and the classic *All Quiet on the Western Front* was painstakingly pieced together for its television presentation. Italian director Valerio Zurlini's critical reputation must also be much more secure now that his two films *A Girl with a Suitcase* and *Family Diary* have been made available on television in a more complete form than they were seen in British cinemas. But there are undoubtedly disadvantages to small-screen viewing. Twentieth Century-Fox developed the Cinemascope process in an effort to counter competition from television and it is hard to reconcile its elongated image with the almost square format of the television screen. Most

continental television companies present cinemascope films in a letter-box format, leaving huge areas of black, or more accurately grey, above and below the picture. The BBC, however, prefers to select the most important part of the image and scan only that area of the frame. In cases where films have received a network transmission in America, "converted" prints already exist but both the scanning and colour values, not to mention the picture and sound quality, sometimes leave much to be desired. Most of the cinemascope films shown by the Corporation therefore are "converted" on their own premises and transmitted on videotape. In simple terms, the special process, developed by Corporation engineers and still undergoing refinement, is operated as follows. There is a choice of nine different picture positions and a metallic dot is applied to the edge of the print wherever a pan or a cut is required. Cuts occur between one frame and the next and are virtually invisible, but pans can take anything between two and ten seconds. The resulting information is coded and then punched on to a paper tape. The tape reader is then "locked" to the television channel and when a metallic dot passes over the detector head, the tape moves on to the next instruction and activates the scanning circuits. At present the resultant images are recorded and transmitted on videotape, but it is hoped that the system will eventually be foolproof enough to permit live transmissions. Colour has also raised additional problems. Many different colour processes have been used in the last forty years, including one or two like Cinecolor which utilised only two component colours. These must all be reconciled with the superb colour quality which can be achieved in a modern television studio. Also colour negatives often tend to fade and prints drawn from older Technicolor masters may suffer from a mottled appearance. Colour changes between one shot and the next can be controlled under some circumstances by adjusting the relationship between the primary colours, but these changes would have to be programmed in the same way as the Cinemascope conversions if one wanted to overcome the problem completely.

Sub-titling presents difficulties on television as well. The titles must be about two-thirds of the length of those used on cinema prints to allow for badly adjusted television receivers and they must be placed far higher on the frame to compensate for vertical misalignment. Legibility is also more critical and it is particularly difficult to read titles against a light background. Recently the BBC has been employing a process which electronically applies a black band around each letter. The lighter the image the darker the band becomes and vice-versa. Unfortunately the extreme contrast between the peak white of the letter itself and the black of the surrounding band sometimes results in an unpleasant buzz on the sound-track. This can only be eliminated by dyeing the letters so that the white of the engraved letters is only fractionally whiter than the peak white in the picture itself.

In the long run the careful presentation of feature films on television must benefit the cinema and television alike and one hopes that in the not too distant future newspapers and magazines will devote the same amount of space to feature films premièred or revived on television as they would if the same films were shown commercially. It must not be forgotten that potentially all television viewers are cinema patrons.

WHERE HAVE ALL THE ORGANS GONE?

Answered by John Mountjoy

New Boy – John Mann. Theatre Organ Club Patron, 1970. Granada Wurlitzer, Clapham.

Nowadays many cinemas look and "feel" as unimaginative and impersonal as a painted parish hall. Which makes it difficult for us to visualise or, for young people particularly, to realise that once upon a time – and it is that long ago – the floor space in front of the silver screen was a wide, deep pit which housed an orchestra and an organ console. The organist provided music for the second feature film and the newsreel. And before the first feature – we called it the "big picture"–started there was a spectacular stage show starring tip-top performers.

We could count on three and a half hours of film and stage entertainment. Luxury presentations in luxury surroundings in luxury seats. Best balcony seats cost one-and-sixpence! *Those* were the cinema days!

A regular feature in the live show was the organist's solo playing. He, sometimes she, got a billing like the stars. And as the white, sometimes illuminated, console rose on its lift out of the pit into view the organist got a star's welcome.

Even when "the talkies" silenced (and sacked) the orchestras and stopped stage shows the organist still provided a feature interlude. Names like Reginald Foort, Reginald New, Reginald Porter-Brown, Harold Ramsay, Bryan Rodwell, Andrew Fenner, Ena Baga, Sydney Gustard, Florence de Jong, Doreen Chadwick and dozens of others still meant something at the box office. Some seeing the red light moved into music hall playing speciality spots. Robin Richmond, now with the BBC, is an example. Foort toured with his giant Moller. Robinson Cleaver played summer seasons at Scarborough, winter at Richmond Sportsdrome by the Thames and promoted concerts at Llandudno.

But slowly and surely the organs have been replaced by silence or records. Like the large picture palaces – remember the Trocadero in the Elephant and Castle or the Regal, Marble Arch; Astoria, Brixton; Commodore, Hammersmith, for instance – they fill no function, hence have no place in the current scene.

There are a few exceptions. Gerald Shaw, the only organist in complete captivity, plays every day at the Odeon, Leicester Square, London. His fine Compton organ rises as it

38

Alec Leader – The Plough pub player in
Great Munden.

used to. But he is never presented as part of
the programme. The very fine Wurlitzer at
the Odeon, Manchester, is played at
weekends. So is the Wurlitzer at the State,
Kilburn, London, from time to time. There
are others principally in the North where
cinema organs have always had much,
much more acclaim than in the slumbering
South. The Tower, Blackpool, is an
outstanding example.

Because they are of such little numerical or
significant consequence I am omitting them
in my reply to this regrettable question. Sad
in a cinema sense. Consoling and pleasing in
another. Certainly surprising I can
promise you. Positively shocking for
musical conservatives. After all, for them,
the intrusion of this instrument purporting
to be an organ into a picture is an affront to
the great comparable, well, almost
comparable, to taking Blessed Mary, Our
Lady, into a strip club. Now, what next?
And since we have mentioned religious
matters it is appropriate . . .

Their first shock is that an increasing number
of Christian ministers are installing them in
church. Furthermore, using them for
recitals as well as for hymns and services.
Gerald Shaw opened the Cosham Odeon
organ at the new church of St. Andrew,
Chorley Wood, near London. Andrew
Fenner occasionally plays "specials" on the
ABC Nuneaton Compton at St. John
Vianney, Ilford. Other churches include:
Chasetown Trinity Methodist – Burslem
Coliseum Compton; Holy Trinity, Prestwood
– ABC Woking Compton; Castle Hill
Congregational – Clacton Essoldo Christie;
Oxley Parish, Wolverhampton – Windsor
Bearwood Compton; St. John, Romford –
Leeds Forum Christie; Beer

Congregational – Walsall Picture House
Wurlitzer. By no means last, press day
limits research time, is St. Francis in
Wormwood Scrubs Prison – ABC Ealing
Compton; Quinton Parish, Birmingham –
Smethwick Gaumont Compton. In most
cases the consoles look the same as they did
in what cinema organ fans describe as
"the golden days".

Not every cinema owner used an organ. On
the other hand, organs weren't confined to
the mammoth movie houses. I discovered one
boxed away at the small Cameo-Poly in
Regent Street, London. Further down the
street I listened to Florence de Jong and
Ena Baga, her sister, play the famous
Wurlitzer each featured many moons back
at the then New Gallery Cinema, now New
Gallery, a Seventh Day Adventists' Chapel
and Reading House. Florence stayed there
13 years, Ena, after a year as her assistant,
switched to the Tivoli in the Strand, now
Peter Robinson's multi-purpose store.
Foort broadcast frequently from the New
Gallery. The Wurlitzer retains its chimes,
snare drum, and all those effects organists
used to back action in the silent films.
During those "golden days" cinema organs –
usually a Compton, a Christie or a
Wurlitzer – and their players enrolled a
large legion of steadfast admirers whose
affection and loyalty has never wavered and
to whom everyone who applauded, say,
Fredric Bayco or Jackie Brown, but did
nothing about it when they were axed, owes
the audible fact that lots of cinema organs
can be and are still being heard in almost
every part of the country.

These very active fans grouped themselves
under the separate banners of the Theatre
Organ Club, whose president is Robinson

Cleaver, and The Cinema Organ Society founded by Hubert Selby, another notable name. They work ceaselessly to either save organs due for the scrap heap or promote concerts where enthusiasts might spend an afternoon in cinema surroundings or wherever the Theatre Organ Preservation Society members have sweated physically to install (hence save) an organ the management agreed to sell.

These determined men and women practice the religious fervour of a Billy Graham and there is a story worth reading, even though it isn't front page news, behind each installation.

The Rawle families in Northolt and Chorley Wood come immediately to mind, principally because I have heard their Wurlitzers – in their houses. The Rawles have always been organ devotees. Their house is named Wurlitzer Lodge. Neither dad nor mum can play, but Len learned before, during and after the Second World War. Dad bought the Wandsworth Granada Wurlitzer, built special chambers within the house and put the console in their extended lounge room. There are frequent formal as well as many informal concerts. George Blackmore and Jack Ferguson are "regulars". Before Len left home to bring up his own family in Chorley Wood, he planned his house to accommodate the Leicester Square, Empire Wurlitzer which Sandy Macpherson used to play. This is where it is now. He has broadcast and recorded two LPs from his home. Getting it out of the Empire and getting it into his house is a story in itself.

But the Rawles aren't unique. There is no telling where you might suddenly find a cinema organ. The Leicester Gaumont Wurlitzer is in Allan Hickling's Dormston House in Sedgley. Michael Candy is putting in a Wurlitzer at his Hemel Hempstead home specially designed to cope. The Leicester ABC Compton is at Derrick Plant's Ashby-de-la-Zouch house. Ricky Hart has bought the Folkestone Pleasure Gardens Theatre Compton, adding it to ranks from other Folkestone cinemas in his house. This Compton started its life at the Cambridge Rex. The Wurlitzer from the Maidenhead Plaza is played by Roy Bingham in his Castle Donington home. Almost as shocking, but certainly as surprising to conservatives, is their acquisition by schools. A *cinema* organ in a school! The Twickenham College of Technology organ is the Wood Green, London, Odeon Compton complete with vibraphone, xylophone, carillon of twenty tubes, glockenspiel, sleigh bells, cymbal, klaxon horn, tom-tom, tambourine, birds and bass drum. There are nine hundred pipes, two thousand magnets, one hundred and fifty-two stop keys, fifty-three thumb and toe pistons, and eight hundred insulated wires in the multicable between console and organ. It was opened in March, 1969. The programme included the Prelude from the Prelude and Fugue in B Minor by Bach, a Vaughan Williams Prelude, Widor's Toccata from the Fifth Organ Symphony and Finale from Vierne's Symphony No 1. Makes you think, doesn't it?

But Twickenham College is not alone. George Blackmore recently returned to Aberdeen to play the Astoria Compton on which he broadcast for many years. But he went to Powis Secondary School in which staff and pupils rebuilt the organ they had removed from the newly demolished cinema.

Ena Baga at the New Gallery Centre Wurlitzer which she played when the Centre was a cinema.

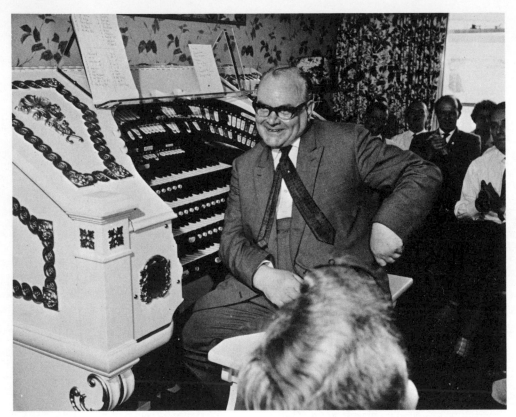

Gerald Shaw at the Leicester Square
Empire Wurlitzer, now part of the furniture
at Len Rawle's home in Chorley Wood.

The Wellingborough Lyric Compton is now at the Wellingborough Technical Grammar School; ABC Harrogate Compton – Taverham Hall Boys Preparatory School, Norwich; Birmingham Rialto Compton – Bishop Vesey Grammar School; Smethwick Princes Hall Compton – Holly Lodge Boys Grammar School; Coventry Forum Conacher – Northampton Grammar School. Golders Green, London, Odeon Compton – New City Grammar School Hall, Sheffield; and London Warner Compton – Christchurch School, Canterbury.

Two particularly popular centres are The Abbey Hall in Abingdon where the Birmingham Gaumont Compton was "opened" in 1966 by the Mayor of Abingdon, and Buckingham Town Hall which houses the London Metropole Wurlitzer using the console from the Stepney Troxy, now London Opera Centre's HQ. In each venue the organ enjoys a little of its former glory. Their installation is another example of blood, sweat and tears because the labour is spare-time. Theatre Organ Preservation Society members travelled five weekends to Birmingham to dismantle it and bring it to Abingdon where the council provided premises for use as a workshop. Members worked every Wednesday checking, renovating, wiring and rebuilding it prior to installation.

George Thorn, Watford civic organist, tells me that the Town Hall organ is the Chelsea Gaumont (now Odeon) Compton completely rebuilt and modified and suitable for serious as well as light music. Such dual-organs as this model give an answer to conservative critics of the cinema organ's flexibility. Windsor owes its Memorial Hall's Compton from the ABC, Old Kent Road, to Ted

Lawrence, a fellow-fanatic whose home is already supplied with organ music by an electronic (no hissing please). The moment he heard it was for sale he started lobbying, and if you'd stayed in Windsor during those days you might have thought conspirators were organising to take over the castle. The removal took three week-ends. At one point it looked like taking three years. The organ chambers were high up in the wall of the cinema. The only access was a spiral staircase. Removing the blower – a weight of 600 lb – was back-breaking. The relay bank refused to negotiate the stairs. It became inextricably jammed for two hours. They got it out by cutting it in half, folding it like a book. Once in a Windsor warehouse they had to recondition it. The work was hard and filthy. All London's grime seemed to have settled into the organ. But with the same dogged drive inseparable from cinema organ following, Ted and his many chums – some of them were committees and councils – saw the evening in January, 1969 when a restored Compton console, new contours, new music desk and "organza and gold" finish fronted the organ they had striven to bring home to Old Windsor.

They have also found their way into pubs, notably The Plough, Great Munden, where Alec Leader is resident every Friday, Saturday and Sunday. Gerald Carrington, mine host and organ expert, extended his lounge to house the massive array of pipes and ancillary instruments of this Finchley, North London, Gaumont Compton. He claims that it is the only pipe organ of its size and kind heard in any public house in the world. Carrington is always scouting round for possible organ venues and he is now a respected name in potential buyers'

quarters. He spells good news for organ fans. Another such pub is The Pontygwindy Inn, Caerphilly, with its Wurlitzer and Roy Tritschler, resident organist.

At Liskeard in Cornwall there is Paul Corin Musical Collection which includes the Bournemouth Regent Wurlitzer first played by Reginald Foort there in 1929, subsequently succeeded by Kevin and Edith Buckley.

The Regal (later Odeon) Marble Arch Christie is said to be stored somewhere in Cornwall. The London Plaza Wurlitzer is also being held pending its installation in someone's Home Counties house. Also the fine Wurlitzer played by Quentin Maclean at the Elephant and Castle Trocadero (now rebuilt as an Odeon) and bought by the Cinema Organ Society will reopen in the sober surroundings of the Borough, London, Polytechnic after the lengthy but essential preparation. The Cheltenham Spa Odeon Compton should by now be in a new Melbourne, Australia, cinema following the success of a Wurlitzer in the district's Dendy Theatre. The Bebbington Rialto Compton is installed in Ossett Town Hall. It incorporates pipes and parts from other organs – Sparkbrook Piccadilly; Bolton Lido Christie; Handsworth Regal and Exeter Savoy. The Aldershot Empire Compton is backing for bingo at the Gorleston Palace. The organ played (and broadcast) by Ronald Curtis in Bolton is a composite Compton instrument made mainly from Odeons in Southend and Bolton; Gaumonts Chester and Preston, also Ritz, Warrington. The console comes from Liverpool Odeon. The Beckenham Regal Wurlitzer known through Reginald New's broadcasts and now owned by Mr. and Mrs.

St. John Vianney, Ilford. New home of the ABC Nuneaton Compton.

42

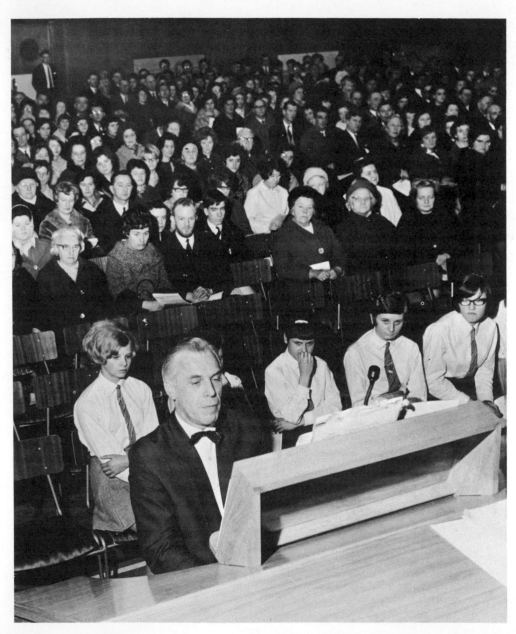

Leslie Kent is in St. Dominic's Hall, Cowley, Oxford. The Wycombe Organ Centre in High Wycombe has a small Wurlitzer from a Grantham club and is temporarily holding the Leeds Odeon Wurlitzer which Claude Birks, the centre owner, is going to have installed in his home.

And where have all the organists gone? An answer as incomplete as my first reply. Sidney Torch is a freelance conductor; Sydney Gustard has retired; Reginald Porter-Brown, now based at the Southampton ABC, plays at the Torquay ABC, where he made his name, in the summer; Felton Rapley is a church organist in Winchester; Fredric Bayco, Holy Trinity, Paddington; Jackie Brown is running organ studios in Shoreham; Noel Briggs switched to cinema management like many others; Terence Casey, semi-retirement in Brighton; Edward O'Henry retired in Jersey; Sandy Macpherson, retired but still broadcasts; Horace Finch now mine host in a Northern pub; Robinson Cleaver, freelancing like Tommy Dando, Stanley Tudor, Dudley Savage, Neville Meale, Florence de Jong, Bobby Pagan; Ena Baga, principal demonstrator at Chiswick Hammond Organ studios.

A never-to-be-forgotten night at Powis Secondary School, Aberdeen. George Blackmore at the organ from the Astoria Cinema.

Reginald Foort lives at Pompano Beach, Florida. He is a church organist, teaches, and occasionally plays a cinema organ in a concert date. At home he has a Baldwin organ. He says he couldn't afford a British tour! Which is salutory food for thought. Several "greats" are dead. Quentin Maclean, Reginald New, Donald Thorne, Lloyd Thomas, G. T. Pattman, Frank Newman, James Bell, Frank Matthew, Dr. George Tootell.

At this press minute I cannot trace Jack Helyer or Harold Ramsay.

In between questioning Tony Moss and Douglas Badham of the Cinema Organ Society, Ralph Bartlett of the Theatre Organ Club, Gerald Carrington, and anyone else on whose tibias I could lay my hands, I let up with Gerald Shaw, that grand, far-from-old man at the Leicester Square Odeon and Alec Leader from The Plough, Great Munden. Each blamed indifferent organists playing indifferent organs for the organ's decline and fall. Each conceded that declining cinema attendances also hastened the day. Shaw is sure that the organ's cinema days are done. Leader fancies their promotion in select cinemas, assuming first class organs played by first class organists, might, nay could, be successful but cannot foresee it happening. It is far better, he argues, to accept that defeat and remove such organs to situations where they can be heard to full advantage. Like The Plough. There is a large public already organ-minded. Prospects are bright – though unlikely in cinemas.

Gerald Shaw agreed. If ever management has a change of heart about organs, they will be electronic, he says. Cinema organ prices are prohibitive. In between his interludes he composes and edits music. He showed me the pressings of The Filsham Mass he composed and played with the church choir at St. Alban, High Holborn. He loathes passivity. That is why he has no spare time even though backstage cinema is empty and deserted. How unlike his first days at the Brixton Astoria in 1936. He recalls two films, news, organ feature and 40 minutes stage with the then famous Ambrose and his Orchestra. All for sixpence before midday! By the time you read this the BBC's change of heart in the shape of a Wurlitzer from a Blackpool ballroom should be in regular use. Robin Richmond's "The Organist Entertains", a BBC weekly feature, has served its double purpose. So everybody is happy! Well, nearly!

Gerald Shaw reacts violently to John Mountjoy's mis-playing of the Compton in the Chelsea (then) Gaumont – now in regular use at Watford Town Hall.

SWEDISH CINEMA POST-WAR

Ingmar Bergman
Alf Sjöberg
Vilgot Sjöman
Arne Mattsson
Bo Widerberg
Lars Magnus Lindgren
Mai Zetterling
Jörn Donner
Arne Sucksdorff
Hasse Ekman
Jan Troell
Hampe Faustman

by Peter Cowie

Per Oscarsson and Bibi Andersson in Vilgot Sjöman's *My Sister, My Love.*

Sinful and soul-searching are two adjectives that are all too glibly used to describe Swedish cinema. It's true that sex is treated as eating and drinking in most modern Swedish films, from *One Summer of Happiness* in the early 50s to *I Am Curious* in the late 60s. It is also undeniable that Ingmar Bergman has appeared to all and sundry a man stretched on a rack of his own creation, striving to solve man's most intimate dilemmas at a time when it would be so much easier – and so much more fashionable – for him to espouse the mealy-mouthed commitment of other directors. But oddly enough film-making in Sweden is enormous fun. It always has been, from the days when Victor Sjöström took his tiny crews out into the magnificent landscapes to shoot a series of classic films far from the "front office". Bergman has spoken of his reluctance to go to Hollywood for this very reason, for fear he should deprive himself of "that unique family feeling which is typical of film-making in Sweden". The budgets are smaller; the stars are less rampant; the *risk* of film-making is altogether diminished (hardly surprising that prickly foreign talents like Peter Watkins and Susan Sontag should be given a free hand by Sandrews, one of the major Swedish producers). There are economic problems nonetheless, and poor attendances at home can make a Swedish film a costly failure – in the context of local production – unless (or even if) it wins a quality prize from the Swedish Film Institute.

The foundation of this Institute is probably the most important event in the post-war Swedish film industry. Feature production had dwindled to a mere seventeen pictures a year (from a 1947 peak of forty-four), and

46

Liv Ullmann and Max Von Sydow in Jan Troell's *The Emigrants*.

Martin Widerberg in Bo Widerberg's *Adalen '31*

the companies were becoming more and more cautious in their choice of projects. Then Harry Schein, an astute chemical engineer who had also served as critic for *BLM* (Sweden's equivalent of *Encounter*) sketched out a masterly plan for the revival of Swedish cinema. In a nutshell, the Government was prevailed on to reduce the taxes levied on tickets and to channel them into a Film Institute instead of the Treasury, and with this sizeable subsidy to endow films of quality as compensation for possible box-office disappointment. Almost at once new producers and new directors jumped at the opportunity of doing adventurous work, with the films that pleased both critics and audiences coming best out of the situation – and rightly so. In the last two years, however, another crisis has begun to build up. Attendances have declined sharply, and especially for Swedish-made films (one recouped less than $5,000 for Sandrews!) and the Institute, which depends on ticket sales for its income, has also been emitting sounds of dismay. A lot depends on the success of Jan Troell's mammoth epic for Svensk Filmindustri, *The Emigrants* and *Unto – Good Land*, and on the durability of directors like Kjell Grede, whose *Gay Harry* has brightened the scene for Sandrews this year.

But in spite of this gloomy lull, Swedish cinema is still immensely strong, both in reserves of talent and in its contacts with foreign markets. A Swedish producer is hardly likely to object to his film's being re-entitled from *The Bathers* to *I, A Virgin*, or from *Burnt Child* to *The Sinning Urge*, if the result is a long run in London's West End or on Manhattan's Forty-Second Street. Ingmar Bergman's *The Silence* grossed close

to half a million pounds in West Germany, but not exactly on account of its artistic stature. Nearly all Bergman's films have been saddled with an "X" certificate in Britain, and several – notably *The Virgin Spring* – have been cut, often upsetting the delicate balance that Bergman strikes between cause and effect. Still, Bergman was undoubtedly the most widely known and "seen" of all foreign-language directors in the decade 1958 to 1968, and, only in his early fifties, he continues to mature artistically and to maintain an unusually prolific output. Inevitably, it is to his work that one turns first in making any qualitative assessment of the post-war era in Swedish cinema. *Sawdust and Tinsel*, *The Seventh Seal*, *Wild Strawberries*, *The Silence*, *Persona*, and *Shame* are all towering achievements, not by virtue of technique or topicality, but because they represent a concentration of human thought rarely found in the cinema. Unlike Godard, Bergman has not tried to assimilate the facia of modern life into his films; instead he has been concerned solely with his own experience and his own fears. "I try to talk to other people through my pictures," he says, "and there is perhaps an idea in my mind that if I talk and tell them about my wounds, tensions and problems, other people might recognise something in that – something of their own – and it may have a relieving effect on them." The fact that his films are Swedish lends them a certain mysterious allure, like the plays of Ibsen or the music of Sibelius; but beyond that Bergman's real accomplishment has been to communicate with his international audience, to strike at least one chord in each spectator's sensibility at some stage in each film. In this he is not typical of the Swedish cinema as a whole, but his career demonstrates just how much a film director can be respected in Scandinavia. Since about 1956 Bergman has been free to direct virtually any screenplay he cares to write, and his last four features have all been bought outright for world distribution by United Artists before they were even completed.

Most other Swedish film-makers have been forced to tread a less uncompromising path to survive in the industry. Arne Mattsson, for instance, a man whose talent graced a few excellent films in the mid-50s (*Salka Valka*, *The Bread of Love* and *The People of Hemsö*), has now completed over fifty features. He failed to make the impact Bergman did, and turned as a result to thrillers and sex-tinged melodramas that may not have endeared him to the critics but have kept Mattsson's name before the public and more than recouped their cost. Mattsson is a journeyman director whose films one is more likely to encounter on a visit to Stockholm than those of almost any other Swede. A few years his senior is Hasse Ekman, son of the legendary Swedish stage actor, Gösta Ekman (Ingrid Bergman's partner in *Intermezzo*), who has now retired. During the post-war years and early 50s Ekman produced a string of solid, gay, amusing and highly polished films, tending somewhat to sentimentality but every bit as entertaining as the work of men like Charles Frend and Robert Hamer in England at the same time. *First Squadron*, *Changing Trains* (a Swedish *Brief Encounter*) and *The Banquet* all suggested Ekman's easy familiarity with the Swedish upper classes, while *Girl with Hyacinths* (1950) was remarkably successful in re-creating the miserable life of a girl

alone in Stockholm. Here the *Angst* of the 40s in Sweden – the unacknowledged guilt at standing aloof from the war, the painful birth of a new social order – was given its fullest expression, with Anders Ek (also the clown in Bergman's *Sawdust and Tinsel*) contributing a memorably bitter portrait of a drunken painter.

Surprisingly, most directors of the late 40s concentrated on either flippant *divertissements* or psychological studies, and Erik "Hampe" Faustman was the one really committed film-maker of the time. In works like *When Meadows Bloom* and *Foreign Harbour* he made no attempt to hide his radical sympathies with the farm workers and sailors of Sweden. Like all propagandist art, Faustman's films have a dated look now, but their good timing, their sense of mood and place, are undeniably exact.

The strong connections between theatre and cinema in Sweden are seen both to advantage and disadvantage in the career of Alf Sjöberg. Now in his sixties, Sjöberg directed one brilliant film (*The Strongest*) during the silent period, but spent most of the 30s producing plays. He returned to film-making in 1939 and since then has been responsible for a number of excellent productions. His classics of the war and post-war eras included *The Road to Heaven*, a most convincing morality tale set in the quaint country villages of Dalarna; *Frenzy*, the first film scripted by Bergman and a pointer to Sjöberg's keen social sense as well as to his fondness for expressionistic technique; and *Iris and the Lieutenant*, an atmospheric and (now) extremely nostalgic description of the Swedish bourgeois family. All these – and even a predominantly outdoor picture like *Only a Mother* (1949) – were shot with

Lena Nyman in Vilgot Sjöman's
I am Curious – Blue.

Harriet Andersson and Thommy Bergen in Jörn Donner's *A Sunday in September*.

48

Bibi Andersson in Ingmar Bergman's
Persona.

Anita Björk in
Alf Sjöberg's *Miss Julie*.

impeccable taste and the concision of fine
stage productions. This scrupulous,
rather academic approach to the cinema
suited Sjöberg so long as he found good
dramatic material to hand. *Miss Julie* (1951),
the only Swedish film to win the Golden
Palm at the Cannes Festival, was a superb
vehicle for his talents. Strindberg the
misogynist and Sjöberg the social inquirer
combined to achieve a plausible analysis of
the class struggle in turn-of-the-century
Sweden, with Anita Björk's "Julie" a
performance distinguished by its arrogance
and barely-concealed hysteria. But it was in
Barabbas and *Karin Mansdötter*, both
adapted from capital works of Swedish
literature, that Sjöberg's theatrical technique
began to pall. The dialogue scenes were
rather too heavy; the staging rather too
formal. It has become increasingly obvious
that while Sjöberg may be as good a
technician as Bergman, he lacks the fierce
personal involvement in his films that would
enable him, like his younger compatriot, to
transcend his theatrical background. It is
perhaps significant that his presentation of
Strindberg's *The Father* at the Royal
Dramatic Theatre at the end of the 60s was
more highly praised than his film version of
the play a short while afterwards. For all
his failure to produce a major picture during
the last decade, however, Sjöberg remains the
portal figure of his generation in Sweden and
Bergman for one professes enormous
admiration for him.

Arne Sucksdorff's career has run parallel to
Sjöberg's in many ways, his finest films
appearing in the 40s and 50s and his most
recent efforts disappointing his followers.
Sucksdorff is as much a naturalist as a
film-maker; a Flaherty of the North who

better than anyone has captured on the screen
the changing seasons of the Swedish year,
the struggle for survival in the animal world,
and the importance of the countryside in
Scandinavian life. Shorts like *Dawn*,
Shadow over the Snow and *People of the
City* have an intuitive rhythm and visual
beauty in the great documentary tradition.
Sucksdorff, like Flaherty, is fascinated by
innocence. He finds it especially in childhood
and nature, and *The Great Adventure* is
probably his finest film. On a farm in central
Sweden, two young brothers find an otter.
They tame him and shelter him through the
long winter, but when spring arrives "Otty"
escapes and the boys realise that "no one can
encage a dream alive for long, however kind
the keeper". Not until Kjell Grede's *Hugo
and Josefin* fifteen years later in 1968 did a
children's film of comparable stature emerge
from Scandinavia. Sucksdorff's subsequent
work, however, has relied more and more on
contrivance. Feature-length studies like
The Flute and the Arrow, *The Boy in the Tree*
and *My Home Is Copacabana* were shot in a
natural environment but fictional elements
were introduced rather artificially into the
setting.

In the early 60s, a new generation of directors
at last made itself heard. There was much
polemic directed at the traditional style of
Swedish film-making, and especially at the
metaphysical preoccupations of poor
Bergman. Bo Widerberg and Vilgot Sjöman
felt that the cinema should reflect contemporary considerations and the shifting
patterns of modern society. But it is curious
that the work of these young progressives
should resemble so much the early films of
Bergman himself, based as they are on the
central idea of young lovers flouting the

conventions of society and suffering as a result. In the final analysis, the Swedish film vision is an individualistic one. The unmarried mother in Widerberg's *The Pram*, the girl in Sjöman's *The Mistress*, even Lena Nyman in the same director's *I Am Curious*, are all at odds with the people and the customs surrounding them, and their guiltiness and defiance stem from this. It has been refreshing to find, however, that Widerberg has such a range of expression – *Elvira Madigan* is the epitome of romance, and *Love 65* a brilliant personal testament about the film-maker's confusion of private desires and professional conduct. In all his pictures, including the more radical like *Adalen '31*, Widerberg has retained a poet's eye for landscape and for the first, delicate steps in a love affair.

Sjöman's work is less appealing to the senses, but in its more muscular fashion it may outlast Widerberg's. Sjöman has had his unmemorable moments (*The Dress*, for example), but throughout his eight years as a director he has displayed a keen desire to tackle controversial issues. This desire is motivated not by the prospect of quick profits so much as by a genuine involvement in such subjects as juvenile delinquency and prison conditions in Sweden (*491* and *You're Lying*), taboos (the revelation of incest in *My Sister, My Love*) and political ignorance and complacency (*I Am Curious*). It was over *I Am Curious*, with its explicit scenes of sexual intercourse, that the last in a series of much-publicised battles with the Swedish Censorship Bureau was fought. Jörn Donner, a Finn, also made four feature films in Sweden during the 60s, but rebelled much less vociferously than either Widerberg or Sjöman. An admirer rather than a critic of Bergman, Donner used

Harriet Andersson in each of his pictures, which were constructed along straightforward lines. A vein of pessimism, of disenchantment, gave each one a peculiarly bewitching quality. There was a sense of relationships changing almost subliminally under the pressure of new surroundings and circumstances (fashion designer Anne Englund's trip to Helsinki in *Adventure Starts Here*, the Hungarian girl Noomi's affair with a married man in Stockholm in *Rooftree*). Certainly Donner is the most lucid and communicative of the new generation, but now it seems as if he has left the Swedish film world for good. Thanks to the stimulus of the Film Institute's award system, a group of even younger directors has been able to enter the cinema in Sweden. Bengt Forslund, a producer and writer at Svensk Film-industri, has fostered the outstandingly lyrical and versatile talent of Jan Troell (*Here's Your Life, Who Saw Him Die?*) and the more orthodox but prolific Jan Halldoff, all of whose entertaining films have been concerned with young people and their problems in Sweden today. At Sandrews, Jonas Cornell made his *début* with a cool and elegant comedy of manners, *Hugs and Kisses*, and followed it with an even more intelligent analysis of the monied class in *Like Night and Day* (1969). Mai Zetterling, the ingenuous blonde heroine of the 40s romances, has matured into an ardent champion of female rights by directing such pictures as *Loving Couples* and *The Girls*, while Lars Magnus Lindgren, elsewhere a pedestrian film-maker, achieved an enormous success with both public and pundits with *Dear John*.

Probably more new directors have entered

the Swedish industry this past decade than in any previous period. The result is a strongly competitive atmosphere and a wide range of themes and styles. Few countries can rival Sweden in this respect and were it not for the limitations or language and finance, Swedish films would be seen by millions more people.

Åke Grönberg and Harriet Andersson in Ingmar Bergman's *Sawdust and Tinsel*.

The Bournemouth Gaumont, now
re-modelled and "twinned" to make two
cinemas where there was one.

CINEMA 69-70

The interior of the 1,150-seater Gaumont cinema at Sheffield.

And the interior of the smaller, 737-seater in the same complex.

The decline continues, though at a slower rate than during 1968. Between January 1 and November 1, 1969, 81 cinemas in the United Kingdom were shut down, leaving a total of 1,636. The saddest closures are probably those which deprive a town of its only source: for example, in September the last cinema in Ilkley, Yorks., was lost to a supermarket, meaning that anyone wanting to see a film must now travel to Keighley, Leeds, or elsewhere.

In the same month it was announced that a redevelopment scheme in Newcastle-under-Lyme will mean that the town will lose both its Rex and Rio cinemas. Blaming falling attendances and rising expenses, the Essoldo group decided not to incorporate a new cinema in the rebuilding.

Hull lost its Criterion to bingo in June after 55 years of showing films, leaving this town – population 301,100 – with 5 cinemas. In November it was announced that Paisley's La Scala was to become a Littlewood supermarket: the same month saw the threatened closure of two "only" cinemas in East Grinstead and Tenterden, Kent. Later news was that East Grinstead's loss will be replaced by a 450-seater, but at the time of writing, prospects for Tenterden are bleak, despite the fact that one in six of its population visits the cinema each week and, in the words of a member of the local council, "the town would suffer terribly if the cinema were closed – you will be able to fire a cannon-ball up the High Street at six o'clock and not hit anybody".

And so, unhappily, it goes on. Tenterden, it may be said, is a small town (5,620), but a survey undertaken in March, 1960 by *Today's Cinema* revealed that there were at least 46 areas in Britain, with a total population of

2½ million people, which had no permanent cinema at all. Districts range from Stoke and Burslem (267,000), Amersham (76,000), Aldridge-Brownhills, Staffs. (83,00), to Rickmansworth (30,000) and Cumbernauld (26,000). That a "planned" town like Stevenage (57,000) should have no local cinema is incredible. As the paper comments, the reason for the fact that more than half the population never visited a cinema at all during the past year may well be simply the lack of a cinema to visit.

On the brighter side, new or refurbished cinemas during the same period of 1969 amounted to 60, leaving a net reduction of 21. Figures for 1968 were 110 closures, 42 new or reopened buildings, a net reduction of 68.

As will be seen from the following selective chronological account, the trend is still towards multiple cinemas under a common roof. Twins and triplets predominate, but from America comes news of a six-in-one at Omaha, others to follow, and even a project for a twelve-in-one in Cincinnati, four halls on each of three levels, planned by American Multicinemas, Ltd.

February was Birkenhead's month, the Plaza reverting from bingo to films (with *The Graduate*) and the former Empire undergoing a transformation by Essoldo into a comfortable 500-seater. In Edinburgh the ABC Ritz reopened with a luxury-lounge – the sixth ABC cinema to adopt this pleasant arrangement.

In March, twin Odeons were opened by Rank in Liverpool, with *Oliver!* and *Chitty Chitty Bang Bang*. The seating capacity is 983 and 1,405 respectively, indicating that multiples do not necessarily imply midgets. An innovation, followed in

52

The new Odeon "Twins" opened in the May of 1959: this is the interior of Odeon L, the upper cinema seating 980 people.

And the ABC which goes beyond "Twinning" – the Triple ABC at Edinburgh

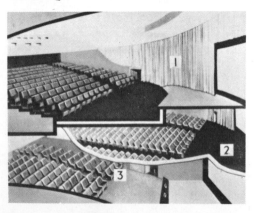

later Rank buildings, is the inclusion of a limited number of super-luxury Pullman armchairs (66 in this instance) wherein the patron may recline in V.I.P. ease on payment of £1. The Liverpool Odeon has since been given the Quigley Award for cinema design – an award won in 1968 by another Odeon, St. Martin's Lane, London.

April saw the opening of Cinecenta twins at Bradford: one a public cinema (seating 238) the other a Penthouse Club for members only (157). The projection system is periscoped through a series of mirrors, a method likely to be increasingly adopted, designed by Dr. Leslie Knopp. In Scotland, the Parade, Dennistoun, Glasgow, returned triumphantly to its rightful use after 7 years as a bingo club, and the Pavilion in Barrhead was completely rebuilt and given new life as the George. "There is a new and vital interest in the cinema," said the owner, George Palmer of G. P. Cinemas. Final April glory – it was stated in Parliament that a cinema was to be built in the Tower of London – a treat for traitors, or a bijou for beefeaters?

May saw another Odeon twin, at Leeds, complete with 28 £1 Pullman seats. Capacities are 980 and 1,290.

The Essoldo, Shepherd's Bush, London, was reopened in June after an extensive £40,000 modernisation, set back by a disastrous fire just before the originally planned completion in August 1968. Once the Shepherd's Bush Pavilion, the handsome building was for years the largest of three entertainment houses lining one side of the Green. Another "new look" Essoldo opened at Huddersfield in August, when the company stated that it was re-styling cinemas at the rate of one every 6½ weeks. Also in June, the 33-year-old

Classic, Erith, reopened after 5 weeks' work (and £20,000 cash) on the provision of a modern appearance and standard of comfort. Two more sets of twins joined the swelling Rank family in July – Gaumonts at Bournemouth and Sheffield – and another, Odeons, at Bradford the following month, the fifth pair of the year. One of the latter is the smallest theatre in the Rank group, seating 450. The company also reopened their Leicester Market Place Odeon as a cinerama theatre.

August saw the inauguration of Scotland's first twin film/bingo combination at Clydebank, on the site of the former La Scala, ABC running a 776-seater cinema on the upper level, and the Star group a bingo hall down below. This could be an example of putting the devil's money to good purpose which might be more widely adopted. The opening film was *Ring of Bright Water*. In the same month the charming little Camelot, Newquay, opened (with *Oliver!*) as an 810 luxury house on the site of the old Pavilion, destroyed by fire twelve months previously. Cinecenta launched a 3-cinema complex in Leicester in September, two houses open to the general public (280 and 198), and a Penthouse Club (136) for members only. Periscope projection is used, an intricate system of mirrors reducing the size of the image to fit the small Cinecenta screens ranging from 19' 6" × 8' 3" to 14' 3" × 6'. On November 13, the former Regal Cinema, Glasgow (now ABC 1), celebrated its 40th anniversary – a link with the opening night being provided by the presence of Miss Ruby Milne – now house manager of ABC 1 – who took the money at the cash box on that historic occasion, in 1929, and has worked at the cinema throughout the entire period.

Prices then: 1s., 1s. 6d. and (circle) 2s.; today, 6s., 7s. and (circle) 8s. The site was formerly occupied by Hengler's Circus, where moving pictures were shown before the First World War. Opening film at the Regal was *The Singing Fool*, followed by *The Broadway Melody*: the biggest "packer-in" was Chaplin's *City Lights*, 39,000 admissions in one week in 1931. The building is now part of the ABC Glasgow Entertainments Centre, which also includes ABC 2 operating as a Road Show. The only major alterations from the original theatre are in the proscenium arch and the front-of-house canopy. Seating capacity has been reduced from 2,359 to 2,059.

Towards the end of the year ABC opened a triple complex in Edinburgh; Essoldo a renovated luxury house at Gerrard's Cross (392 seats all at 10s.); and the Star group, bringing 1969 to an end with a flourish, the first London suburban twin (on the site of the Rex, Lewisham) and new houses at Ripley, Derbyshire, and Thirsk, Yorks. In January 1970 the Paisley Kelburne (Caledonian Associated Cinemas) reopened after extensive modernisation, the second cinema in western Scotland (outside Glasgow) to boast a 70 mm installation: the other being the Cinema, East Kilbride, also run by Caledonian Associated Cinemas. During the period in review the Gala Cinema group largely refurbished their London show places – the two old-timers Berkeley and Continentale in Tottenham Court Road, and the Gala Royal near Marble Arch.

The British Film Institute regional theatres reached a total of 33 with the opening, in January, 1970, of that at Reading. The theatre is a 350-seater in the Palmer Building of the University: opening film, the British première of Mai Zetterling's *The Girls*. Others launched during the period were at Brighton (full time), at Leatherhead (regular Monday showings at the Thorndike) and at the little town of Corsham, Wiltshire (population 9,300). This enterprising venture is due to the enthusiasm of a local man, Norman Jefferies, who rebuilt and re-equipped the former Regal as a modern cinema. Financial assistance is provided by the local council, and the B.F.I. has given a guarantee against loss. It is an example one would happily see followed in many other districts. Some of the film performances will be connected with the Bath Festival. Opening film was *Elvira Madigan*, and the inauguration ceremony was performed by Sir Michael Tippett. Work is well under way on the National Film Theatre's smaller sister on the South Bank, which should be flourishing well before this review appears. Seating will be for 165, and the hall will be used mainly for very specialised material, of limited appeal, and with the accent on education, though regular feature films will also be shown. Projection facilities will be even more elaborate than in the larger theatre, and will include provision for four-way language translations. Meanwhile, as part of the scheme, a new approach and entrance hall has opened for the present N.F.T. One may, perhaps, be permitted a passing regret for the bright, bustling, friendly old entrance (a regret doubtless unshared by those responsible for manipulating the milling multitudes on crowded occasions), but the new arrangement, though dimmer and of a more formal dignity, undoubtedly affords more room and better opportunities for displays. The old

bar is to be turned into a further display hall, and much roomier and wider-ranging catering facilities are planned to serve the two theatres jointly.

Major future plans for London include the "twinning" of the Carlton, Haymarket, and the Warner in Leicester Square. The Carlton is one of the few major houses remaining which were originally built to the old live-theatre format. It opened, in fact, with a musical comedy, *Lady Luck*, in 1927, turning to films the following year with William Wellman's air epic *Wings*, starring Clara Bow and featuring Gary Cooper. The Carlton at present seats 1,157, and a change to the more modern style is obviously due. One may, however, regret the passing of the handsome and comfortable Warner in its present form.

In the first of these surveys, two years ago, I mentioned the possibility that the Cameo-Poly, formerly the Polytechnic Hall, where the first commercial film in London was given by Lumière in 1896, would be closed to accommodate the growing number of Polytechnic students. Last year, happily, I was able to announce a reprieve. Now, once again, closure seems a definite possibility – probably during the coming summer. It is tragic that a building of such historic importance in film history should be lost to the cinema.

JUNIOR CINEMA

A quarter of a century ago last year, the first film to be made especially for children was produced by J. Arthur Rank. From this modest beginning there developed an organisation unique in the world, devoted entirely to such productions – the Children's Film Foundation.

Special programmes for children were not, of course, new. As long ago as 1927 Granada Theatres set up regular weekly shows for young film-goers. These, however, were made up of films which, though suitable for all ages, were originally produced for general distribution, aimed primarily at all-the-family audiences. A picture made *primarily* for children was a rarity.

A disturbing side-effect of the Second World War was the growing delinquency and truancy among children whose parents were absent, and whose lives had perhaps been disrupted by evacuation – by being removed from their homes and set down in strange and sometimes unwelcoming surroundings. The cinema could prove both a link with their old and familiar ways of life, and a meeting-place for enjoyment and letting off steam by participating in vicarious thrills, rather than wandering aimlessly and in the end destructively through the streets. But the number of films which pleased both adults and children was limited. Most were too long, too full of static dialogue, dealing with emotional situations too complex and outside their experience, for children to share. The Rank Organisation therefore decided to provide them with films of their very own. The Children's Entertainment Films Division was founded under the direction of the late Mary Field, O.B.E., M.A., and in 1944 produced an unpretentious picture which combined amusement, entertainment, thrills and – as might be expected – a well-concealed moral: the leading characters were children, and the film's title was *Tom's Ride*.

For seven years the Division continued to produce such films, many of them very successful: but though the demand continued to grow, it became clear that one company could not be expected to shoulder an obviously uneconomical burden on its own. In 1951, therefore, the British film industry as a whole most commendably combined to take on the responsibility, and set up the Children's Film Foundation, on a non-profit-making basis, to ensure that the supply of suitable films should be maintained. Since that year the C.F.F. has received grants totalling £2½ million from the industry, the whole of which has been applied to the production of pictures especially for children. The directors are nominated by the trade associations of the industry, and consist of leading representatives of production, distribution and exhibition, all serving without remuneration. The whole organisation is an achievement of which the British cinema industry can well be proud.

At present there are roughly 800 cinemas in the United Kingdom running special matinees, catering for nearly half a million children each week, and the task of providing suitable material is both a formidable and (bearing in mind the all-pervasive influence of the medium) a responsible one. Films come from various sources now, but the chief provider is still the C.F.F. About six feature films a year are produced by the Foundation, in addition to one or more serials and series of six to ten episodes each. Distribution in the U.K. is by the C.F.F. for 35 mm and Rank Film Library for 16 mm. There is also a wide international demand: C.F.F. productions are to be seen in over thirty countries, including Russia, Czechoslovakia and East Germany. Foreign distribution is handled (for both 35 mm and 16 mm) by the Rank Organisation Overseas Division.

Four rough and elementary guide lines are followed by the makers: plenty of action, no romance, a minimum of dialogue, and children as the central characters. Within these elastic limits the range is wide. The aim expressed by the Foundation is "to keep standards high and encourage a discriminating appreciation of the cinema". The extent of their success in this direction may be measured by the fact that their films have won more than forty major awards at International Film Festivals, particularly at Venice.

The main object, however, is "to provide good entertainment". The children's cinema matinees would never accept anything else, for the audience are lively youngsters with a keen critical appreciation and their reaction to a milk-and-water story would be loud, emphatic, and far from complimentary!

"Basically they are films of action. Action often calls for conflict, but this conflict is usually the rivalry between groups of children. Violence is avoided, but if any form of violence is essential to the telling of an exciting story, it is always kept within bounds so that it will not be disturbing to the more sensitive members of the young audience. Animals, naturally, are very popular with children and have been the "stars" of many films . . . new scenes and new places also have great appeal . . .

56 historical adventures are usually winners and the current 'space' trend is not neglected." Suitable foreign films are included when available, and are dubbed into English. It is unfortunate that this practice must be resorted to : even in a children's film, a character is lost if his voice is taken over by someone speaking in a different language. Both sub-titling and overlaid commentary have been tried by the Foundation, however, both failed to gain acceptance by the young audience and have had to be abandoned. A magazine series, which dealt with subjects ranging from square-dancing to money-boxes, from tennis tips to making bagpipes, has now been discontinued because of the availability of television programmes of a similar nature which have the advantage of keeping more up-to-date with their subjects.

An average Saturday morning programme lasts about two hours and usually consists of a cartoon, a short, a serial episode, a comedy or travelogue and the feature film – the latter usually running just under one hour. Exhibitors often sponsor competitions or stage shows which the children themselves help to organise. The audience (approximate age range 7–12) is frequently consulted by surveys and opinion polls. Much, but not all, of the information gleaned is fairly predictable. "Comedy remains the most popular ingredient, being voted equally enjoyable by children of both sexes and all ages. Children like their films to consist of a series of vivid incidents with as much excitement as possible. The major roles should be taken by characters with whom the children can identify themselves, or that children would like to know and be with in real life." But they like to see the familiar characters in unfamiliar settings. Nine out of ten C.F.F. audiences live in towns but prefer films set in the countrysides of Scotland, Wales or foreign parts. The failing most certain to cause criticism is lack of action. Adult characters are only tolerated if they are really "characters", i.e. well-defined types, or superhuman such as Hercules or Captain Marvel. Another point is that the shock technique so fashionable at present does not go down well with a young audience, which appreciates rather the slow build-up. "If the parents in a film depart on urgent business admonishing 'Now don't get into trouble', the audiences settle down with relish to enjoy the chaos they know must come." And where adult dialogue is necessary " it is best to have a listening child present, otherwise attention wanders." Childhood memory being short and powers of concentration erratic, a character in a film must not disappear for a long time : if he does, the audience will forget him, and treat him on his reappearance as a newcomer to to the plot.

An obvious point of concern is the question of moral tone. Rightly, the C.F.F. realises that children will not stand being preached to, and this has never been its intention. Equally rightly, however, it endeavours to encourage tolerance, a sense of responsibility, a feeling for fair play. The sense of justice in young people is strong, and they want to see the villain get his due deserts, in a way they can understand, but also if possible with a touch of humour. "By all means take the villain to prison, but make sure he falls into a puddle on the way!" On the other hand, a most interesting survey among seventy-five London schoolchildren aged between seven and twelve showed that, while they had no difficulty in distinguishing between the "goodies" and the "baddies" in real life, in their choice of screen characters the villains came out easily on top, in terms of popularity. "Some of the reasons for this . . . may appear to be obvious. There is, for example, especially among the boys, the appeal of bravery and masculine daring, and also of a rejection of authority. But research has shown that children also recognise and accept the basic premises of conventional morality when these are illustrated on the screen. . . . Indeed, it would be completely unacceptable to a children's audience for a 'baddie' to go unpunished. Part of the answer may lie in the fact that young children secretly fear the villains. While they enjoy this sensation from the safety of a cinema seat, they also derive satisfaction from seeing the source of their fear overcome in the last reel."

The development through the years of a more subtle recognition of the complex intermingling of "right" and "wrong" in human behaviour was demonstrated in a special questionnaire held in connection with the film chosen to mark the C.F.F.'s 25th anniversary. The film, entitled *Lionheart*, concerns a lion that escapes from a circus and causes general alarm in the neighbourhood. The Army is called out to shoot it, but a boy called Andrew and his friends hide the animal in a stable, eventually saving its life and receiving congratulations on their courage when the lion is once more safely in its cage. The children were asked how they felt about this situation. Predictably, the great majority "like Andrew best", and an even higher proportion actively disliked the soldiers. Even so, many felt that Andrew was wrong, and that the soldiers were right to try to kill the lion. And this, as the C.F.F. comments, "in a situation where total solidarity with Andrew, a little boy who stood out alone against the big adult world, might have been expected. This reaction may reflect children's recognition of the need for law and order, even at the expense of their natural sympathies. This would appear to be borne out by the fact that this tendency was far more marked among the older children in the sample. The findings may also instance the growing sophistication of children's approach to the 'goodies' and 'baddies' of the screen. For children today, the 'goodies' are perhaps no longer infallible, and the 'baddies' no longer wholly and irretrievably bad."

Economically the C.F.F. has one advantage over other production companies in that their films have a longer working life than the majority of adult movies. As each generation of children grows up another takes its place, and the same film can be repeated three to four years later to an entirely fresh young audience. They are not so liable to become dated by changes of fashion, and their themes – being perennial ones – are not so tied to contemporary events or transitory topics. On the other hand, film techniques have altered considerably during eighteen years and, particularly since the all-embracing advent of television, children are accustomed to, and expect a more sophisticated and advanced approach than was the case with the first films, with their appeal of sheer novelty. On their more modest scale, as much care, ingenuity and skill goes into their making as into any commercial production. Period stories are carefully researched.

Locations have ranged from Cornwall, the Lake District and other parts of the United Kingdom, to Malta, Libya, East Africa, Australia, Morocco, Tunisia and Gibraltar. A quick glance through the titles indicates the wide variety of feature subjects: *The Piper's Tune* (refugees from the Napoleonic Wars), *Blow Your Own Trumpet* (brass band conflicts), *Bungala Boys* (Australian surf life-saving), *Calamity the Cow* (children's strange pet), *Countdown to Danger* (trapped with a time bomb), *Runaway Engine* (children renovate an old railway engine), *Wings of Mystery* (pigeons and secret alloys), *The Salvage Gang* (comedy of an old bedstead) and *Supersonic Saucer* (a Venusian at school). Three of the most popular titles in the list have been *Lionheart,* referred to above (directed by Michael Forlong), *All At Sea*, a sea cruise adventure (directed by Kenneth Fairbairn) and *On the Run*, directed by Pat Jackson. This last film concerns the attempted kidnapping in this country of the son of a visiting African potentate. The boy, helped by two young white friends, escapes and eventually reaches safety. The film demonstrated that differences in colour count for nothing when it comes to people working together in moments of danger or anxiety. In fact, it went further in showing the irrelevance of such boundaries for, as Henry Geddes, executive producer of the C.F.F. remarks, "the interesting thing is that the villain, the boy's uncle, is black too". Among the credit lists of C.F.F. productions are to be found such well-known names as: (players) Jon Pertwee, Gordon Jackson, Terry Scott, Jimmy Edwards, Judy Geeson, Warren Mitchell, Peter Butterworth, Michael Crawford and Maurice Denham: (directors)

Pat Jackson, Charles Frend, Don Sharp, John Krish, Muriel Box, Don Chaffey and Gerald Thomas: (musicians) Anthony Hopkins, Philip Martell, Tristram Carey, Eric Rogers and Muir Mathieson. Leading technicians in all aspects of film making frequently work for the Foundation, invariably for fees considerably below normal commercial rates.

The guiding rule of the C.F.F. is that no film should ever play down to its audience: no film for children should ever be unacceptable to adults. With this in mind, the Foundation no longer thinks of its productions as "children's films", but rather as "junior features".

And the future? "It would appear that priority will be for features or series of short comedies which can be booked either as individual shorts or in lieu of a serial; but the C.F.F. does not intend to lose sight of the fact that it is part of the entertainment business and that the only constant feature in entertainment is change. . . . Its films will always be made first and foremost to entertain. To engage children's attention, to arouse their sympathies, to capture their imagination, to fascinate and delight – that remains the purpose of everyone who works on a C.F.F. production." The extent of the Foundation's continuing success may be measured by the fact that, despite the fall in the total number of cinemas in the country, on January 1, 1970 thirteen more houses were running children's matinees than was the case a year previously.

Note: The quotations in the above survey are from the C.F.F. booklet and catalogue: *Saturday Morning Cinema.*

RELEASES OF THE YEAR IN PICTURES

(You will find more detailed information about the films illustrated in a later section of this volume—The Year's Releases in detail)

You really didn't have to be a child to enjoy Albert R. Broccoli's lavish screen adaptation of the late Ian Fleming's fairy tale, *Chitty Chitty Bang Bang*, with one of its central characters the car of the title, a fabulous, gleaming monster capable of taking to the air – or sea – in emergencies. Among the humans involved, Professor Dick Van Dyke and Sally Ann Howes (shown "disguised" as puppets) and Gert Fröbe (left, as the bad old Baron).

This has been quite a vintage year for Westerns, with plenty on show, among which there have been quite outstanding examples of the genre. Towards, if not actually right at the top must come Henry Hathaway's movie for Paramount of *True Grit* in which John Wayne gave one of the performances of his lifetime as the one-eyed, whisky-swilling, rough and callous lawman who is persuaded by a very determined young girl to go searching the wilderness for her father's killer. (Incidentally, the girl, newcomer Kim Darby made a most promising début.)

John Wayne also starred in *The Undefeated*, Fox's Western (based on historical fact), about a few of the various groups of characters who at the end of the American Civil War drifted towards Mexico rather than stay in what to them was conquered territory. Also in the film, Rock Hudson – shown dealing with a carpetbagger who has offered him a ridiculous amount of money for his plantation.

62

Another favourite Westerner, Gregory
Peck, starred in Carl Foreman's Columbia
film *Mackenna's Gold*, in which he played
a man with a map (of a golden fortune)
in his mind, who is "persuaded" by bandit
Omar Sharif to lead an expedition to the
canyon where the treasure is supposed to
lie buried.

In Universal–Rank's *Death of a Gunfighter*,
Richard Widmark starred as the old-style
marshal of a small Western town who won't
admit to progress, and won't quit his job
when asked, and in the end is shot down
by the community he has served so well –
just because they can't find any other
way of removing him!

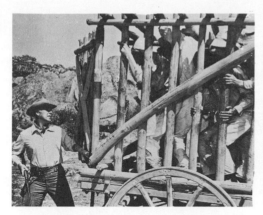

That knight-errant Western septet were back on the screen for the third time (even if played by different actors now) in U.A.'s *Guns of the Magnificent Seven*. This time it was George Kennedy (shown) and James Whitmore who were among those defending the poor and the down-trodden – some of them paying with their lives for interest.

More thoughtful than many of its kind, Paramount's modest Western, *Buckskin*, was about a frontiersman who accepts the job of town Marshal and then proceeds to weed out the local bad elements, a sometimes dangerous – and even deadly – job!

Telly Savalas (left) was the big bad boss in Columbia's *Land Raiders*, lording it over the small town that he calls his realm and from there trying for his own selfish ends to force the redskins off their territory, fighting them – and his more reasonably-minded young brother – to the death, in attempting to achieve his aim.

There was a nice vein of comedy running through Warner–Pathé's *The Good Guys and the Bad Guys*, starring George Kennedy and Robert Mitchum (right) in a story about a very conscientious town marshal (the latter) who even when he is sacked carries on the job of bringing in the bad men, a task in which he is – amusingly – assisted by his former enemy.

The Europeans generally, and the Italians in particular, continued to offer a pretty steady stream of Westerns, one of the best of which was *Once Upon a Time . . . In the West*, a leisurely, superior, relating of a brutal, violent struggle for a parcel of land across which the railroad is planned to be built. Henry Fonda (inset) played the ruthless villain, tracked doggedly down by a mysterious stranger (Charles Bronson) who, in the scene illustrated, comes to the aid of the lovely widow-victim (Claudia Cardinale).

Paramount's *Revenge in El Paso* was another made-in-Italy Western – more amusing and less violent than some – about three bad characters who are all jointly or separately seeking a "thefted" golden fortune.

Another Robert Aldrich thriller in the "Baby Jane" series was C.I.R.O.'s *Whatever Happened to Aunt Alice?* which was highlighted by a duel of wits between Geraldine Page, as the woman who buries the bodies at the bottom of the garden, and Ruth Gordon, who suspects her of doing it. Illustrated: unconscious, likely next victim Rosemary Forsyth.

Stella Stevens and Shelley Winters in the Columbia murder thriller *The Mad Room*, in which Miss Stevens played the paid companion of a woman brutally murdered – and becomes one of the main suspects of the crime.

Rock Hudson and Claudia Cardinale as the somewhat unlikely team of crooks in Warner–Pathé's *A Fine Pair*; he, being a New York cop who is conned into helping her to pinch a jewelled fortune in Austria.

Boris Karloff, King of the monster-makers, in Paramount's thriller *Targets*, notable largely for the fact that it was the last role that Karloff played prior to his death last year.

Carol White and Scott Hylands, victim and victimiser in Mark Robson's thriller for Warner's, *Daddy's Gone A-Hunting*, which concerned a young wife pursued by her revengeful, nut-case ex-lover, who's determined to kill her because she has aborted his child.

Roger Moore shows there's more than one way of dealing with a pointed gun, or a woman (Martha Hyer), in U.A.'s *Crossplot*, a thriller about a plan to assassinate the President of a foreign country . . .

Raymond Chandler's famous Private Eye,
Philip Marlowe, was back on the screen in
M-G-M's fast, furious (and commendable)
detection thriller called, aptly enough,
Marlowe. On this occasion his search for an
attractive lady's vanished brother leads him
into a dirty mess of murder, dope and
blackmail.

Frustrated British Secret Service man Fred
Astaire, his American pen-friend Richard
Crenna and girl-friend Anne Heywood –
the trio involved is the former's "foolproof"
plan to steal fifteen million dollars'-worth of
gold in C.I.R.O.'s *A Run on Gold*.

Gregory Peck – *The Most Dangerous Man in the World* in the Fox thriller of that title. And he's that because on his secret mission into Red China to find out and bring back the details of a newly-discovered enzyme, he carries a transmitter – and miniature atomic bomb – in his head!

Professional killer James Coburn finds his Achilles' heel in Lee Remick, whom he meets in Spain while on one of his murderous missions, and who penetrates his hard-shell defences, with explosive result.
And it all happens in Fox's *Hard Contract*.

The Disney Studios' contribution to the the year's thriller list was *Guns in the Heather* which, set in Ireland, was about an American plot to smuggle out of the country a defecting Iron-Curtain scientist. Among those involved, Glenn Corbett (right).

70

Paramount's *The Italian Job* was a jokey little thriller about a cockney crook (Michael Caine) who takes over the operation of a large-scale robbery of Chinese gold which had been planned by his Italian pal but dropped when the latter is bumped off by the Mafia, the latter taking a very dim view of Britishers stepping into their particular area of crime.

The fantastic city beneath the sea which is home to the "Nautilus's" owner in M-G-M's *Captain Nemo and the Underwater City*, which was a (sort-of!) sequel to the famous Jules Verne story about that submarine – the previously filmed "20,000 Leagues Under the Sea".

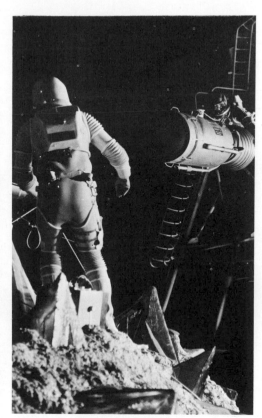

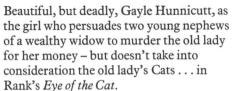

Beautiful, but deadly, Gayle Hunnicutt, as the girl who persuades two young nephews of a wealthy widow to murder the old lady for her money – but doesn't take into consideration the old lady's Cats . . . in Rank's *Eye of the Cat*.

Hammer's *Moon Zero Two* was a topical science-fiction thriller set in a decade or so in the future, when there's a kind of spaceship shuttle service between the Earth and Moon, and James Olson as a veteran astronaut becomes involved in all sorts of stellar skulduggery in his search for a vanished moon-miner!

An unusual kind of duel between man and antediluvian animals in Warner–Pathé's fantasy *The Valley of Gwangi*, about the discovery of yet another "Lost World".

David Warner played the rather glum hero of the title in Columbia's *Michael Kohlhaas*, a story of 16th-century rebellion in Germany. With him (he's on the left), Anita Pallenberg.

Tommy Steele (with Fiona Lewis?) as the – very considerably whitewashed – young varlet Jack Sheppard in Paramount's *Where's Jack?* which emerged as a largely fictional biography of the highwayman brought to the gallows by crooked crook-catcher Jonathan Wild.

James Mason and Ava Gardner as Emperor and Empress of the Austrian Empire in Warner-Pathé's sad tale from Hapsburg history: *Mayerling*, the tragedy of the double suicide at his shooting lodge of the Archduke Rudolf and his pretty little mistress, Maria Vetsera.

David Hemmings as the young king *Alfred The Great* in Clive Donner's slam-bang cinematic version of a chapter of early British history.

Dany Robin and George Sanders share a highly decorative bed in M-G-M's presentation of the Carlo Ponti comedy *The Best House in London* – which was about the one-day-and-night existence in London of a lush, Paris-style brothel.

Miss Brodie shows some of her favourite "gels" around Edinburgh and teaches them how to face up to life in Fox's delightful screen adaptation of the play, which in turn was an adaptation of the Muriel Spark novel *The Prime of Miss Jean Brodie*: about a dedicated schoolmistress whose egotism is suddenly pricked by one of her own pupils and finds herself without a job and past her "Prime". Wonderful performance by Maggie Smith as Miss Brodie and an outstanding one by Pamela Franklin (on her direct right) as a precocious pupil.

Emma Hamilton had never previously been so prettily, certainly nakedly revealed on or off the screen, than lovely luscious Michèle Mercier presented her in the – sometimes intentionally – amusing film about her, directed by Christian-Jaque. Richard Johnson played Lord Nelson.

Ben Gazzara and George Segal as two of the Americans in the struggle to gain control of *The Bridge At Remagen*, in the U.A. film of that title, which covered the Allied capture of this key point during the final Allied advance during the Second World War.

The best, most original war film of the year, and most other years, was Richard Attenborough's stylish, imaginative musical, *Oh ! What a Lovely War* which, an adaptation of the stage show of the same title, presented a moving, disturbing picture of the First World War (and, indeed, all wars) through a succession of the 1914–18 "Tommy" songs. And marked a triumphant directorial début by actor-producer Attenborough. In this scene John Mills as (Field Marshal Sir Douglas Haig), enjoys a moment of dubious triumph. Inset: Ralph Richardson, Kenneth More, Frank Forsyth, Ian Holm and John Gabriel.

Hywel Bennett (foreground) as one of *The Virgin Soldiers* in Carl Foreman's Columbia film which amusingly described the adventures of a group of young and innocent National Service soldiers during their training in Singapore in 1950.

Rod Steiger, as the be-medalled Second World War veteran in Warner's *The Sergeant*, starts to knock into shape the lax-disciplined company of American soldiers in France in the winter of 1952, and there becomes revealed as a latent homosexual as his friendship for one of the men, John Phillip Law (near to camera), grows more and more demanding.

Rod Steiger played the title role in the bizarre little Warner–Pathé fantasy *The Illustrated Man*. His whole body has been lavishly tattooed, with the exception of one small part, and if anyone looks at that too long they find themselves in the future!

Among the films aimed directly at the younger movie-goers, and very firmly anchored in today's permissive period, was American International's *Three in the Attic*, a story of three girls who, finding they are all girl-friend dupes of the same smart philandering male – Christopher Jones – get together and decide to teach him a lesson by imprisoning him in an attic where they take it in turns to love him to – if not death, at least to exhausted desperation! One of the trio of temptresses was played by Yvette Mimieux.

Having had to wait a long time for it, M-G-M's *Mrs. Brown, You've got a Lovely Daughter* won a general release last August. Made largely to exploit the charm and talent of Herman (of the Hermits Pop Group fame), this is a story about a greyhound which wins races, is lost, turns up again – by which time our hero has learnt a little more about life (one hopes!).

Something along similar lines was the story of the not over-successful Fox film *The Touchables*, which was a gimmicky sort of treatment of a story about four girls (one of them the delectable Judy Huxtable shown here with equine friend) who capture a pop-singing idol – played by David Anthony – and take him to their "Pleasure Dome" for their pleasure!

Where It's At was a U.A. film about a father and son relationship seen against a Las Vegas background, where "Pa" David Janssen runs a gambling house and his idealistic son finds dad's mistress attracting him too much for his peace of mind. Shown, son and mistress: Robert Drivas and Rosemary Forsyth.

Less charming, more doggedly with-it, was Avco Embassy's *A Nice Girl Like Me*, about a young lady called Candida, played by Barbara Ferris, whose several lovers leave their mark on her, so to speak, but is finally persuaded to let Harry Andrews take legal care of her and her brood.

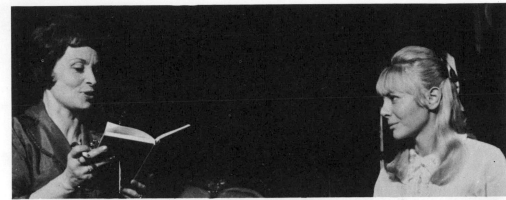

Mirisch-U.A.'s titillatingly titled *You Don't Need Pajamas at Rosie's* was another film about growing up – in this case three American sixteen-year-olds whose boyish search for sexual experience, if never touching, was at least amusing. Jacqueline Bisset played the girl who – quite sweetly – teaches Wes Stern, playing the leading boy, a thing or two.

Opposite page
One of the warmest and easily the best of the year's teenager comedies was Warner–Pathé's *Me, Natalie*, in which newcomer Patty Duke gave a delightful performance as the Jewish girl growing to maturity in the Bronx and in Greenwich Village and having to fight her conventional family to achieve it.

True to the Walt Disney "family film" tradition, sex didn't rear its head in the charming *Rascal*, which in superb colour and with endless charm told the story of a glorious summer in the life of a young man – Steve Forrest – which he spends with his dog and a pet racoon (the creature which gives the film its title) in the woods of Wisconsin.

Another film in which animals played a large – and winning – role, was Rank's *Ring of Bright Water*, an adaptation of the Gavin Maxwell book about pet otters. Bill Travers played the man who finds that with all their charm, the animals have certain drawbacks, including coming in from their icy pond and snuggling under the bed-clothes with him.

Again it was an animal, a pony in this case, which played an important part in the motivation of Irving Allen's *Run Wild, Run Free*, which, set against and photographed in the wild Dartmoor country, told a story about the friendship between a horse and a boy which, in the stress of the rescue of the beast from a swamp-trap, restores to the boy his lost speech. Mark Lester played the boy, John Mills and Fiona Fullerton his friends.

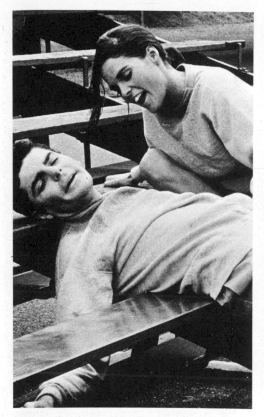

As in "Me, Natalie", the background to Paramount's *Goodbye, Columbus,* was a warmly observed and incidentally amusing one of Jewish-American family life, against which was told the quietly and richly amusing story of boy-meets-girl, boy-sleeps-with-girl – and then shies away when he realises just what he is getting himself into! Richard Benjamin and Ali MacGraw charmingly played the youngsters.

The Jewish Family provided more material for humour, though somewhat black-spotted in this case, in Warner–Pathé's *I Love You, Alice B. Toklas,* in which Peter Sellers played a Los Angeles lawyer lured away from his wife-to-be, and conformity, into a wild life with the hippies by a prettier example of their kind – delightful newcomer Leigh Taylor-Young.

Christopher Robin presides over a tea party for his animal friends, including, at the opposite end, that great A. A. Milne creation Winnie the Pooh–a scene from the second of the Walt Disney long–short cartoon movies based on the author's famous books – *Winnie the Pooh and the Blustery Day*.

The Love Bug in the Walt Disney film of that title was a car, a German Volkswagen, with a mind very much of its own, helping its young owner – Dean Jones – to win the victories in the races he has previously never been able to gain, and so win, too, the pretty hand of his girl-friend Michele Lee.

The Gerald Thomas'–Peter Rogers' "Carry On" series carried on all sorts of box-office records, emerging, in fact, as some of the greatest British money spinners of the year. With the usual double-meanings, *Carry On Camping* was a pretty good example of the broad British fun purveyed – of which this scene by Barbara Windsor, whose physical jerks have had an unexpected (?) result, is typical.

Playing the dastardly villain, determined to win by fair means or, preferably, foul, rally competitor Terry-Thomas, with his assistant Eric Sykes, plans a further example of skullduggery in the Paramount comedy *Monte Carlo or Bust*, relating the – wholly fictional – events of a Monte Carlo Rally of the 20s.

Featured in last year's "Film Review" as one of "The Neglected Ones", Paramount's *Diamonds for Breakfast* was at long last given a general release in December, 1969. A light and loosely constructed comedy, it presented Marcello Mastroianni as an ex-Russian Grand Duke, now a Hampstead boutique owner, who embarks on a plan to recapture the Crown Jewels of the Czars.

Julie Andrews (in Noël Coward's "Parisien Pierrot" number) in *Star!*, the large-scale Fox musical about the life and career of that bright British theatrical star Gertrude Lawrence, which in spite of its subject, and its cast, and its music, failed to repeat the tremendous success of the previous Fox musical spectacular with Julie, "The Sound of Music".

The daddy of all the pop singers, Elvis Presley, surviving all the changes of fashion in style and music, continues to turn out a steady stream of successful musicals, one of them being last year's M-G-M film *The Trouble With Girls*, in which his co-star was Marlyn Mason.

If the actual story of M-G-M's *The Gypsy Moths* was familiar enough, about small-town boredom and the break in routine brought about by the advent of a group of dare-devil sky-divers, it was made unique by the magnificent, spectacular air sequences in which Burt Lancaster and his men dance in the sky as they plunge to earth at 100 m.p.h.

As spectacular beneath the earth as "The Gypsy Moths" was above it, M-G-M's *Ice Station Zebra* was a rattling good thriller-spectacular about a race to the North Pole between an American submarine and Soviet airplanes, both seeking a canister, the contents of which could completely change the world balance of power. In charge of the sub. – Rock Hudson.

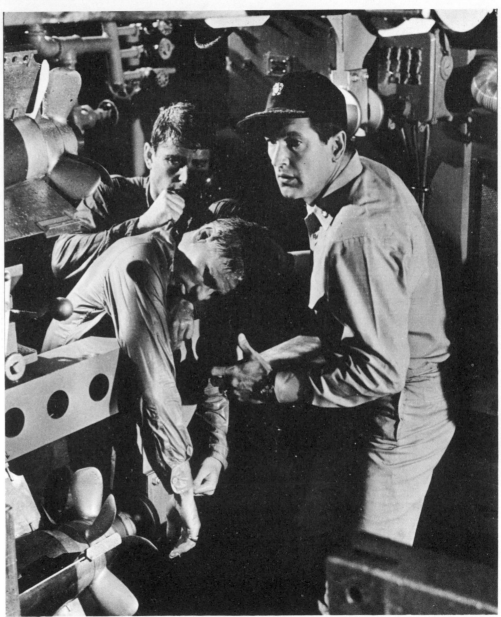

Fox's *Che!* was the first of a number of films planned about the late Cuban revolutionary. In this case Omar Sharif took the title role, with Jack Palance as an equally unlikely Fidel Castro.

90 Fox's *Justine* was a gallant but hardly successful attempt to condense Lawrence Durrell's vast Alexandria Quartet of novels into a single film. Here British diplomat Dirk Bogarde – who came out of the venture with considerable credit – introduces his blind sister (Elaine Church) to "Justine" (Anouk Aimée) and the young British poet (Michael York).

If Michael Powell and James Mason's co-production *Age of Consent* did not meet with exactly universal approval, it certainly saw the critics united in their appreciation of Mason's own performance and that of new star Helen Mirren, playing the girl who models for the artist (Mason) and eventually gives him a new interest in life. Background was Australia's Great Barrier Reef.

Marcello Mastroianni and Faye Dunaway in M-G-M's *A Place for Lovers*, a cinematic "weepie" in the old tradition about a woman's last love affair, a romantic interlude prior to her return to America and inevitable death.

Husband Rod Steiger, and Judy Geeson, the latter as the little tramp he picks up and who deliberately ruins his marriage, discuss the best way to tell the wife (played by Claire Bloom) that they intend to go off together – in Universal's convincingly thorough examination of a failing marriage, *Three Into Two Won't Go*.

Made in Italy, with English dialogue, Cinecenta's *She and He* was Laurence Harvey's contribution to the sex cycle, with its story about a woman (Sylva Koscina) and her lover (that's Harvey) and their love-hate relationship.

Another movie which might be labelled – perhaps just a bit unfairly – as a "Woman's Picture" was British Lion's *A Touch of Love*, the story of a girl (Sandy Dennis) who becomes pregnant as a result of her sexual initiation and then decides not to tell the man responsible but to have the child and go it alone! Also in this scene, Eleanor Bron and Michael Coles.

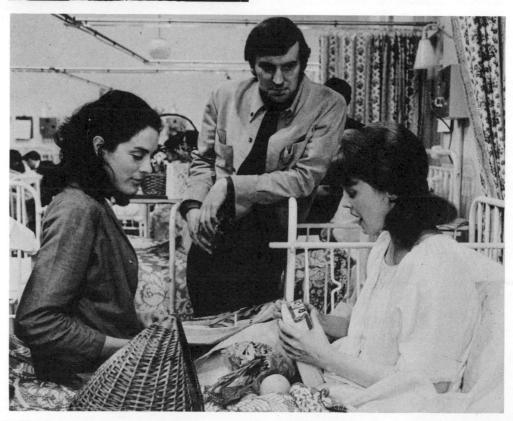

Cleo Goldstein in a dubious position in Miracle's *A Promise of Bed*, a collection of three short erotic films about three men and their (real or imagined) erotic adventures with the girls.

Fox's *The World of Fashion* was a 23-minute Fashion Parade, with Geneviève Gilles as the model who dreams herself into a wide variety of outfits, past and present and – possibly – future.

If it contributed little to the art of the screen, Harrison Marks' *Nine Ages of Nakedness* did offer quite a lot of sly humour—and as vast an array of bared female bosoms as any other movie of the period could boast.

It's obvious that some literary works will never be satisfactorily transcribed into terms of the cinema and, as obviously, James Joyce's *Finnegans Wake* is one of them. But if Mary Ellen Bute's attempt to bring some of this classic's pages to the screen in visual terms finally didn't add up to success, it did represent an imaginative, brave and commendably spirited attempt.

Cinerama's *Changes* was yet another in the cycle of movies about youngsters finding out about life: in this case a young American who comes out of college and whose refusal to accept any sort of lasting responsibility makes him reject the open arms of a series of warmly welcoming young women. In this case it is Manuela Thiess; Kent Lane played the young man.

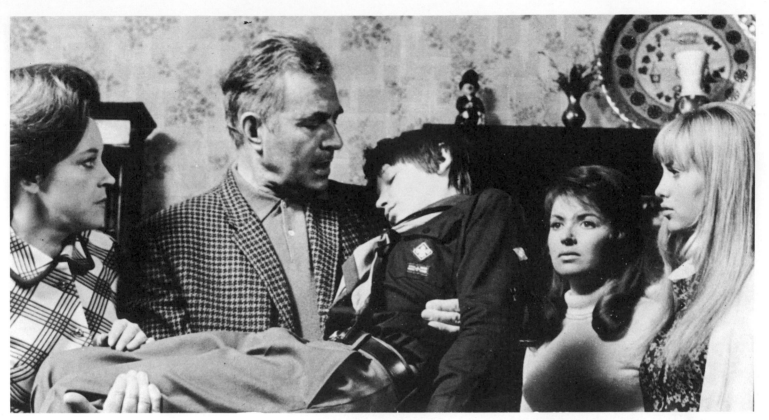

If *Spring and Port Wine* was "old-fashioned"
it was certainly so in the best possible way:
its object and achievement being to entertain.
A straightforward adaptation of the warm and
beautifully observant North Country family
play by Bill Naughton, it offered plenty
of acting opportunities, brilliantly realised
by James Mason, Diana Coupland, Adrienne
Posta and many others.

The new "007", George Lazenby (who, incidentally, was making his quite successful acting début in the film) at the gambling tables in the latest, and certainly one of the best and most exciting James Bond thrillers, U.A.'s *On Her Majesty's Secret Service*. Inset, one of the remarkable shots from the attack on the snowy "Spectre" headquarters high in in the Alps.

Cornered, with no way out, the last (and leader) of *The Wild Bunch*, William Holden, shoots it out to the death against the Mexican bandit army in the bloody, but very good, Warner–Seven Arts Western which, set in the year 1914, took as its wider theme the plight of the old frontier badmen faced by the changing conditions which made their way of life more and more impossible.

Peeping George (Christopher), playing the hero back from the wars who finds a horrid mess of murder, intrigue and mystery waiting for him in Commonwealth United's thriller *Tiger by the Tail*.

Tense moment from M-G-M's large-scale spectacularly violent, quite incredible but consistently entertaining "war escape" thriller *Where Eagles Dare*, with Derren Nesbitt, Mary Ure and Ingrid Pitt. Inset, Clint Eastwood, as the cool American killer who helps Richard Burton to break into and out of the "impregnable" Nazi stronghold high in the German Alps.

Worried wife Dany Robin pleads with
French agent Frederick Stafford not to let
his American friend involve him too deeply
in the latter's search for facts about the
installation of Russian rockets in Cuba – in
Alfred Hitchcock's Universal espionage
thriller *Topaz*.

Robert Stack and Bibi Andersson realise
that what started as a light-hearted affair in
Rome has become serious enough to disrupt
both their marriages and bring misery to a
number of people: in the Universal film
Story of a Woman which Leonardo Bercovici
wrote, directed and produced.

100 *Prologue* was a Canadian film about a couple of hippy types who clash about the way one should go about achieving world-wide peace, with one opting for the aggressive, protest procedure, the other convinced that the passive way is the right one.

Peter Watkins' "The War Game" is now a matter of film and television history, but it is unlikely that his follow-up, *The Peace Game*, will make anything like the same historical impact. A story set in the future, it was concerned with a war game organised internationally in order to satisfy man's aggressive instincts.

One of the great, award-winning successes of this film year was John Schlesinger's *Midnight Cowboy* which, set in the sleaziest quarter of New York, was about two oddly assorted characters (Jon Voight, an impressive newcomer, as the Cowboy, Dustin Hoffman as his unscrupulous friend) who team up because of their desperate need for human contact in a world of cold decadence.

Another of the year's biggest-surprise-successes was Peter Fonda's superbly photographed *Easy Rider*, which he himself wrote and produced and in which he took one of the main roles: an off-beat, mini-budgeted film based on a motor-cycle trip across America made by two hippy types and their pleasant – and less pleasant – experiences along the way, it was directed by the film's co-star Dennis Hopper.

Rank's *Twinky* was a comedy (which from one point of view might be considered to be in dubious taste) about the romance, wooing and marriage of 38-year-old American writer Charles Bronson and 16-year-old British schoolgirl Susan George, and the final realisation of the failure of their relationship.

One of the most unusual films of the year, also produced on a – comparatively – tiny budget was Leonard Kastle's *The Honeymoon Killers*, a reproduction of the notorious New York Lonely Heart Killers case of the early 1950's, when a fat nurse (played by Shirley Stoler) teamed up with a handsome young Spanish immigrant (played by Tony Lo Bianco) and took over the actual murders from him.

Looking like something which has escaped from "Easy Rider", Jeremy Slate and supporting members of the cast of Anglo's *Hell's Angels '69*, in which two rich brothers plan a big Las Vegas robbery, to be covered by the activities of the gang of young motor-cycle thugs of the title.

Johnny Cash – The Man, His World, His Music was the title which explained all in the Crispin feature film about that famous folk character.

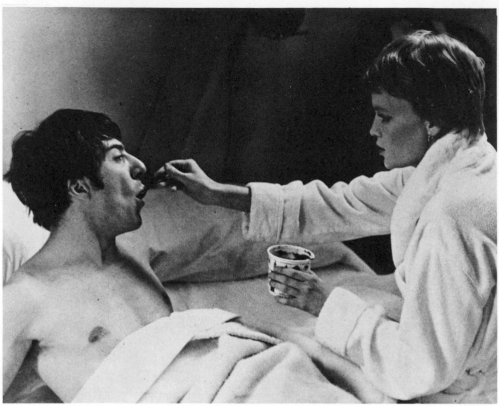

Young British director Peter Yates, after his brilliant thriller "Bullitt", showed his versatility in Fox's amusing, sympathetic and intimate comedy about two young people *John and Mary*. With Dustin Hoffman as the picker-up who finds the girl picked-up, Mia Farrow, intends to extend their night of love to a lasting solid relationship.

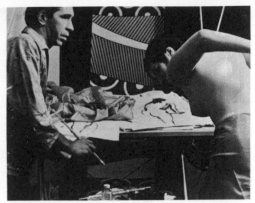

Another in this category of movies was Border's *The Queer . . . The Erotic*, a collection of odd and incidental erotica from around the world, including the German girls who, ashamed of their virginity, hunt down their male prey in packs!

From the same company came another "interest" film, *Legend of the Witches*, an exploration of the oldest of Pagan religions, tracing its history, explaining its rites and practices and showing how it has persisted and is actually growing again in today's world.

Richard Schulman's *Love is a Splendid Illusion* was one of the new kind of films which sprang from the relaxed censorship, with plenty of "daring" scenes in its story about a young man in the interior decorating business tempted into near-disaster by some of his pretty-and-willing customers. Simon Brent played the man.

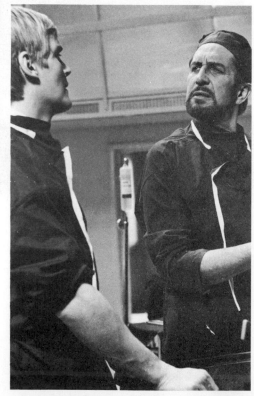

Opposite page
Barbra Streisand does a little extempore entertaining in Columbia's musical *Funny Girl*, in which she repeated her stage triumph in a typical theatrical success story – from back-yard rags to limelit riches – based on the life of yester-year Ziegfeld star Fanny Brice.

Premièred quite a time ago but not subsequently seen (except for one or two isolated showings), Paramount's oddly titled *Situation Hopeless – But Not Serious* presented Alec Guinness as a German shop assistant who, hiding a couple of shot-down American air-crew in his boss's cellar during the war, becomes so happy about the situation that he continues to keep them in hiding (and in ignorance of the march of events) long after the war has ended.

Vincent Price (with assistant Christopher Matthews) headed a team of celluloid shiverers including Christopher Lee and Peter Cushing in Warner–Pathé's aptly titled *Scream and Scream Again*, the action in which starts when the cops find the bodies of two girls sucked dry of their blood!

108

Short (just over the half-hour) and to the comic point, Anglo's *Rhubarb* was very much of a one-man movie, for Eric Sykes wrote, directed and himself played in it. A crazy, goonish comedy, it adapted the old silent techniques, using one word, that of the title, as dialogue, repeated and repeated again for every circumstance! Also starring (l. to r.) Harry Secombe, Hattie Jacques and Jimmy Edwards, it enhanced Sykes' comedy reputation as a creator of comedy.

There's very little one can say about the apparently eternal "Carry On" comedies except to record the title of the latest addition and list the cast taking part in these popular, broad, blue, British funfests. Here in *Carry On Again, Doctor*, Doctor Jim Dale makes a somewhat bemused examination of Barbara Windsor, watched by disapproving matron Hattie Jacques.

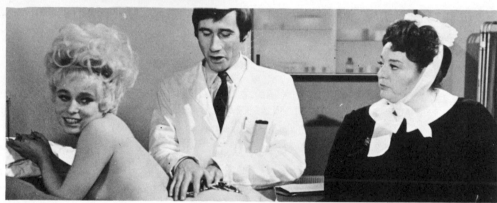

Barber Roman Polanski and barbered André Katelbach in the former's 16-minute comedy based on the master and slave relationship, *The Fat and The Lean*, made way back in 1961 (in France) but seen in Britain for the first time this year.

Cesar Romero (right) and a Rolls-Royce in Disney's family comedy *The Computer Wore Tennis Shoes* – the story of a boy who accidentally takes over from a computer and is able to answer its problems but becomes involved in comic crook complications.

Spike Milligan, as the traffic warden persuaded, at a price, to eat his own parking tickets – one of the more genuinely funny sequences in Commonwealth United's otherwise rather specialised comedy *The Magic Christian*, based on the Terry Southern book about a millionaire who sadistically and callously uses his wealth to degrade his fellows.

Not so serious as it looks – merely a part of the training of the amateur agent and half-crazy Polish boy (Christopher Jones), sent by a couple of nostalgic MI5ers on a dubious mission into East Germany which, always inevitably, ends in disaster and death. From typical John Le Carre anti-romantic spy story, *The Looking Glass War* was brought to the screen by Frankovich for Columbia.

William Forman's film for Cinerama, *Krakatoa – East of Java*, never pretended to be more than it successfully was, a large-screen spectacular, with all the various individual story threads leading to the climax of the great volcano eruption of 1883. Fighting the flames below decks, Diane Baker and John Leyton, while the boat (inset) sails its way through fire, flame and spurting lava!

III

Gloomy Irishman Patrick Magee and cheery Jew Sydney Tafler, the two mysterious persecutors of scruffy, failed and frightened pianist victim Robert Shaw, who is finally driven off his trolley by their mysterious threats, accusations and actions in Harold Pinter's word-intoxicating adaptation of his ambiguous stage play *The Birthday Party*.

The moment of revenge: Nicol Williamson as the Liverpool–Irish lad who has made good in the London business world in a big way, comes back to his old home to see that the death of his "Da'" at the hands of a long-haired lout is properly, and lethally, revenged. A fine performance in Columbia's adaptation of the Patrick Hall novel "The Harp That Once", screened as *The Reckoning*.

An understandably frightened Karin Dor pursued with evil intent by knife-wielding Carl Lange among the twelve dead virgins in New Realm's grisly ghoulie *The Blood Demon*, which also starred Christopher Lee as the ghost of the 40-year-dead Count Regula.

The joy of victory, and the agony of defeat – expressed in the faces of the runner in this scene from Columbia's record of *The Olympics in Mexico*, preserved highlights of more than the one and a half million feet of film exposed in coverage of the 1968 Olympic Games.

The accused's legal representative Barry Newman (right, a most impressive screen début), secretary Diana Muldaur and sheriff Ken Swofford at the murder trial which is presented like a miniature State Fair in Paramount's *The Lawyer*, a thoroughly expert story about prejudice in a small, primitive Middle West cow-town.

Robert Viharo, chaired by luscious Gina Lollobrigida, as the athletic, unscrupulous anti-hero of Paramount's *Stuntman*.

Emlyn Williams, Dame Edith Evans, Pamela Franklin and Robin Phillips – the last in the title role in Fox's version of the Dickens classic *David Copperfield*.

Anthony Quinn and Irene Papas in Warner–Pathé's *A Dream of Kings*, in which Quinn played a Chicago–Greek, a gambler and womaniser, whose dream is that his ailing son will be restored to health if only he can raise enough money to take him back to bask in the Grecian sun.

Cathy Burns, thunder stealing in Warner–Pathé's *Last Summer*, as the victim of a cruel and callous game played by a group of rich American teenagers whose characters the film observes in frightening depth.

Opposite page
Dirk Bogarde, Helmut Berger and Helmut Griem, playing the power game against a background of the Nazis' rise to power in Germany in Luchino Visconti's powerful and gripping drama about a depraved steel family of the Reich, *The Damned*.

Ex-slaver Stephen Boyd, now a plantation owner, whose coloured mistress Dionne Warwick holds a grudge against him because he has separated her from her husband, and lives for the revenge she one day intends to have in *Slaves*.

Robert Forster and Marianna Hill in Haskell Wexler's sensational first large-screen feature, *Medium Cool*, a story of personal and political violence seen against an entirely and terrifyingly authentic background of the riots in Chicago in the summer of 1968.

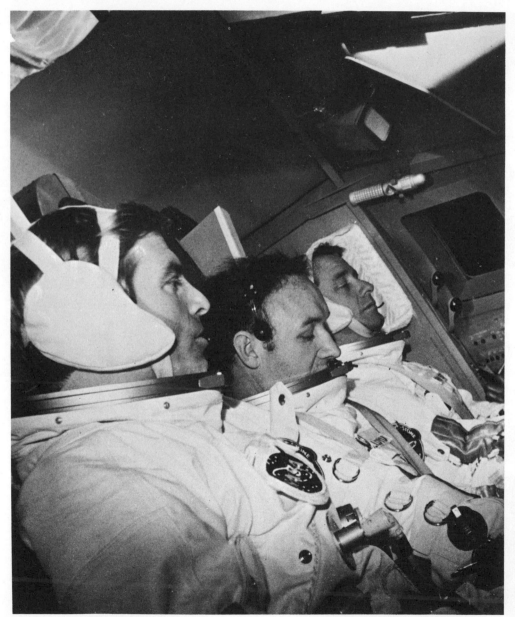

Most suddenly, and unhappily, topical release of the whole year was Columbia's *Marooned*, which duplicated fictionally to a great extent what was actually happening in space when it was released last April. The story of three astronauts whose spacecraft fails, and are left uncontrollably sailing through space with ever diminishing supplies of oxygen while ground control struggle to bring them back alive, it was uncomfortably close to truth. The three astronauts were played by Richard Crenna, James Franciscus and Gene Hackman – while Gregory Peck led the worried crew of technicians on earth.

Another space film, this time wholly factual, an actual documentary account of the first landing on the moon, was Fox's *Footprints on the Moon – Apollo II*.

Very firmly on earth, very firmly bedded
in fiction, was Paramount's *The Adventurers*,
a gargantuan film based on Harold
Robbins's equally gargantuan novel, which
amidst the welter of incident – rape,
massacre, orgy, nude love-making, gory
battle, duplicity, lesbianism, dope – the lot
(in fact, you name it, and this film had it,
in jumbo size too!) – told a story of a South
American revolutionary leader corrupted
by power into becoming more rigidly
and ruthlessly dictatorial than the dictator's
régime he has overthrown. In this scene

Rossano Brazzi, returning home, is
understandably surprised at some of the
decorations he finds in his drawing room.

Long, too – but not so long, or even too
long – filled with (somewhat less
melodramatic) incident was Norman
Jewison's film for Columbia of the semi-
autobiographical Ben Hecht story "Gaily,
Gaily" (the film's American Label) re-
titled *Chicago, Chicago* in G.B. Beau
Bridges (right, most promising newcomer,
son of Lloyd Bridges) played the naïve
youngster from out of town who finds
under ace newspaperman Brian Keith
(a lovely performance), life rich and
corrupt in the big city.

While M-G-M's musical re-make of that great romantic screen yesteryear success *Goodbye, Mr. Chips* may not have been an unqualified success, it certainly gave Peter O'Toole the – eagerly seized – opportunity to turn in one of the outstanding performances of the year as the quiet, dedicated schoolmaster of the title. Petula Clark was the surprise choice for the old Greer Garson role of his actress wife.

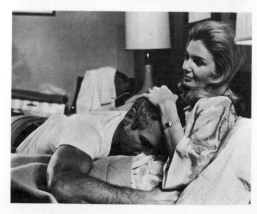

More romance, this time among the car racers and their wives and girlfriends, in Universal's *Winning*, in which Paul Newman finds driving easier than living, even with real-life wife Joanne Woodward as his understanding little woman.

Romantic, too, Francis Searle's small (half-hour) feature for Planet, *The Pale Faced Girl*, in which Kevin McHugh finds the P.F. girl – Fidelma Murphy – quite unlike all the other girls he has picked up during his Saturday night Dublin excursions.

Gambling his way, with Mafia (Lando Buzzanca) help, past the suspicious customs officer, British oil engineer Peter McEnery finds on arriving in Italy that he's warmly ensconced between two warring factions of the Italian crook society in Universal's *Better a Widow*.

Already something of a small-screen darling, screenwriter-comic Marty Feldman was given his first large-screen opportunity in Ned Sherrin's British Lion comedy *Every Home Should Have One*, a satire aimed at the world of advertising, in which Mr. Feldman was cast as the genius selected to lead a campaign to put sex into porridge. Sharing this snarling scene, glamorous Julie Ege.

120 Tense gambler, left, is Jean Simmons, whose performance in U.A.'s *The Happy Ending* (the film directed by her husband Richard Brooks in which she played a young wife whose marriage goes wrong and sends her to the bottle) brought her a 1970 Oscar nomination.

More gambling, in Fox's *The Only Game in Town*, the gambler being casual piano-player Warren Beatty, whose addiction to the vice of the dice almost, but not quite, loses him lovely – but disillusioned – Las Vegas showgirl Elizabeth Taylor.

Undoubtedly one of the most commercially – and to a considerable extent – artistically successful Westerns of the year was Fox's highly entertaining (and often extremely amusing) *Butch Cassidy and The Sundance Kid*, a story based on the true exploits of a couple of high-spirited badmen who roamed and robbed the Old West between 1880 and 1900. It produced two grand performances in the title roles by Paul Newman and Robert Redford (also inset), shown nearing the end of their finally bloody story.

122

There was almost as mucn story behind as in Abraham Polonsky's Western for Rank, *Tell Them Willie Boy is Here*. For Polonsky, claimed as a past victim of political discrimination, this was a pretty useful celluloid comeback which below the surface story of the chase and cornering by a white lawman of a redskin who has killed his father could be read all sorts of significant undertones.

Typically deadly scene from Miracle's tough Italian-made Western, *No Room to Die*; in which a band of outlaws, the crooked banker who is using them, and a couple of bounty hunters come to final confrontation along the Mexican border.

Henry Fonda lives, Aldo Ray dies; in M-G-M's Western *Killer on a Horse*, a tale of a man who kills a town and then one day, when it is beginning to live again, rides in to certify the corpse – this time at his cost.

The Indian – John Yesno – saving a grizzly bear cub from its parents' fate and so beginning the strange story of animal memory in Walt Disney's nature film *King of the Grizzlies*.

Don Knotts, getting the full treatment in Universal's comedy *The Love God?* a film about a bird-watcher conned by a crooked pornographic editor into turning his magazine over to another completely different sort of bird!

Universal's *The Lost Man* might be described as a colour-conscious "Odd Man Out", for the main character, a negro, becomes more or less innocently involved with some coloured militants, with them commits a crime leading to accidental murder and from then on, wounded and dying, is always just a few steps ahead of the cops. With Sidney Poitier (left), Al Freeman Jr. and Joanna Shimkus, as the former's white and faithful girl-friend.

Look out, Lady! The sort of incident which was to be found many times in U.A.'s *Matchless*, a spy story with a difference, the difference being that the main spy had when in a tight corner the ability to make himself invisible, always a useful asset of course! Moving across large areas of the world, always gaily incredible, it was directed by, of all people, Alberto Lattuada.

Not always to be taken too seriously was C.I.R.O.'s rather old-fashioned-style adventure thriller *The Last Grenade*, in which a grim Stanley Baker played the soldier of fortune whose life is dedicated to obtaining revenge for the way he has been double-crossed and his men murdered by his erstwhile pal during the Congo War. Rafer Johnson, here with Baker, played one of the renegade's victims.

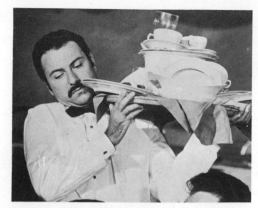

Alan Arkin as the Puerto Rican pappa
in U.A.'s *Popi*, doing one of the three jobs
he takes in order to raise the money to
send his sons away from their New York
slum surroundings to get a better education
and, he hopes, a better life than he himself
has had.

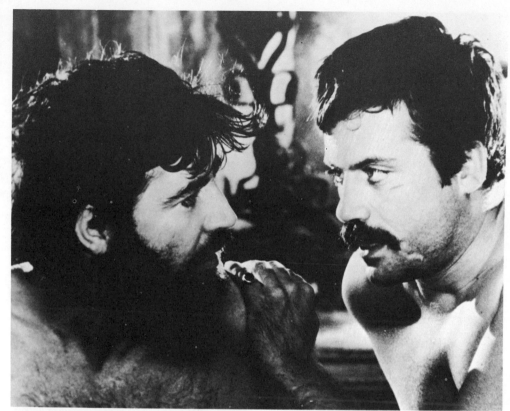

Rudolf Nureyev and Dame Margot
Fonteyn in the A. B.–Pathé film of the
Tchaikovsky ballet *Swan Lake*.

Alan Bates and Oliver Reed in the famous
nude wrestling scene in U.A.'s *Women in
Love*, Ken Russell's pretty faithful-to-the-
original adaptation to the screen of the
famous D. H. Lawrence story: hailed by
some as one of the most completely sensual
films of the year.

Among the stranger films of the year – and certainly among those competing in the longest-titles stakes! – was Anthony Newley's *Can Heironymus Merkin Ever Forget Mercy Humppe and Find True Happiness?*, which turned out to be as confused but nevertheless as interesting as its title. Newley, taking on the coats of director, writer, composer, producer and star, presented 107 often erotic minutes of what looked like self-examination, through which talent sometimes bubbled. Among those helping him out were Margaret Nolan (left) and Milton Berle (right).

With an even longer and more (B.O.) poisonous title was Paramount's *Oh Dad, Poor Dad, Mamma's Hung You in the Closet and I'm Feeling So Sad*, in which it really was sad to see Rosalind Russell (right, with son, Robert Morse) caught up in such a welter of unpleasant black comedy about a wife who takes her late, stuffed husband everywhere she goes and has a mentally retarded offspring who murders the girl who introduces him to sex.

Not so way out, not so black, was Fox's *Joanna* which, intended or not, presented a pretty unflattering picture of today's permissive young people in its story of a girl (Joanna, of course) who after sleeping around becomes involved with a negro murderer and in the end is left with his child. Baby-voiced Jo was played by Genevieve Waite, the negro by Calvin Lockhart (the latter illustrating his method of dealing with cop callers!).

Some of the year's best acting was to be seen (if you could find it – for this was one of the films which never had a general release) in Paramount's *The Dance of Death*, a completely straightforward filming, without any real concessions to the changed medium, of the National Theatre Company's stage production of the great, grim August Strindberg play, with Laurence Olivier giving one of the finest performances of his career as the man chained by a terrible love-hate relationship to his bitter ex-actress wife, played impeccably by Geraldine McEwan. Robert Lang, in the background, played the third main role, that of the friend.

Another filmed play was Sidney Lumet's almost reverent and fine transcription to the screen for Warner–Pathe of Chekhov's *The Seagull*, with a distinguished cast including Simone Signoret (in hammock) and Vanessa Redgrave (right); and James Mason (not in the scene).

Not from a play, but based on a Bernard Malamud novel about Russia, John Frankenheimer's *The Fixer* for M-G-M contained a number of outstanding performances, including those of Alan Bates in the title role (here fixed!) and Dirk Bogarde as the lawyer who defends him when the government attempt to divert the hatred of the people for the aristocrats by pinning a murder on this Jewish handyman; who, innocent, subsequently refuses in spite of all that the authorities can do to break his spirit, to admit his guilt.

Quite outrageously sentimental but also – thanks considerably to a notable performance by Bourvil – often amusing was Fox's *The Christmas Tree* in which William Holden played the doting millionaire father of a small boy (Brooker Fuller, right) who, exposed to atomic radiation when a plane carrying atom bombs crashes into the sea, is doomed we know to die; the only question being when?

128

A strange, fascinating and visually exciting film was Joseph Losey's *Secret Ceremony*, with its wandering cameras, its rich décor and its carefully nursed atmosphere hiding a very slim – and psychologically suspect – story about a dolly off her trolley (Mia Farrow right) who picks up a prostitute (Elizabeth Taylor, left) takes her into her home and insists that she's her mother, a course of action which eventually leads to murder and suicide.

Another out-of-the-rut film which never won a general release was Noel Black's *Pretty Poison* for Fox, in which Tuesday Weld gave a very neat performance indeed as a sweet, blonde 17-year-old girl (seen here with Joseph Bova) who, joining up with a restless young dreamer (Anthony Perkins), becomes the evil motivating force behind him as they carry on a career of murder and sabotage.

A direct product of the screen's new "freedom" was Stanley Donen's *Staircase* for Fox, an adaptation (by the playwright) of Charles Dyer's play about a couple of bitchy homosexuals who find that though life is hardly perfect together it is hell apart! Part of the joke was that Richard Burton and Rex Harrison played the leading roles!

With some of the screen's best performances of the period coming from the suddenly much sought-after Nicol Williamson, not many of them were in films which obtained a general or even wide release. One that only had a floating release was U.A.'s *Laughter in the Dark*, a rather odd piece based on the Nabokov novel in which Williamson played a rich man fascinated by a nasty little tart, an obsession which leads to his downfall, degradation, blindness and finally, death.

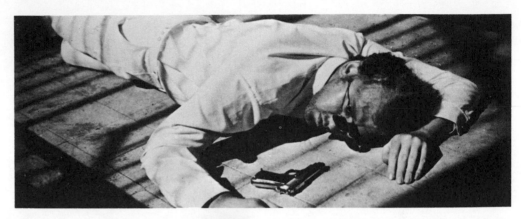

Inclined to be type-cast now, Alan Arkin in Warner's *The Heart is a Lonely Hunter*, played a deaf-mute who goes to his sad suicide's grave unaware that the girl he loves, loves him, in spite of her grievous rejection of him.

Zero Mostel eats his ice-cream in Avco Embassy's *The Producers*, a pretty crazy comedy based on the stage play about a theatrical producer who finds after constant disaster that he can make more money out of deliberate flops than from successes – but then in trying to produce the biggest flop of all, finds he's got a tremendous (and unwanted) success on his hands!

130 It was nice to see Jane Wyman back on the screen when she co-starred with Bob Hope in C.I.R.O.'s *How to Commit Marriage*, playing his wife in a story about a couple whose divorce plans are more or less wrecked when their daughter announces *she* is getting married!

Brought into this section now because it is unlikely that after years of "special releases" it will ever get a "general one" (as we know the term) comes M-G-M's *Doctor Zhivago*, David Lean's often exquisitely visual 3½-hour adaptation of the Pasternak novel about life in Russia prior to and during the Revolution. In a long cast Rod Steiger's performance, as Komarovsky, stood out.

132

Sandy Dennis and the boy she takes pity
on when from her flat window she sees
him sitting forlorn on a wintry Vancouver
park seat and invites him in – a relationship which mounts steadily to disaster in
Commonwealth United's *That Cold Day
in the Park*.

Vanessa Redgrave's performance as the
great dancer in Universal's *Isadora*, the
autobiographical film about the
unconventional Isadora Duncan which
won quite a lot of critical acclaim.

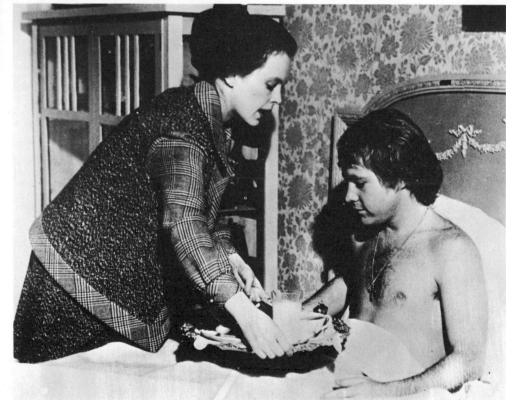

Now at last safely steered away from Bond and all that, Sean Connery played a militant, saboteur coal-miner, at the heart of the struggle of the Pennsylvania anthracite-hewers in 1870, in Paramount's *The Molly Maguires*.

Daria Halprin in Antonioni's visually fascinating but otherwise less than outstanding first American film, M-G-M's *Zabriskie Point*.

134

The macabre, black – very black – ending to Warner–Pathe's release of the screen version of Joe Orton's sick comedy *Entertaining Mr. Sloane*, when the young lodger (Peter McEnery) is blackmailed by a threat of exposure as a murderer to take part in a double wedding ceremony, with sister and brother Beryl Reid and Harry Andrews (a trio of really outstanding performances) who agree to share the young man's favours in six-month periods.

A scene from U.A.'s hippy folk-music movie *Alice's Restaurant*; among the considerably long-haired cast was Arlo, son of Woody Guthrie.

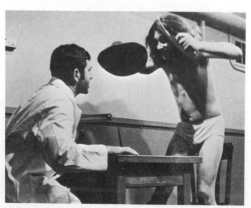

Paul McCartney makes music, in U.A.'s
Let It Be, a documentary about the group,
collectively and individually, at work and
at play.

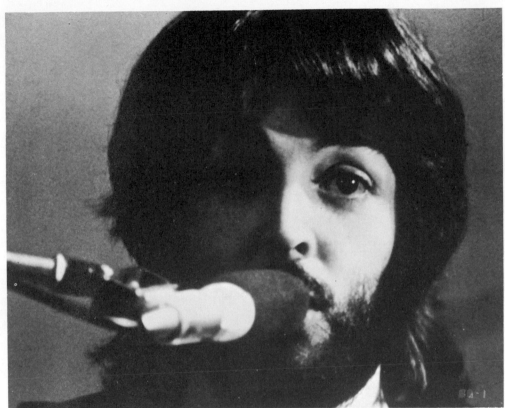

In view of the great financial success of
Fox's *The Planet of the Apes* it's not so
surprising that a sequel was put in hand
pretty quickly. Called *Beneath the Planet of
the Apes*, it starts where the last film ended
and follows Charlton Heston's adventures
into the Forbidden Zone after he has
realised that he's in post-atomised world.
And don't let that banner fool you!

THE CONTINENTAL FILM

CZECHOSLOVAKIA

Jiri Menzel's *Capricious Summer* was entirely conventional in style and content and reminiscent in style and treatment of the classic pre-war French film, telling with wit and great charm the story of three friends living in a tiny broken-down spa town who each in turn try their luck with the lovely young partner of a visiting showman, each in turn being made to realise his age and limitations.

FRANCE

Karen Blanguernon and Leslie Bedos in *Gentle Love* which was certainly a slight and gentle story about a photographer and fashion model who part and years later come together again.

Ulla Jacobsson and Jean-Claude Dauphin in Bernard T. Michel's *The Tender Age*, the tragic-ending romance of a movie-maker and the woman he selects to play his heroine.

One of the year's best erotic films, *Thérèse and Isabelle* told with discretion and considerable beauty the Violette Leduc story about a lesbian love affair between two very pretty and precocious schoolgirls: played by Essy Persson and Anna Gael.

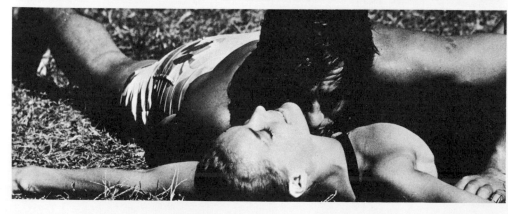

Alain Delon and Romy Schneider played two of the characters, the lovers, most closely involved with the murder that changes so much (and so little!) in Jacques Deray's *The Sinners*.

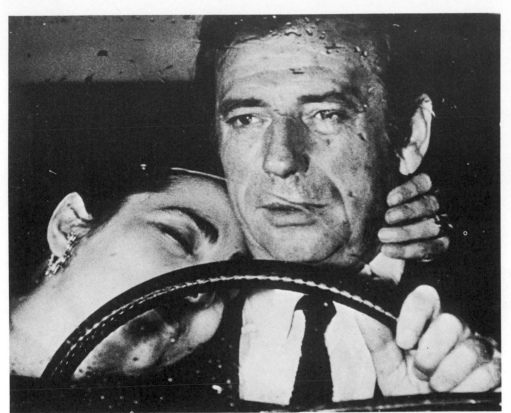

Terry Torday, as Susan in *Sexy Susan Sins Again*, in the new adventure leads the girls of her native town in a mass strip-tease in order to defeat a plot to assassinate the Emperor Napoleon.

Last in alphabetical order, but very nearly if not quite first in merit order, Costa-Gavras's *Z* was a brilliantly made story of political murder in Greece and its aftermath, based on an actual historical case. Yves Montand played the leading role of the victim.

Ma Nuit Chez Maud (*My Night With Maud*) was a delicate and witty story about the night spent in bed – and largely passed in conversation! – by a strict catholic young man (Jean-Louis Trintignant) and a willing young girl (delightful newcomer Françoise Fabian) when they are marooned in a winter snowstorm.

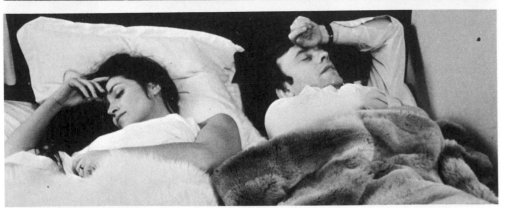

Pierre Brasseur as the King, in Polish poet Walerian Borowczyk's *Goto, L'Ile d'Amour*, grim French film about an isolated island community living under totalitarian conditions, and, more especially, about a nasty little character who, by means of lies and murder, climbs from the lowly position of official "Killer of the Flies" to the throne itself.

Marcel Carné's *Les Jeunes Loups—Young Wolves* was his attempt to deal with the problems of today's youth but it received little critical attention and lukewarm public interest. Christian Hay played one of the young wolves, Haydée Politoff one of his two mistresses.

Claude Chabrol has seldom done better than his *La Femme Infidèle – The Unfaithful Wife*, in which with great polish and superb expertise he told the story of a man who, kills the threatener of his marriage and then, with his wife's co-operation, tries to avoid the consequences of the crime. A deep examination of the relationship between man and woman; with Stéphane Audran and Michel Bouquet giving superb performances as the pair.

Louis de Funès played the leading role of the French cop in both *The Gendarme of St. Tropez* and its sequel *Gendarme in New York*. The first was all about his triumphant recovery of a stolen painting and the daring young nudists of his home town (inset) and the second was about his official visit across the Atlantic, complicated by his daughter's stowing away to accompany him.

L'Astragale is the French word for a bone in the ankle and it is by breaking this during her escape from jail that Marlène Jobert meets passing motor cyclist Horst Buchholz and so begins the passionate, sad-ending love affair related in the film.

A nasty moment for small-time crooks: Jean-Paul Belmondo and Bourvil in Gérard Oury's English-dubbed *The Brain*, the story of another – French – Great Train Robbery.

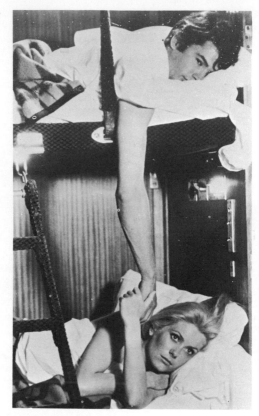

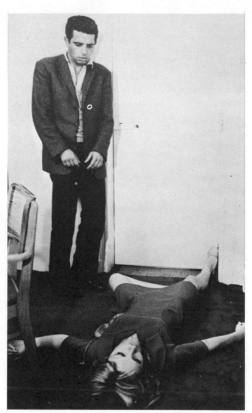

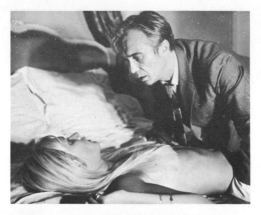

Philippe Lemaire leans over one of the two stripper girls – Agnès Ball – he keeps prisoner while he tries to raise the money and the means to get abroad and finance his defence of the charge that he has murdered his wife in *Night of the Outrages*.

A nubile group of girls involved in New Realm's *Sex is a Pleasure*, a film which sets out to prove the point of its statement in its story about a very sex-conscious group of people romping around in a chateau.

Catherine Deneuve with the young man (Roger Van Hool) for whom she leaves her wealthy lover, only to realise eventually she cannot live without the luxury which he can give her, so she goes back to him in this adaptation of a typical Françoise Sagan novel, *La Chamade – Heartbeat*.

Amidou with one of his prostitute victims in Claude Lelouch's cry of outrage against the death penalty, *Life Love Death*, a technically smoothly presented story of the trailing, capture, trial and judicial decapitation of a sex multi-murderer which only in the final minutes revealed its propagandic motive with a direct and impassioned appeal to the audience.

Gina Lollobrigida and Ewa Aulin as the two women – wife and mistress – in Giulio Questi's aptly titled *A Curious Way to Love*, in which a farmer and his mistress set a trap for his wife, who, with her lover, sets up a trap for them!

The really complicated character in Damiano Damiani's *Complicated Girl* was the man, Jean Sorel, who draws his girl-friend Catherine Spaak into his complicated fantasy world and allows his illusions to drive him to murder.

ITALY

The ubiquitous Jean-Louis Trintignant turned up again in the Italian-made *The Libertine*, which avoided being pornographic, in spite of its highly erotic content, by knowing exactly when to draw the line and by a neatly injected vein of humour: Catherine Spaak played the sex-seeking young widow finally tamed by the "doctor" Trintignant.

Cinderella – Italian Style: Sophia Loren played the leading role in this fairly amusing fairy tale in which Omar Sharif played the Prince – who is not always so charming.

M-G-M's *Five Man Army*, though actually made in Italy, had something of an international flavour about it, for it was English speaking and directed by American Don Taylor. It was all about a 1914 plan to rob a military train in Mexico of some half-million dollars which four of the holders-up want for themselves and the fifth wants for The Revolution.

Also with an international flavour was Alberto de Martino's *The Insatiables*, for while it was Italian-made, it was given English dialogue, and the story of an investigation of the murder of a pal by a reporter was set in Hollywood. The co-stars also were non-Italian, Dorothy Malone and Robert Hoffman.

Maker of cinematic enigmas, Pier Paolo Pasolini has never been more "difficult" than he was in his new film *Pigsty–Porcile* which told two stories, one set in the 17th century, the other in post-war Germany, and told them simultaneously, jumping from one to the other without any obvious rhythm or reason! In the first story Pierre Clémenti was

SWEDEN. SCANDINAVIA
Though this scene may look amusing
enough there was certainly little enough
comedy in Susan Sontag's *Duet for Cannibals*,
a pretty sombre Swedish psychological
sex drama about a man drawn with his girl-
friend into a strange and symbolic quartet
which is full of ambiguous meaning. The
quartet consisted of Agneta Ekmanner
and Adriana Asti as the women and Gösta
Ekman and Lars Ekborg as the men.

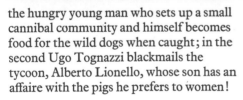

the hungry young man who sets up a small
cannibal community and himself becomes
food for the wild dogs when caught; in the
second Ugo Tognazzi blackmails the
tycoon, Alberto Lionello, whose son has an
affaire with the pigs he prefers to women!

Chosen to open a new London film club, *As
the Naked Wind From the Sea* was an
erotic story about a young violinist who
doesn't let his musical studies interfere
with his sensual studies during a holiday by
the sea with several nubile young girls. The
young man was played by Hans Gustafsson.

146

Another superior Scandinavian exhibit was Bo Widerberg's critically highly acclaimed *Adalen '31*, in which, in a very leisurely, consistently poetic way, he presented the story of a strike at the little North Swedish town of the title, a dispute which ended in violence and death for some of those involved. But visually at least as important were the glorious backgrounds, bathed in spring sunshine.

Though the direction was French, by Cécil Saint-Laurent, *48 Hours of Love* was an otherwise wholly Swedish sex film, about a young architect who dreams up an odd practical exercise to prove the loyalty of his fiancée – an exercise which ends in disaster. Tester and tested : Francis Lemonaier and Thelma Ramstrom.

Sex played a comparatively minor part, however, in the best Danish film of the period: Palle Kjaerulff-Schmidt's completely captivating and deceptively simple film (almost documentary in character) *Once There Was a War*, about a boy growing up in occupied Denmark. It was almost like a flip through an animated family album. The boy was played with superb confidence by Ole Busck – the girl in the picture is Yvonne Ingdal.

MacAhlberg's *The Voyeur* carried on the story of the permissive young woman, Siv (played now by Gio Petre), we met previously in "I A Woman", this chapter relating the events of her marriage, her gradual realisation that her husband is a pervert and her leaving him to return to her casual relationships while he goes down the hill.

Gunnar Björnstrand as the nasty doctor who runs a clinic and uses it as a cover for his unpleasant habits in *The Sadist*. Personable Essy Persson played one of his victims.

Bibi Andersson in not very gentle-sex mood in Mai Zetterling's *The Girls*, a not too convincing protest about the unequal place of woman in modern society, revealed in a story about three actresses touring in a production of "Lysistrata" who find their own and their theatrical problems becoming inextricably mixed.

GERMANY

A scene from *Walk the Hot Streets*, a German gangster thriller about a municipal prosecutor who battles bravely against the racketeers who have taken charge of the city.

Following the fantastic success of the original German sex-education film "Helga", a whole flood of similar pictures came out of Germany, including a sequel to the original: *Michael and Helga*, which examined the sexual problems of the young married couple of the title, played by Ruth Gassman and Felix Franchy.

Angel Baby was a rather heavily-weighted comedy about a young provincial teen-age Miss who comes to the big city (of Munich) determined to lose her virginity there, but finds it not so easy, after all, even when she is apparently prepared to throw herself at any one of a rather unprepossessing group of males. Gila von Weiterhausen played the "baby".

Along very similar lines was *Sexual Partnership*, a "medical" sex film about marriage and its problems as seen through the case of a young couple, played by Petra Perry and Michael Maien.

Reflecting the world-wide interest in Britain's *Great Train Robbery* of a few years back was the careful, documentary-style reconstruction of the crime, in the John Olden and Claus Peter Witt film with that title.

HUNGARY

Ferenc Kósa's rather grim and gloomy *Ten Thousand Suns* presented a view of modern Hungarian history seen through the memories of an old peasant farmer, as he looks back on his unremittingly hard-toiling life.

Silence and Cry was the third in Miklós Jancsó's great trilogy of films about the dehumanising and degrading effect of war and revolution, this one being concerned with the brutally repressive period which followed the defeat of the communists by the Admiral Horthy regime – seen against an almost hypnotic, wonderfully photographed background of the seemingly limitless plains of Hungary – resulting in an uncomfortable but unforgettable movie.

CUBA

An interesting cinematic curiosity, T. G. Alea's *Memories of Underdevelopment* was a curiously liberal Cuban film which with sympathy and understanding told the story of a young man who, coming from a firmly conservative background, finds that though he attempts it he cannot finally come to terms with Castro's revolution.

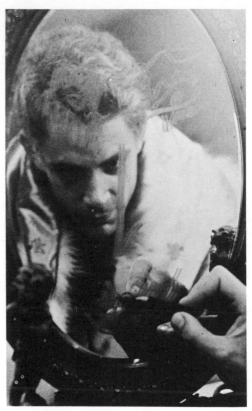

YUGOSLAVIA

Dusan Makavejev's *The Switchboard Operator* in unconventional manner (making periodic excursions away from the matter on hand, with such asides as a lecture on phallus worship and discussions on criminal investigation and pornography), but amusingly and captivatingly, told the story of a gay little telephone operator who falls in love with a rat catcher, an affair that leads to her pregnancy and death.

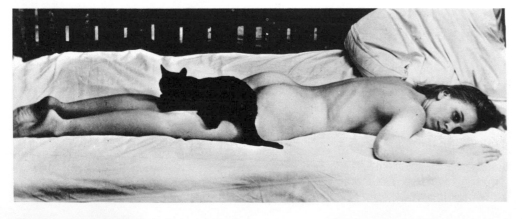

More highly unconventional in treatment and presentation was the same director's *Innocence Unprotected*, which "framed" within itself, so to speak, another complete movie, a sort of home-movie type of picture made clandestinely during the war by an acrobat-strongman.

SOUTH AMERICA

At one time threatened as his last movie, Luis Buñuel's *La Voie Lacteé* saw him back at his favourite film pastime of baiting the holies, in a movie which was in fact a sort of anthology of heresies, presented during a pilgrimage by two characters from France to Spain.

A scene from Glauber Rocha's Brazilian Cinema Nuova sensation, *Black God, White Devil*, which was a fictional account of the history of a barren area of Brazil in the late 19th century.

LATE ADDITIONS

FROM FRANCE

Michel Duchaussoy, after a moment's hesitation, stretches out a life-saving hand to Jean Yanne, as the man who has killed his small son in a hit-and-run incident and whom he has tracked down with the object of coldly executing in Claude Chabrol's *Killer! – Que La Bête Meure*, a magnificently (if always unobtrusively) directed suspense thriller.

Brigitte Bardot and Michel Piccoli in Jean-Luc Godard's *Contempt – Le Mépris*, based on an Alberto Moravia novel about the break-up of a once almost perfect marriage.

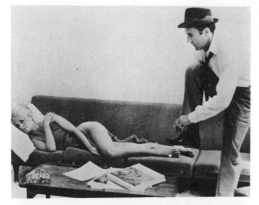

Anouk Aimée as the girl in *The Model Shop* (in the Jacques Demy – he wrote, directed and produced – Columbia film) who gives draftee Gary Lockwood a new purpose in life with their one night of love!

FROM RUSSIA

Lenin's centenary was celebrated in London at the Paris-Pullman cinema by two films based on periods in his life: the first, *Heart of a Mother*, concerned Lenin's family life between his 14th and 23rd years, was directed by Mark Donskoi and starred Elena Fadeyeva as the Mother: the second, *The Sixth of July*, was about a later part of Lenin's life, when he had just come to power in 1918. In the latter movie the role of Lenin was played by Yuri Kayurov.

FROM ITALY

Nathalie Delon and Susan Strasberg in Roberto Malenotti's *Le Sorelle – The Sisters*, a story of two women so closely tied by their relationship that they feel impelled to share everything, even their lovers!

UNDERGROUND CINEMA

by Ralph Stephenson

Dwoskin's *Alone*

One can hardly expect a neat, systematic thesis on such a long-haired, untidy subject as "Underground Cinema". By its nature, it is sprawling, anarchic, unsystematic. The films are thrown on to an old sheet in cellars, converted warehouses, or college lecture rooms borrowed for the week-end. There are no Press shows, no credit-titles, no actors' biographies, no stills, no interviews with promising young directors. The films themselves, put together with a borrowed camera, a second-hand tape-recorder and a blunt razor-blade, after being kicked around by amateur projectionists, scratched and worn into inaudibility and invisibility, end up in the dustbin, unmourned by their improvident, prolific authors.

Underground cinema is akin to self-destructive art, and appropriately there is an underground film, Robert Breer's *Homage to Tinguely's Homage to New York*, about the self-destructive machine Tinguely built for the New York Modern Museum. Another underground film-maker (Jerry Joffen) does not exhibit his films and is said to destroy them as soon as he makes them. It is as difficult to be precise about length, style or subject-matter, as about dates and credits. As Sheldon Renan says in *An Introduction to American Underground Film*, "there are underground films in which there is no movement and films in which there is nothing but movement. There are films about people and films about light. There are short, short underground films and long, long underground films. There are sexy films and sexless films, political films and poetical films, film epigrams and film epics . . . Underground film is an *explosion* of

Emshwiller's *Image, Flesh and Voice*

cinematic styles, forms and directions."
However, if the anarchistic underground
anti-establishment regard the historian, the
archivist, the cataloguer, as irrelevant if not
mischievous, if it is not possible (or
desirable) to present an impeccably
documented dossier of the underground
with dates, titles, critical assessments, at
least one can make a few notes. One can
discern origins, one can describe general
characteristics (even if the most characteristic
characteristic is that there are no general
characteristics) – and perhaps most

important of all one can locate the movement
as part of the new art world (itself part of a
new non-conformist society) with a new
formal, disrespectful, explosive
relationship between the vociferous,
free-style artist in whatever medium, and
his quiet-eyed, tatterdemalion audience.
One can record, too, the full official
registration marks of recent films in which the
underground as it spreads out comes (like
London Transport) to the surface – in such
films as Agnès Varda's *Lions' Love*, Robert
Frank's *Me and My Brother*, Brian de

Palma's *Greetings* and Jim McBride's *David Holzman's Diary*.

"Underground" is a recently popular word, and, though said to have been first used before the war, no doubt owes its present vogue to real or imagined connections with anti-Nazi liberating movements. But the type of film it represents goes back under such names as *Avant-garde*, *Symbolist*, *Surrealist*, *Expressionist*, to the beginning of cinema. Sheldon Renan somewhat over-inclusively traces early influences from Méliès, Feuillade, Delluc, L'Herbier, Kirsanov, etc., in France; Eggeling, Richter, Rutmann and Fischinger in Germany, Ince and Sennet in America. Then in later stages mentions a good hundred names and many times that number of films. In America he traces four distinct *avant-gardes*. The first in the 20s and 30s with the work of Paul Fejos, Ralph Steiner, Robert Florey, Lewis Jacobs and Mary Ellen Bute. The second over the war period and up to 1954 with Maya Deren (*Meshes of the Afternoon*), Kenneth Anger (*Fireworks*), Gregory Markopoulos (*Psyche*, *Flowers of Asphalt* and later *The Iliac Passion*, 1965) and James Broughton (*Pleasure Garden*). The third, the underground avant-garde, was started in the 50s, and its film-makers include Jonas Mekas, Robert Breer, Stan Brakhage, Bruce Connor, Jack Smith, Ron Rice, Ed. Emswhiller and Andy Warhol. This third movement, the underground, had less of the formality and nightmarish despair of the earlier schools and more flow and lyricism. There was a strong sense of identification between the vision of the film-maker and the eye of the camera. The people in the earlier movements were artists, actors or writers who made one or two films; now they were (or became) film-makers for good and all – rebellious, experimental and unconventional into the bargain. Finally, in the third phase there were far *more* film-makers and far *more* films: the movement was larger and more influential.

In 1960 the new American Cinema Group met in New York and two years later founded the Film-Makers Co-operative. They issued a statement which said, "We don't want false, polished, slick films – we prefer them rough, unpolished but alive; we don't want rosy films – we want them the colour of blood", and the Co-operative distributed all films submitted to it with nobody ruling as to their quality. Finally, the fourth *avant-garde*, only now beginning its development (though again it stretches back to earlier days) is "expanded cinema" in which the conventional film form is expanded by use of multiple and unconventional screens (e.g. a pile of white cardboard boxes later thrown at the audience) by the use of both film and live action, by television image techniques, by computer films, stroboscopes, liquid projections, the colour organ, kinematic sculpture and so on.

Turning back to the origins of underground cinema one can select from the crowd of titles mentioned by Sheldon Renan a few key films which have survived as personal creations and influenced all serious, dedicated later film-makers. Such are Méliès' *Trip to the Moon* (1902) an astonishing little masterpiece of comic invention; René Clair's *Entr'acte* made as an accompaniment to an experimental ballet in which there is a frenetically tripping set of mourners at a

Leacock Pennebaker's Bob Dylan film *Don't Look Back*

158

lop-sided funeral and the only ballet-dancer is seen upside down. Then in 1928 there were Delluc's *Seashell and the Clergyman*, a surrealist fantasy, and Buñuel's *Un Chien Andalou*, intended to be a brutal rebuttal of surrealism (the eyes that floated mistily in other films are here sliced with a razor) but hailed by the surrealists themselves as a masterpiece. *The Seashell and the Clergyman* was banned in England with the comment, "The film is so cryptic as to be almost meaningless. If there be a meaning it is doubtless objectionable." Then there was Metzner's *Uberfall* (1929), a late German expressionist film, the story of a robbery with distorted images. Buñuel's *L'Age d'Or* (1930) full of iconoclastic and shocking symbolism, and Man Ray's *Etoile de Mer* (1928), an abstruse love story photographed through distorting glass. Cocteau made his strange *Sang d'un Poête* in 1930. All these have been individual films, poems of the cinema, difficult sometimes to understand but with a depth and quality which has given them permanent value.

The nature of the cinema has in the past been against the production of these

K. Anger's *Fireworks*

individual films for two main reasons – the cost and the technical complexity of making a film. It is to be noted that all the films that have been mentioned were made by artists who were already successful, or on the way to a successful career, in film or another artistic medium. Man Ray was a painter and photographer, Cocteau a poet and author, Buñuel made *L'Age d'Or* with Dali, the surrealist painter. Clair and Delluc made more popular films as well. The present flood of individual underground films owes its prolific nature to technical advances in film-stock, equipment and processing, which have made it both cheaper and easier to make good films without great technical expertise. Another important and related factor is that there is a whole new younger generation, especially in America, to whom film-making is a familiar hobby, and what was a technical mystery to their parents is to them an everyday pastime.

The largest collection of underground films shown in England was presented at the National Film Theatre in April 1968 when 63 films, varying in length from a few minutes to several hours, were included in a season called *The New American Cinema*. Each session was devoted to one or more film-makers as follows: Bruce Connor and the West Coast School: Andy Warhol and Ron Rice; Gregory Markopoulos and the New York School (films by Shirley Clarke and Jonas Mekas were included); Harry Smith and his Magic Cinema; Breer, Kubelka and Van der Beek and the world of Stan Brakhage.
Since the N.F.T. season the New Cinema Club has shown Emswhiller's *Relativity*,

Anger's *Scorpio Rising*, Warhol's *The Chelsea Girls* and the New Arts Laboratory has shown Warhol's *Lonesome Cowboys*. *Scorpio Rising* is a film of the motor-cycle cult mixed with glimpses of comic-strip characters, Hitler, James Dean, Marlon Brando (shown on a TV set in *The Wild One*) and Jesus Christ – from a religious movie. *The Chelsea Girls* has been a key underground film, a side-by-side movie, in which two cameras stare fixedly at groups in the rooms of the Chelsea Hotel in New York, groups of drug-takers, lesbians and homosexuals, sitting, lolling, chatting and making-up. The cameras stare at them minute after minute until we begin to count the wrinkles under their eyes, or admire the folds of their dress. *The Chelsea Girls* owes its popularity partly to its risqué subject, but equally to the success of its original technique.
The N.F.T. season and subsequent club showings are admittedly a random selection, but common features emerge. First, style is pushed to extreme limits. For instance:
(*a*) The flow of images is so rapid that the eye can hardly follow it. The most extreme exponent of this is Robert Breer who uses a radically different image for every frame of the film. Or alternatively:
(*b*) the action is so slow as to seem completely static. The camera fixes on the same scene or objects for minutes and a tracking shot may move at the rate of a few inches an hour.
(*c*) There are variations of light so violent as to be an assault on the eye like torture methods used in political brain-washing – a technique now copied by advertising films and (for instance) in the trailer to *The Thomas Crown Affair*.

(*d*) There is frequent and gratuitous use of technical tricks such as double exposure, reverse motion, upside-down shots, negative images, swinging camera, and so on.
(*e*) Sound tracks are sometimes deafening, sometimes inaudible, sometimes blurred with garbled dialogue, distorted sounds and over-lapping words.
A second feature of underground films is to have little or no formal plot. They may show incidents dealing with the same characters but not in any meaningful sequence. They may merely be a series of random images. Time is irrelevant or jumbled, and shots taken for the film may be inter-cut with scenes from old silent movies or patterns on coloured celluloid. Like the artist who presents *objets trouvés* the film includes *images trouvés* – bits of newsreels, old silent film, photographs, picked up from anywhere.
Allied to this is a third common trait – the mixing of the real and the fictional. Many short films are full of newsreel material – parades, riots, bomb explosions, accidents, fires and war casualties. One of Bruce Connor's most effective films is a pastiche of television sound and image on the Kennedy Assassination. Often there is a mixing of real and fictional characters. In Robert Franks' *Me and My Brother*, Alan Ginsberg, the poet, appears preparing a lecture tour, reading his own poetry. In *Lion's Love*, the director, Agnès Varda, after some persuasion, appears in the film herself. In *David Holzman's Diary* the film-maker is the camera, and he lives his life through its lens, endlessly photographing strangers, friends, the girl-next-door and his own girl friend, alienating them all in the end with his camera mono-mania.

Andy Warhol's *Lonesome Cowboys*

A fourth feature of underground films is that the images, like the style, are ostensibly violent and shocking, but are not presented naturalistically so that the edge is taken off the violence. In style, the film makes shouts at the audience, in content he uses rude swear-words. But because he does it with such naïvety the violence is unreal as if it were bad language copied by a child from grown-ups. In Andy Warhol's *Lonesome Cowboys* there is an exotic scene of three nearly-naked young men fighting, and another in which a cowboy mob strips the skinny heroine and peeps at her genitals. She crawls away and swears at them. These scenes show far more than, say, the fight between Gregory Peck and Robert Mitchum in J. Lee Thompson's *Cape Fear*, or the rape scene in *Virgin Spring*, yet in the two latter films every resource of skill and suggestion is used to make us believe in the *reality* of the situation and the effect is far more powerful. The same applies generally to sex in underground films. As Sheldon Renan says, "There is more nudity but less sex than in commercial films. What sex there is tends to be less licentious, but the representation tends to be more uninhibited." It is perhaps nearer to say it is more juvenile, light-hearted, with less force of depth and passion. In one of Bruce Connor's films there is a shot of a couple in side silhouette in a vertical frame simulating frantic copulation while the girl shouts in a rhythmical climax, "*What does* this thing do? *What does* this thing do?" The scene is too detached and clinical in its effect to be very strongly emotive. Far stronger is Alf Sjöberg's Swedish film *Hets* (*Frenzy*) in which a young girl is seduced, corrupted, and turned into a drunken wreck, by a sadistic, middle-aged school-master. More shocking – though we never even see them in bed together.
It is tempting to think that expanded cinema, the fourth *avant-garde*, the latest manifestation of the underground, is the thing of the future. But these extensions of the cinema are rather additional enrichment than any real substitute for the central art of the story-teller, the dramatist, the master of visual poetry and vivid imagery. Computers may help in lightening the labour of animated drawing or making complex abstract patterns, but they must be under the control of a human artist. Side-by-side films are an enrichment but their quality depends on the quality of the individual films, not on the gimmick of showing them together. The liquid projection of colours can produce interesting effects as in psychedelic discothéques, and they can enrich credit sequences but they are not a substitute for the pattern of human behaviour presented by conventional movies. Nevertheless one must welcome all these experiments as one welcomes the underground film, for like all extreme fashions the underground style will be partially absorbed into the mainstream of cinema, will nourish it and keep the cinema flexible, fresh, interesting and alive.

AWARDS AND FESTIVALS

I have, you will notice, made some amendments to these features on this occasion, combining both under one heading. The reason for this is that, logically, one is an extension of the other and at least one of the objects of most of the many Festivals which are now held is to hand out awards. Moreover, as Peter Cowie, who in the past has contributed introductory notes to the Festivals feature, said when requested to do the same this year: there is little to say about them now. After all, no frothing, left-wing director has swung on the proscenium curtain to stop his film being shown during the past twelve months (at least as far as I know), nobody has even suggested singing the Internationale to drown the sound-track and there haven't been any other – recorded – childish goings-on as there have been at some news-making Festivals in the past. So, without anything like this upon which to comment, here are the bare bones of the various Awards, starting with the high-spot of the Prize-giving year, the "Oscars", awarded by the American Academy of Motion Picture Arts and Sciences in April of this year – 1970.

Best Picture of the Year
MIDNIGHT COWBOY, Jerome Hellman-John Schlesinger Production for United Artists. Jerome Hellman, Producer.

Best Foreign Language Film
Z, Reggane-O.N.C.I.C. Production (Algeria). Directed by Constantine Costa-Gavras.

Best Director
JOHN SCHLESINGER for *Midnight Cowboy*.

Best Actor
JOHN WAYNE in *True Grit*, Hal Wallis Production, Paramount.

Best Actress
MAGGIE SMITH in *The Prime Of Miss Jean Brodie*, 20th Century-Fox.

Best Supporting Actor
GIG YOUNG in *They Shoot Horses, Don't They?*, Chartoff–Winkler–Pollack Production, ABC Pictures Presentation, Cinerama.

Best Supporting Actress
GOLDIE HAWN in *Cactus Flower*, Frankovich Productions, Columbia.

Best Screenplay
(*based on material from another medium*)
MIDNIGHT COWBOY, screenplay by Waldo Salt.

Best Story and Screenplay
(*based on material not previously published or produced*)
BUTCH CASSIDY AND THE SUNDANCE KID, Campanile Productions, 20th Century-Fox. Story and screenplay by William Goldman.

Best Cinematography
BUTCH CASSIDY AND THE SUNDANCE KID, Conrad Hall.

Best Costume Design
ANNE OF THE THOUSAND DAYS, Hal. B. Wallis–Universal. Margaret Furse.

Best Film Editing
Z, Françoise Bonnot.

Best Art Direction
HELLO, DOLLY! Chenault Productions, 20th Century-Fox. John DeCuir, Jack Martin Smith and Herman Blumenthal. Set Decoration: Walter M. Scott, George Hopkins and Raphael Bretton.

Best Sound
HELLO, DOLLY! Jack Solomon and Murray Spivak.

Best Special Visual Effects
MAROONED, a Frankovich-Sturges Production, Columbia. Robie Robinson.

Best Score of a Musical Picture
(*original or adaptation*)
HELLO, DOLLY! music adapted by Lennie Hayton and Lionel Newman.

Best Song
(*Original for The Picture*)
RAINDROPS KEEP FALLIN' ON MY HEAD, from *Butch Cassidy And The Sundance Kid*. Music by Burt Bacharach. Lyrics by Hal David.

Best Original Score
(*For a Motion Picture not a Musical for which only the composer shall be eligible*)
BURT BACHARACH. *Butch Cassidy And The Sundance Kid*.

Documentaries
(*a*) Feature: *ARTUR RUBINSTEIN – THE LOVE OF LIFE*, Midem production Bernard Chevry, producer.

(*b*) Shorts: *CZECHOSLOVAKIA 1968*, U.S. Information Agency, Denis Sanders and Robert M. Fresco, producers.

164

John Wayne, left, who won this year's "Male" Oscar for his performance in *True Grit* (in particular, but also, surely, in general, for many years of fine performances). Incidentally the girl, in the film, Kim Darby, though no Oscar winner, will surely be a star of the future after her delightful performance in this movie.

The Oscar for the best "Foreign-language" film of the year went to *Z*, the highly praised French production.

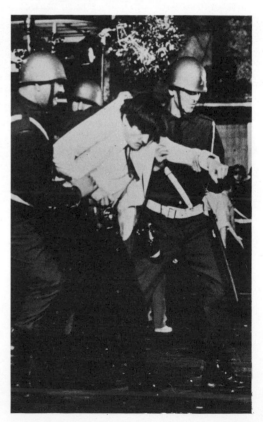

Winner of the year's best actress award was Maggie Smith, Oscar-ed for her outstanding work in *The Prime of Miss Jean Brodie*, the Fox film in which she played an Edinburgh teacher who teaches her gels about life as well as the more routine subjects.

Voted by the Academy of Motion Picture Arts and Sciences as the best *film* of the year was John Schlesinger's *Midnight Cowboy*, in which Jon Voight made a most impressive and highly praised large screen acting début.

Shorts
(*a*) Live Action: *THE MAGIC MACHINES*, Fly-by-Night Productions, Manson Distributing, Joan Keller Stern, producer.

(*b*) Cartoons: *IT'S TOUGH TO BE A BIRD*, Disney Productions, Buena Vista, Ward Kimball, producer.

Just about five weeks previously we had the British equivalent, those prizes distributed by The Society of Film and Television Arts Limited: the "Stellas". These, on March 8, were announced and presented to the following:

SFTA 1969 Awards
On Sunday, March 8, 1970, the following film and television Awards were announced

and presented:

Film Awards

Best Film: *MIDNIGHT COWBOY* (U.S.A.)
United Nations Award: *OH! WHAT A LOVELY WAR* (G.B.)
Best Specialised Film: *LET THERE BE LIGHT* (G.B.)
Best Short Film: *PICTURE TO POST* (G.B.)
Robert Flaherty Award: *PROLOGUE* (Canada)

Film Craft Awards

Best Direction: JOHN SCHLESINGER – *Midnight Cowboy*
Best Screenplay: WALDO SALT – *Midnight Cowboy*
Best Cinematography: GERRY TURPIN – *Oh! What a Lovely War*
Best Art Direction: DON ASHTON – *Oh! What a Lovely War*
Best Costume Design: ANTHONY MENDLESON – *Oh! What a Lovely War*
Best Film Editing: HUGH A. ROBERTSON – *Midnight Cowboy*
Best Sound Track: DON CHALLIS, SIMON KAYE – *Oh! What a Lovely War*

Film Performance Awards

Best Actress: MAGGIE SMITH in *The Prime of Miss Jean Brodie*
Best Supporting Actress: CELIA JOHNSON in *The Prime of Miss Jean Brodie*
Best Actor: DUSTIN HOFFMAN in *Midnight Cowboy* and *John and Mary*
Best Supporting Actor: LAURENCE OLIVIER in *Oh! What a Lovely War*
Most Promising Newcomer: JOHN VOIGHT in *Midnight Cowboy*

The Anthony Asquith Award

Presented by the Anthony Asquith Memorial Trust, for original film music: *Z* – directed by Costa-Gavras, music by Mikos Theodorakis.

The Variety Club, after giving – last March – their Show Personality of the Year Award to Danny La Rue went on to name Nicol Williamson (*Inadmissible Evidence*, *The Bofors Gun* and *The Reckoning*) and Glenda Jackson (*Women in Love*) as the two best film performances of the year.

The *Motion Picture Herald*'s December issue announced the list of "The Top Ten Money-Making Stars of the Year, 1969", voted into their various positions by a poll taken from American and Canadian exhibitors, was as follows:

1. Paul Newman. 2. John Wayne. 3. Steve McQueen. 4. Dustin Hoffman. 5. Clint Eastwood. 6. Sidney Poitier. 7. Lee Marvin. 8. Jack Lemmon. 9. Katharine Hepburn. 10. Barbra Streisand. 11. Dean Martin. 12. Joanne Woodward. 13. Walter Matthau. 14. Richard Burton. 15. Raquel Welch. 16. Jane Fonda. 17. Elizabeth Taylor. 18. Peter Fonda. 19. Julie Andrews. 20. Faye Dunaway. 21. Mia Farrow. 22. Elvis Presley. 23. Sandy Dennis. 24. Warren Beatty. 25. James Garner.

It's interesting to compare this list with the one later issued by the same film newspaper, in which similar ratings (compiled by averaging the previous nine years' lists) were given for "The Decade's Top-Ranking Money-Making Stars": 1. John Wayne. 2. Doris Day. 3. Cary Grant and Rock Hudson – a tie. 4. Jack Lemmon. 5. Julie Andrews. 6. Paul Newman. 7. Sean Connery. 8. Elvis Presley. 9. Sidney Poitier. 10. Lee Marvin.

Now to the Festivals.

Berlin 1969

Golden Bear for best feature film: *EARLY WORKS* (Yugoslavia) directed by Zelimir Zilnik.
Silver Bears: *I AM AN ELEPHANT MADAM – ICH BIN EIN ELEFANT MADAME* (Germany); *BRAZIL A.D. 2,000* (Brazil); *A LONELY PLACE* (Italy); *GREETINGS* (U.S.A.); *MADE IN SWEDEN* (Sweden).

Moscow 1969

Golds to: *LUCIA* (Cuba); *SERAFINO* (Italy); *UNTIL MONDAY* (U.S.S.R.).
Special Jury Prize: *OLIVER!*
Best director: CAROL REED.
Best actor: RON MOODY.

Rio De Janeiro 1969

Golden Seagull: *MARTIN FIERRO* (Argentina). Dir: Leopold Torre-Nilsson.
Silver Seagull: *LA PISCINE* (France). Dir: Jacques Deray.
Special Jury Prize: *JOANNA* (G.B.). Dir: Michael Sarne.
Best actor: AMIDOU in *La Vie, L'Amour, La Mort* (France).
Critics' Prize: *PODNE*.

Trieste 1967

Golden Seal: *THE LAST MAN* (France).
Best actor: TOBIAS ENGELIN – *Can*

You Imagine Robinson (Finland).
Special Jury Prize to *WHY MAN
CREATES* directed by Saul Bass.

New Delhi 1969
Grand Prix: *THE DAMNED* (Italy).
Dir: Visconti.
Silver Peacock to KAREL KACHYNA for
best direction – *The Funny Old Man*.
Best actor: CHRISTOPHER
SANDFORD.
Best actress: LUCIA BOSE.
Golden Seashell for Best Film:
L'AMANTE DI GRANIGNA (Italy).
Silver Seashell: *UNE FEMME DOUCE*
(France).
Silver Seashell: *LOS DESAFIOS ZERT*
(Czechoslovakia).
CIDALC and OCIC Prizes: *PIERRE ET
PAUL* (France).
CEC and Guipuzcoa Prizes: *THE
ITALIAN JOB*, also Special Golden Prize.
Juvenile Prize: *UNE FEMME DOUCE*.
Best Actress: *STEFANIA SANDRELLI*
in *L'Amante di Granigna*.
Best Actress: *LUDMILLA
TCHOURSINA*.
Best Actor: *NICOL WILLIAMSON*.

Cracow (International) 1969
June 17–22
Grand Prize: *THREE LESSONS*
(U.S.S.R.).
Award of the President of the Cracow
City Council: *THE INCIDENTAL BOMB*
(France).
Silver Lajkoniks: *MADIN-BOE* (Cuba);
OPERATION V-2 (Poland); *THE HOLE*
(France); *THE NAME OF MAN*
(Yugoslavia).
Hon. Diploma: *RICEFIELDS UNDER*

FIRE (N. Vietnam).
U.N. Food and Agricultural Organisation
Award: *SKETCHES FOR A FILM ON
INDIA*.
CIDALC: *WALKING* (Canada).
Hon. Mentions: *THE DECORATION*
(Yugoslavia); *DROUGHT* (Poland);
FILM, FILM, FILM (U.S.S.R.).
Commendation: *ONE OF THE MISSING*
(U.K.).

Berlin 1969
June 25–July 6
Golden Bear and Grand Prix as best film:
EARLY YEARS (Yugoslavia).
Berlin Senate's Youth Film Prize to
Director ZELIMIR ZILNIK.
Silver Bears: *BRAZIL YEAR 2000*;
MADE IN SWEDEN (Sweden); *I AM
AN ELEPHANT, MADAME* (FRG);
GREETINGS (U.S.A.); *A QUIET PLACE
IN THE COUNTRY* (Italy).
OCIC Prize: *MIDNIGHT COWBOY*
(U.S.A.).
Gandhi Prize given by CIDALC Jury:
THE BED-SITTING ROOM (U.K.).
UNICRIT Prize to Director GERARD
PIRES for *Erotissimo*.
International Film Prize: *THE MILKY
WAY* (France).

Moscow 1969
July 7–22
Gold Prizes: *LUCIA* (Cuba); *SERAFINO*
(Italy); *SEE YOU MONDAY* (U.S.S.R.).
Other Prizes: *THE BROTHERS
KARAMAZOV* (U.S.S.R.); *OLIVER!*
(U.K.); *A GERMAN DIARY* (W.
Germany); *PLAYTIME* (France); *WHEN
YOU HEAR THE BELLS* (Yugoslavia);
COLONEL WOLODYJOWSKI (Poland);

A WOMAN FOR A SEASON
(Rumania); *A STRIP OF SKY* (Argentina)
2001: A SPACE ODYSSEY (U.S.A.);

Performances: Actors: RON MOODY,
TADENCZ LOMNICKI (Poland).
Female: ANNA MARIA PIKKIO
(Argentina).

Trieste 1969 (Science Fiction)
July 12–19
Gold Asterisk (Grand Prix): *LE DERNIER
HOMME* (France).
Gold Seal (Best Short): *COSMIC ZOOM*
(Canada).
Special Prizes: *RUUSUJEN AIKA*
(Finland); *WHY MAN CREATES*
(U.S.A.).
Best Actor: RITVA VESPA in *Ruusjen
Aika*.
Best Actress: TOBIAS ENGEL in *Tu
Imagines, Robinson*.

Venice 1969
Aug 24–Sept 6
Critics Prize for best domestic: Fellini's
SATYRICON (Italy).
Other Awards: *SIERRA MAESTRA*
(Italy); *PIGSTY* (Italy); *UNDER THE
SIGN OF THE SCORPION* (Italy);
BENITO CERENO (France); *PIRATE'S
FIANCEE* (France); *PAULINE IS
LEAVING*; *HONOUR AND GLORY*
(Czechoslovakia); *THE DEVILS*; *THE
TRAP* (Yugoslavia); *THE ADVENT*;
THE INHERITORS (Brazil); *YARVAR
MALIKU* (Bolivia); *THE FIRST
MACHETE CHARGE* (Cuba); *OF LOVE
AND OTHER SOLITUDES* (Spain);
CARDILLAC; *THE BOY* (Japan);
WINTER-WIND (France–Hungary);

FORBIDDEN ZONE (Hungary); *TWO GENTLEMEN SHARING* (U.K.); *SWEET HUNTERS*; *THE FATHER* (Sweden); *CHILREN'S GAMES* (U.S.A.); *DAY STAR* (U.S.S.R.).

Edinburgh 1969
Aug 24–Sept 13
Films listed as shown (no entry of Awards)
THE FALL (U.S.A.); *MADE IN SWEDEN* (Sweden); *DILLINGER IS DEAD* (Italy); *EASY RIDER* (U.S.A.); *THE BED-SITTING ROOM*; *SHOCK CORRIDOR* (U.S.A.); *THE GLADIATORS* (U.K.); *GOTO, L'ILE D'AMOUR* (France).

Bergamo 1969
Sept 7–14
(*Suspended Sept 8. Feature Prize not awarded*)

Mannheim 1969
Oct 6–11
First Prizes: *322* (Czechoslovakia); *MEDIUM COOL* (U.S.A.).
Other Awards: *EIKA KATAPPA* (Germany); *SALESMAN* (U.S.A.); *ITALIAN CAPRICCIO* (FRG); *SISTERS OF THE REVOLUTION*; *THE GALLONS* (Czechoslovakia); *GERMANY DADA* (FRG); *HEY, MAMA.*

7th Kodak Teenage Awards (U.S.A.)
First two Prizes to animation: *THE WAD AND THE WORM*; *THAT'S HOW IT IS*

Costa Del Sol (Spain) 1969

International Week of Author Films
Nov 3–9
1st: *LA MANZANA DE LA DISCORDIA* (Mexico).
2nd: *TROPICI* (Italy).
1st by Public Vote: *ANTONIO DAS MORTES* (Brazil).
2nd by Public Vote: *HET COMPROMISS* (Holland).
Shorts: 1st: *GOSPEL* (Spain).
2nd: *CABASCABO* (Nigeria).

Chicago 1969
Nov 8–19
Feature Winner: *EENY MEENY MINY MOE* (Sweden).
Actor Prize: Silver Hugo: PER OSCARSSON, in *Eeny Meeny Miny Moe.*
Best Director: HARRY KUMEL for *Horoscope* (Yugoslavia);
Other Prizes: *SIEGE* (Israel); *FLASHBACK* (Italy).
Special Prize: *AKRAN* (U.S.A.).

Shorts: *THE SPRING OF LIFE* (Yugoslavia); *WALKING* (Canada, for animation); *ANNABEL LEE* (U.S.A.); *ANIMA MUNDI* (Sweden); *MAESTRO KOKO* (Yugoslavia); *THANKYOU, MARSHALL MAN* (U.S.A.).

Hemisfilm 1969
Best Film: *ALEXANDER* (France).
Best Director: DUSAN VOKOTIC for *Seventh Continent* (Yugoslavia).
Best Actress: SUZY KENDALL in *The Gamblers* (U.S.A.).
Best Actor: NICOLO in *Der Findling* (Germany).
Best Photography: ALFRED TAYLOR

for *Soft* (U.S.A.).
Best Shorts Subject: *STALKED* (U.S.A.).
Best Underground: *MESSAGES, MESSAGES* (U.S.A.).
Best Commercial: *EVERYONE* (U.S.A.).
Special Jury Awards: *THE SUPPER AND SCENE POLITIC, '68* (U.S.A.); *THE CLOSING CENTURIES* (India); To N. YAKHONTOV for *MAN TO MAN* (U.S.S.R.).

Mar Del Plata (Argentina) 1970
March 5–15
Best Picture: *MACUNAIMA* (Brazil).
Best Director: FRANK PERRY for *Last Summer* (U.S.A.).
Best Actor: UGO TOGNAZZI in *Il Commisario Pepe* (Italy).
Best Actress: LIZA MINELLI for *The Sterile Cuckoo* (U.S.A.).
Best Screenplay: KRYSZTOF ZANUSSI (*Struktura Krysztalu* (Structure of Crystals)) (Poland).
OPERA PRIMA (First Work): RAUL DE LA TORRE for *Juan Lamaglia y Senora* (Argentina).

Cartenga (Colombia) 1970
March
Best Latin American Picture: *JUAN LAMAGLIA Y SENORA* (Argentina).
Best Actress: BERYL REID for *The Killing of Sister George.*
Best Actor: BABA KIKABIDZE in *Don't Worry* (U.S.S.R.).
OCIC Award: *TELL THEM WILLIE BOY IS HERE.*

Oberhausen 1970 (Shorts)
April 12–18
(*By policy no prizes. Awards in Cash*).

Cannes 1970
May
Grand Prix: *MASH* (director: Robert Altman).
Special Jury Prize: *ABOVE SUSPICION* (director: Elio Petri).
Male Acting: MARCELLO MASTROIANNI in *Drama of Jealousy*.
Female Acting: OTTAVIA PICCOLO in *Metelo*.
Director: JOHN BOORMAN for *Leo The Last*.
Jury Prizes: *THE BALKANS* (Hungary); *STRAWBERRY STATEMENT* (U.S.A.).
First Film Prize: RAOUL COUTARD for *Hoa Binh*.

Oberhausen 1970
No Prizes instead Premiums mostly awarded to political pictures: 3 Premiums $1,350: *OLLAS POPULARES* (Argentina); *MOLES OF REVOLUTION* (W. Germany); *GUIDE FOR BONN AND SURROUNDINGS* (W. Germany).

4 Premiums at $540: *METHODS* (Hungary); *42nd ST* (U.S.A.); *INVASION* (Poland); *SOBOTA GRAZYNA* (Poland) (Split Premium) *OXI-NEIN* (E. Germany).

2 Premiums at $405: *SILENT WEEK IN THE HOUSE* (Czechoslovakia); *WE* (?).

1 Premium at $270: *BONDAR* (U.S.S.R.).

Carmen d'Avino Prize ($540): *NOT EVERYTHING THAT FLIES IS A BIRD* (Yugoslavia).

International Film Critics Association Prize: *THE GARDENER OF LANDSCAPES* (Switzerland); *LE PEUPLE ET SES FUSILS* (France); Four Shorts by Frans Zwartjes (Holland); *THE TRENDSETTER* (U.K.).

Melbourne 1969
(May 6–21)
Grand Prize: *PAS DE DEUX* (N. Maclaren, Canada NFB)
Silver Boomerang: *THE VOICE OF THE WATER* (The Netherlands)
Special Prizes: *THE APPLICANT* (U.S.A.); *FAITHFUL DEPARTED* (Ireland); *SAN FRANCISCO* (U.K.); *MAGIC LIGHT* (Germany); *THE TALGAI SKULL* (Australia); *DREDGING* (The Netherlands); *SIRENE* (Belgium); *FLOWERS ON A ONE-WAY STREET* (Canada, NFB).
Diplomas of Merit: *ABOUT THE WHITE BUS* (U.K.); *AND THEY NAMED IT HOLLAND* (The Netherlands); *THE DROVER'S WIFE* (Australia); *END OF A REVOLUTION* (U.K.); *THE OTHER SIDE* (Belgium); *THE RED ARROWS* (U.K.); *SANDCASTLES* (U.S.S.R.); *WHY MAN CREATES* (U.S.A.); *WINDY DAY* (U.S.A.).

Cracow 1969
9th Festival of Polish Shorts (June 14–17)
Principal Awards: *HIS NAME IS BLAZEJ REJDEK*; *HE LIVES AT ROZNICA*; *JEDREJOW COUNTRY*.
Other Awards: *FOR OUR FREEDOM AND YOURS*; *KRZYSZTOF PENDERECKI*; *JUST SOLDIERS*; *TARDIGRADA*; *THE STAIRS*;

SALOME; *OPERATION V-2*.
Best Film on Social Problems: *THE OLD MINERS*.
Critics Award: *SIXTEEN YEARS OLD*.

San Sebastian 1969
June 16–24
First Award: *THE RAINBOW PEOPLE* (U.S.A.).

Mar Del Plata 1970
Best film: *MACUNAIMA* (Brazil). Dir: Joaquin Pedro de Andrade.
Best director: FRANK PERRY for *Last Summer* (U.S.A.).
Best actor: UGO TOGNAZZI for *Il Commisario Pepe* (Italy).
Best actress: LIZA MINELLI for *The Sterile Cuckoo* (U.S.A.)
Best screenplay: KRYSZTOF ZANUSSI for *Struktura Krysztalu* (Poland).

Coming now to commercial successes, the following films were announced by *The Daily Cinema* as being the biggest British box-office successes of 1969: *Oliver? Till Death Us Do Part, Carry on Camping, The Love Bug, Bullitt, Carry On Up The Khyber, The Virgin Soldiers, Three Into Two Won't Go, Oh! What a Lovely War, The Italian Job, Ice Station Zebra.*

The *Motion Picture Herald*'s 1970 list of exhibitor-voted "Stars of Tomorrow" put *Midnight Cowboy* co-star JON VOIGHT in first place, followed by: Kim Darby, Glenn Campbell, Richard Benjamin, Mark Lester, Olivia Hussey, Leonard Whiting, Ali McGraw, Barbara Hershey and Alan Alda in that order.

WORLD ROUND-UP

by Peter Armitage

If the popular press is to be believed, world cinema is in a parlous state. It is partly true, of course: at least, everywhere American finance plays a significant role. In the States, the selling of old properties, not least the nostalgic relics of old Hollywood, attracts understandable attention and brings out the professional mourners. In Britain, the high unemployment of ciné-technicians, principally caused by the American withdrawal, deservedly is a suitable topic for concern and not only from the unions. But stand back, or sit back and look at the screen and the commercial cinema is not on its last legs. There is quite a lot to cheer about.

Some reports make it sound as if the blockbuster is dead. Again, not altogether true since there are still some in the pipeline and others projected, and the notion of safety in massive insurance and investment will die hard. But the blinding truths that small-budget films can make money and that the essential thing is youth appeal have been rediscovered yet again – the constant citing of *Easy Rider* is becoming unbearable. Wild hopes that the days of the great comedian or the small, exhilarating musical might come back will, no doubt, be dashed, but there is much pleasure to be found in the new, low calorie cinema of *Butch Cassidy and the Sundance Kid*, *Goodbye, Columbus*, *The Graduate* and *Midnight Cowboy*.

Look at the world cinema and many contrasting pictures emerge. One optimistic view was admirably put in a National Film Theatre brochure: "the young people of the world have seized upon cinema as their personal art form. Creative minds that once would have written novels now make films and they are circumventing the traditionally expensive ways of making them. Not just the young people of the major countries either but the youths of the 'third world', the countries without a film tradition from Cuba and Brazil to Algeria and Senegal who have created a 'new cinema'. Films have become the weapons of the young – the revolutionary weapons . . ."

In so-called advanced countries the young film-maker is mainly an underground worker. Elsewhere, paradoxically, opportunity can be much easier. In Cuba the régime favours the cinema, whereas in Brazil they may be permissive until the film is finished. The result is that we suddenly become aware of the cinema in these countries, of films like Gomez's *The Charge of the Knives* or Rocha's *Antonio das Mortes*. It is no longer a surprise to find a vigorous and vital cinema where previously one was not known to exist.

While more serious observers may notice that film-makers in many countries are fascinated by the problems of social change from mild protest to revolution, the popular view is that the cinema is currently obsessed with sex. Apart from "adult information" from the Germans and such national variants as the Swedish vicar troubled by his inexhaustible virility, the Japanese *Prisoner of Lust*, the Italian *Sacred, Pure and Uncontaminated by Woman*, there is nudity everywhere. Perhaps the cinematic novelty will soon wear off though there is little sign yet. Perhaps Mike Nichols will transport the whole subject of sex to comic heights with

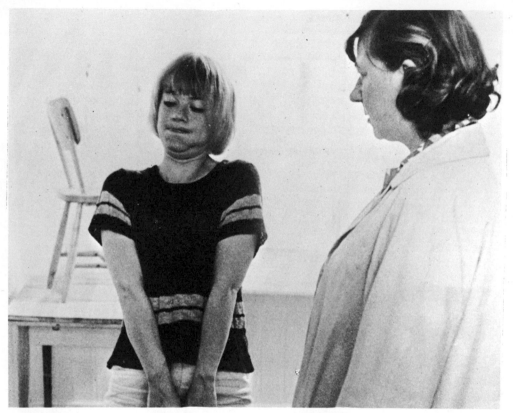

Anita Ekstrom is the star of Lars Farsberg's *Yankee*, the story of a young girl's life in a Gothenburg slum, based on the best-selling novel by Martin Weiss. Another Svenska Fiminstituet production released in G.B. by Gala Films.

Carnal Knowledge. In the meantime, one can only sympathise with the straight-forward reaction of the Sengalese director Ousmane Sembene:
"It is really rather stupid. You go to a ninety-minute movie and ten minutes is spent in credits, one half-hour is spent on sex, and then the camera starts searching and searching, endlessly searching. It doesn't leave much time for the story."
It is, of course, quite impossible to make, let alone present, a full and proper survey of world production. Annually several

thousand films are produced and registered and innumerably more stay underground, so that one person, even if he never emerged from the cinema and watched several screens at once, could not see it all. And watching fragments, as we all know from trailers and television clips, can be highly deceptive. What we do see is the small biased sample of films which gain international currency through festivals, and we read about the films which are vigorously promoted and which are made by recognised film-makers and stars. The best that can be done is to survey most of the European countries and one or two of the major industries outside Europe, noting some of the works of merit already made and speculating upon some of the intriguing prospects still in the making. Even so, there may be major omissions: Luis Buñuel filming in his native Spain for only the third time in his long career, *Tristana* with Catherine Deneuve; Jerzy Skolimowski, as before with *Le Départ*, in Belgium to make *The Suicide*.

FRANCE
There is such a wealth of top film-makers in France that one would expect a good haul even in a lean year. The older generation goes on and on: at eighty Abel Gance works on a film about Christ and a two-part *Christopher Columbus*; Clouzot on *Le hotu*; Carné on *Les enbrumes* with Sylvana Mangano and Leonard Whiting; Delannoy on a re-make of *L'eternal retour* with Jean Marais; Autant-Lara on *Les patates*; Cayatte on *Les chemins de Khatmandu*; Melville on *The Red Circle* with Delon, Montand and Bourvil; Franju on *C'est la faute de l'abbé*

Alf Sjöberg's film of the famous Strindberg play *The Father*, with George Rydeberg in the title role and Gunnel Lindblom as his wife. A Svenska Filminstitutet production released in G.B. by Gala Films.

Mouret from Zola; Clément has apparently regained form with *Le passage de la pluie*; and even Renoir makes a TV film, *Le petit roi d'Yvetot* with Arnoul to be seen later in the cinema. Even more active, of course, are the generation of directors who came up with the new wave and in the early 60s: Demy, *Peau d'Ane* with Deneuve; de Broca, *Les figurants du nouveau monde* with Noiret, Gravey, Perier and Valentina Cortese; Doniol-Valcroze, *La maison des Bories*; Colpi, *Ulysses Come Home* with Fernandel; Deville, *L'ours et la poupée* with Bardot and Cassel; Allio, *La noce chez les petits*; Molinaro, *Mon Oncle Benjamin* with Jacques Brel; Drach, *Elise ou la vie vraie* with Marie-José Nat; Moussy, *Three Men on a Horse* with Robert Dhéry; Delouche, *Man of Passion* with Riva; and Rohmer, *Le genou de Claire* with Brialy.

Most important is the sustained current peak of Chabrol and Truffaut. Since *Les Biches* Chabrol has not had to fall back on potboilers and after *Le Boucher*, a thriller about a butcher who falls in love with the schoolmistress, he went on to *Le jour des Parques* with the same team of Jean Yanne and Stephane Audran. Truffaut, who has not been as prolific as Chabrol over the years, has not looked back since the success of *Stolen Kisses*, and has moved on to a sequel *Domicile conjugal* with Léaud, and *L'enfant sauvage*, set in 1798, the story of the education of the virgin mind of a child grown up in the wild, with Truffaut himself playing a leading role.

It would appear that Costa-Gravas has attempted to repeat the success of *Z* with *L'aveu*, a political biography of a former Czech Minister of Foreign Affairs which was originally to have been shot in Czechoslovakia but was overtaken by events. Lelouch has begun a trilogy with *Un homme qui me plaît* with Belmondo and Girardot and *La femme de quarante ans* with Signoret and Brialy. He is also the producer of two features shot in Brazil, one by Glauber Rocha, the other Jean Pollett's *Le maître du temps*.

Others seem to have reached turning point in their careers. Reichenbach, who has made many documentaries, most recently

Kara Juro in Nagiha Oshima's *The Diary of a Shinjuku Thief*, which although shown in Britain at a special screening has yet to have a commercial release here.

Artur Rubinstein with *The Yehudi Menuhin Story* and *Violence in Houston* planned, is due to make his first fictional drama, *Massacre* with Natalie Delon. Etaix, after *Le grand amour* and a string of comedies, has turned to a documentary, *Cocagne*, on the consumer society with no script and no actors, not even himself. Rossif, a specialist in historical compilations, is making his first fictional work, *Aussi loin que l'amour*. Malle, who tries to change with every film and who seems to have undergone a personal

revelation with *Calcutta*, has declared that he does not want to make any more fictional films and plans a feature on the social behaviour of bees, a documentary, *The Machine*, on a small tribe in a remote valley, and he is expected to direct *Did Gulliver Ever Come Home?*, the preparation for which involved a symposium of international scholars held in Denmark. Malle has also turned actor in Nelly Kaplan's first feature *La fiancée de Pirate* and *The Friends*, also a first directorial assignment of comedian Gérard Blain. At the same time, new talent is emerging and developing: Luc Mollet, *The New Adventures of Billy the Kid* with Léaud; Raoul Coutard, *Hoa Binh*, the cameraman's first feature as a director; Claude Sautet, *The Little Things in Life* with Piccoli, Romy Schneider and Lea Massari; Jean Cayrol, *Prière de ne pas déranger*; and Gérard Brach, Polanski's scriptwriter, has directed *The House* with Michel Simon. All this does not exhaust the list of promising titles. Just three more: two gangster thrillers, Verneuil's *Le clan des Siciliens* with Delon, Gabin and Ventura and Jacques Deray's *Borsalino* with Delon and Belmondo, and Georges Lautner's *La route de Salina* which stars Robert Walker Jr., Mimsy Farmer and Rita Hayworth.

ITALY
The largest film industry in Europe does not seem to have suffered greatly from the withdrawal of U.S. finance. At least it is possible to reel off a long list of interesting new works from the many talented film-makers. After *The Damned*, Visconti turned to Thomas Mann's *Death in Venice*

with Bogarde and is lined up for a version of Proust's *Remembrance of Things Past* with four or five adaptors working on the script and a cast reported to include Delon, Girardot, Helmut Berger, Bardot and Olivier. Another heavy gun, Pasolini, went from *Medea* with Callas to a life of *St. Paul* and a film inspired by *The Decameron*, and he has also assisted one of his favourite actors Franco Citti (*Accattone*, *Oedipus Rex*) to direct his first feature, *Ostia*. Marco Ferrari's *The Seed of Man* stars Girardot, Anne Wiazemsky and Marco Margine in a story which moves into a dead world and final annihilation. Further strange visions can be expected from the director of *Escalation*, Roberto Faenza, with another ironic fantasy *H2S* and Bernardo Bertolucci whose *Il Conformista* is based on a Moravia story and features Jean-Louis Trintignant and Stefania Sandrelli.

There are numerous other satires and comments on the conflict between the generation from Luigi Zampa's *La Contestazione* (Gassman and Manfredi), and Yves Allegret's *The Invasion* (Gastoni and Piccoli) to Liliana Cavani's *The Cannibals* (Ekland and Clémenti) and Bruno Baratti's *La Marcusiana* (Prevost and Olga Linka). Other films by directors whose work usually attracts attention: de Sica, *Il Giardino dei Finzi Contini*; Mauro Bolognini; Francesco Rosi, *Uomini contro* with Mark Frechette; Pietro Germi, *The Chestnuts are Good*; Patroni Griffi, *Gli Amanti*; Carmelo Bene's *Edward II*; Lina Wertmuller's *Dranghetta*; and Renato Castellani's *Leonardo*. Lina We and Sophia Loren in *Mother Courage*, Lisa Gastoni in *Maddalena*, directed by the Pole Jerzy

Kawalerowicz and Clémenti in *Teste Tagliate*, directed by Brazilian Glauber Rocha, are plans that will excite varied expectations.

WEST GERMANY

For a national cinema with a glorious past, the progress of West German film production is nothing to shout about. The sex film is still dominant and going strong with *Helga and Men*, *Sex is a Pleasure*, *Sexual Partnership*, *Can I Make a Mother of You?* *Your Husband the Unknown*, *Living Together, Poppet: Or How Do I Tell My Daughter?* and many more. Even the film which won the 1970 Ernst Lubitsch prize for the best German-speaking comedy had the title *Don't Fumble Darling*. There have been a few artistic successes. Alexander Kluge's *Artists at the Top of the Big Top: Disorientated* received the highest critical praise as well as provoking bitter critical argument. *I am an Elephant, Madam*, the first film of a leading theatrical director Peter Zadek is one of the more successful attempts at a Brechtian cinema. Werner Herzog's *Signs of Life*, shown at the London Festival, which dealt with the breakdown of a young German soldier in Greece in the Second World War, marked an impressive début. Werner Schroeter's *Eika Katappa*, an underground film with affinities with Warhol, won the Josef von Sternberg prize.

There are some hopes for Rolf Thiele's *Ears Boxed* with Curd Jürgens, Gila von Weitershausen, Nadja Tiller and Alexandra Stewart and a version of Turgenev's *First Love* directed by Maximilian Schell. The programme of Rob Houwer who produced

Johannes Schaaf's *The Delinquent* includes Michael Verhoeven's *The Orgy* and Helmut Förnbacher's *Who Bit the Apple First?*, photographed by Jakubisko's cameraman, Igor Luther.

SWEDEN

Thirty-two features were made last year and there was a big increase in the number that were wholly Swedish, though co-productions are still going strong. *Man from the Other Side* has Bibi Andersson as a Swedish woman in love with a Soviet engineer, Slava Tichonov. Arne Mattson's *Anne and Eve* is being shot in English in Italy and Yugoslavia with an international cast headed by Francisco Rabal. Gunnar Högland's *Swedish Sin – Is There Any?* is a comedy about the investigations of a German sociologist.

Turning to the purely Swedish, Bergman's thirtieth film (but only his second in colour), *A Passion*, is described as a psychological chamber play with the performers Liv Ullman, Bibi Andersson and Max von Sydow stepping outside their roles to comment on the characters. Vilgot Sjöman has followed his *Curious Yellow* film with a strong indictment of the purely punitive penal system, *You're Lying*. Jan Troell is back home from the U.S.A. editing *The Emigrants* and Bo Widerberg is reported to be following his footsteps by making his next film about the Swedish syndicalist Joe Hill, in the States. Kjell Grede has moved on from the world of the children in *Hugo and Josefin* to the emergence of the adolescent into the adult world in *Harry Munter*.

Bo Vibenius, Grede's unit manager on

176 *Hugo and Josefin*, has made a children's feature for his first film, *How Marie Met Frederik, Rebus the Donkey, Ploj the Kangeroo and . . .* , with Frederik Becklen who played Hugo. Another film graduate and assistant to Bo Widerberg, Roy Andersson, has made his first feature, *A Love Story*, working with Jorgen Persson the photographer of *Elvira Madigan* and *Adalen '31*.

The new films of Jan Halldoff and Jonas Cornell are social satires. Cornell has moved some distance since *Hugs and Kisses* to *The Pig Hunt*, which is about a state drive to eradicate all the pigs in Sweden and which has allegorical overtones. Halldoff's *A Dream about Freedom* shows how society, first by indifference and then by over-dramatisation, turns two young minor delinquents into major criminals.

JAPAN

The world's largest industry continues to pour out films though its condition remains troubled. Most of the output deals with some aspect of war or sex. The war films range through history from *Samurai Banners* set in ancient Japan to *The Battle of the Japan Sea* based on the Russo–Japanese War of 1905 and *Gateway to Glory* and *Admiral Yamamato*, both set in the Second World War. The sex films sound "typically Japanese": *Secrets of a Women's Temple* ("the nunnery becomes a nest of sadism, violence and murder"); *The Blind Beast* ("she sinks uncomprehendingly into a world of unending sadism and masochism"); *The Joys of Torture* ("the lovers prefer death and the abbess is later crucified"). A highly popular strain can be seen in such titles as

Mini-Skirt Lynchers, Womens Police, Lefty Fencer (a one-handed, single-eyed heroine) and *Crimson Bat, the Blind Swordswoman* which has spawned a series.

On the other hand there is the continued inability of Kurosawa to find finance for numerous projects. He has declared that he has no interest in war pictures or pornography and has been quoted as saying "I am hoping to get together a small group of directors who think as I do – we plan to call ourselves 'The Four Samurai' – to build our own fortress inside the film

Another film shown by Derek Hill's New Cinema Club but still awaiting the certificate which will give it a wider showing is the Danish production, *Det Kaere Legetoj – Danish Blue* as it was called in G.B.

industry". Everyone, except Japanese producers, must hope that they will be endowed with the samurai's invincibility. New works from other well-known directors are noticeably absent, but a director like Kaneto Shindo continues to thrive with *Odd Affinity* (the latent, mutual sexual attraction of mother and son) and *Heat Wave Island* (poverty, morals and the love of two women). Three more films likely to have international appeal are Hani's *Aido*, a gothic story based on a popular play about a student and a mysterious lady; Masumura's *A Thousand Cranes*, based on a novel by the Nobel laureate Kawabata; and Shinoda's *Double Suicide*, a period drama in the highly clinical style. There may be numerous good films and directors hidden in the long list of releases, but with three of his films – *Boy*, *Death by Hanging* and *Diary of a Shinjuku Thief* – all reaching us hard on each others' heels the major recent discovery has been director Nagisha Oshima.

U.S.S.R.

The centenary of Lenin's birth has seen a surge in the number of films celebrating his life and Soviet history. Apart from a ciné-anthology and documentaries such as *Lenin, Documents, Facts, Reminiscences* and *Leader, Teacher and Friend*, Lenin is portrayed in dramatic features such as Yarasik's *Lenin, the Year 1903* and events related to his life are depicted in Pogodin's *Kremlin Chimes* and Azarov's *A Train for Tomorrow*. In addition, Mosfilm timed the release of other major features such as Ozerov's 70mm epic, *The Capture of Berlin*, and Saltykov's *The Director* to be part of the celebrations.

The successful collaboration with the Italians on Bondarchuk's *Waterloo* has led to further co-productions on works of high cultural pedigree. Bondarchuk moved on to direct and appear as the Tsar in *Boris Godunov*, Gregori Chukrai directed Pushkin's *Dubrovsky* and de Sica made *Sunflower* with Mastroianni, Loren and Lyadmila Savelyeva (who played Natasha in *War and Peace*) using Russian locations. In similar vein, co-production with the East German Defa has resulted in a two-part film on the Spanish artist *Goya*, directed by the East German, Konrad Wolf, and scripted by the Bulgarian Angel Wagenstein.

The whole Eastern bloc would appear to have collaborated on Oserov's trilogy *Liberation*. Other versions of literary masterpieces include Tolstoy's *Living Corpse* and Dostoievsky's *Crime and Punishment*, directed by Kulijanov with Georgi Taratorkin as Raskolnikov and Smoktunovsky also starring.

Of modern subjects, Rostotsky's *Till Monday*, a school drama about pupil–teacher relations, has had considerable domestic success. *In Love*, made by the Uzbek director Ishmukhamedov in Tashkent may place him alongside Konchalovsky (*The First Teacher* and *A Nest of Gentlefolk*) as a film-maker working far from Moscow whose work is eagerly anticipated. Among other films of international interest: Yutkevich's *Plot for a Short Story* which reconstructs the history of Chekhov's "Seagull"; a full-length biography of the great film-maker Dovzhenko called *Golden Gate* and made by his widow Yulia Solntseva.

YUGOSLAVIA

In its modest way, the Yugoslav cinema is prospering more than most, and of the annual record of thirty-five features produced last year, one third were by new directors. Two of the more important newcomers are Boro Drašković and Želimir Žilnik, both of whom are deeply concerned about the contemporary human condition and anxious to use film to change people. Drašković's *Horoscope* deals with the inactivity of purposeless youth and Žilnik's *Early Works*, which won the Golden Bear at the Berlin Festival, is an attempt to examine social illusions and to analyse the causes of the shallowness and resistance to revolutionary movements.

Youth has not stolen all the limelight, though the notable films from older hands are not so hotly topical: Mimica's *The Event* is a modernisation of Chekhov; Petrovic's *It Rains in My Village* is also up-to-date but inspired by Dostoievsky's "Evil Ghosts"; Pavlović's *Ambush* is set in the first days of liberation after the Second World War; and Škubonja's *Downstream from the Sun* is the story of a town girl who as a teacher is sent to a remote mountain village.

One of the most intriguing film titles, unlikely to come from anywhere but Yugoslavia, is Mitrović's *Murder Committed in a Sly and Cruel Manner and from a Low Motive*.

HUNGARY

Miklós Jancsó is still the foremost Hungarian director in international esteem. His pre-occupation with form and his attack on sentimental romanticism do

Jan Nilsen, stars of Sweden's *Harry Munter*, directed by Kjell Grede and selected as this year's Swedish entry for Cannes Film Festival honours. Described as a bitter-sweet story of a young boy growing into adulthood, it will be released in England by Gala Films.

not make his films universally attractive, but both *The Confrontation* and *Winter Sirocco* with Marina Vlady and Jacques Charrier are charged with interest. Jancsó has not encouraged imitation but there would seem to be some elements similar to his work in *Palm Sunday*, the first feature of Imre Gyöngyössy.

István Gaál may gain international recognition as a major director with *High School*. This story of a village where falcons are trained to dispose of bird pests is concerned with discipline and inhumanity and it marks a change of style from his earlier *Current*. In *Love, Emilia*, the tragedy of a schoolgirl at the turn of the century, Pál Sándor has confirmed the talent of *Clowns on the Wall*. Another director whose stature grows is Andras Kovács whose latest, *Relay Race*, is about university students today.

Hungary is making a strong contribution to the growing ranks of women directors with Judit Elek's *The Lady from Constantinople*, Márta Mészáros's *Binding Sentiments* and Livia Gyarmathy's *Do You Know "Sunday-Monday"*? Apart from Gyöngyössy and Elek, first features have come from Pál Gabor (*Forbidden Ground*) and Isolt Kézdi-Kovacs (*Temperate Zone*). There is also the hope that the vein of satire – Rényi's *Krebs the God*, Revész's *Voyage Around my Skull* and Ferenc Kardos's *A Crazy Night* – will throw up a masterpiece.

POLAND

A resurgence in Polish cinema appears to be on the way. Andrzej Wajda found a new lease of artistic life with *Everything* for Sale and he has since made *Hunting Flies*, an anti-feminist comedy, and *Landscape after the Battle*, about a young poet in a displaced persons camp in 1945. Both films have something in common with Wajda's earlier work, but there are developments in both viewpoint and style. While other established directors may appear to be working along familiar lines – Kutz's *The Taste of Black Earth*, Lenartowicz's *The Red and the Gold*, Passendorfer's *Day of Remission* – there has been another crop of promising debutants. Following the success of Witold Leszczyński's *Days of Matthew*, a number of young directors have started their feature careers with films which have the common aim of a more personal cinema. Krzysztof Zanussi's *The Structure of Crystals*, Wladyslaw Slesicki's *Shifting Sands* and Wojciech Solarz's *The Pier*, all attempt a more profound understanding of human relationships and are anti-decorative in their renouncement of sets and make-up. The films make no compromise, so much so that Zanussi says that he intended a difficult film and even chose the title to be "provocatively non-commercial".

Two other new films of interest: *No Return for Johnny*, a drama which confronts a Vietnamese and an American, is directed by an Iranian, Kaveh Pur Rahnama, who graduated from Lódź film school; *Zbyszek*, another film which takes its inspiration from the life of Cybulski, draws on sequences from ten of the features in which he starred, but is fashioned by his former co-worker, Jan Laskowski, into a portrait of a hero of the generation who grew up during the War and were unable to settle to a normal life for many years afterwards.

CZECHOSLOVAKIA

It is still difficult to know the true state of affairs two years after the events of summer 1968. Some reports tell of severe restrictions upon film-makers with loyalty oaths and past successes disclaimed: others say that things are near-normal. Certainly the flow of films has not been interrupted, few sound as if they are limited to safe themes and the only missing names are Forman, Paser and Weiss. In *Genius* by Štefan Uher, one of the pioneers of the new Czechoslovak cinema, men and devils exchange roles, with the devils spreading good and love to reform the world so that they may corrupt it afresh. Pavel Juráček's *A Case for the New Hangmen* is a free adaptation of Gulliver's visit to Laputa. There is no spurious hope in František Vláčil's *Adelheid*, the story of a pathetically doomed love, nor Karyl Kachyna's *A Funny Man*, about an elderly man, seriously ill, who has lost all interest in life. The veteran Otakar Vávra's *Witch Hammer* is an historical drama but hardly innocuous, being concerned with the cruelty and indifference of the witch trials. Juraj Jakubisko, who revealed the most harrowing version in *Deserter and the Nomads*, has completed *Birds, Orphans and Fools* which has love, happiness and death as its themes. Jakubisko is also the co-author of *The Party in the Botanical Garden*, a philosophical comedy marking the début of Slovak director, Elo Havetta. Another first feature, *The Saint from the Outskirts of Town*, is a tragicomedy on the limits of goodness by Petr Tučei, an admirer of Evald Schorm whose latest *The Seventh Day, the Eighth Night* shares the same leading man, Václav Kotva. Several comedies stand out. The latest from Poskalsky is *Men About Town*, three provincial plasterers determined to have a night out in Prague, and Jaroslav Papoušek's second feature is another comedy, *Ecce Homo Homolka*. Ladislav Rychman's *Six Black Girls* is a crime comedy and Oldrich Lipsky's *Gentlemen, I Have Killed Einstein* is a science fiction comedy with all women bearded in the year 2000.

Other new films by directors with reputations are: Juraj Herz, *The Cremator*; Ladislav Helge, *Fever*; Jaromil Jireš, *Valerie and a Week of Wonders*; and Jiří Menzel's *Larks on a String* is again based, like *Closely Observed Trains*, on a literary work by Bohumil Hrabal. *The Shop on the High Street* team, Kadar and Klos, have completed the U.S. co-production *A Handful of Water*, a psychological drama with Rade Markovitch and Josef Kroner. Kadar had previously shot *The Angel Levine* in the U.S.A. with Harry Belafonte, Ida Kaminska, Zero Mostel, Eli Wallach, Anne Jackson and Milo O'Shea. Further co-productions have been made with France, the U.S.S.R., Belgium and Bulgaria: Yves Campi's *Too Late by a Few Days*; Robbe-Grillet's *Eden and After*; Jan Schmidt's *Lanfieri Colony*; Chytilova's *The Fruits of Paradise*; and Rangel Vanchanov's *Aesop*.

180 LATE ADDITIONS

SWEDEN

Scene from Ingmar Bergman's The Rite, which is due to open later in 1970 at the Academy cinema in London.

U.S.S.R.

Battle scene from Sergei Bondarchuk's Waterloo.

POLAND

Scenes from Witold Leszczynski's The Days of St. Matthew (A) and from Krzysztof Zanussi's The Structure of Crystals (B).

BRAZIL

A bandit in Glauber Rocha's Antonio
Das Mortes.

JAPAN

Toshiro Mifune in Samurai Banner—
Furin Kazan.

FRANCE

Brigitte Bardot in Michel Deville's L'Ours
et la Poupée. *Romy Schneider and Michel
Piccoli in Claude Sautet's* Les Choses
de la Vie, *Jean-Pierre Cargol and François
Truffaut in the latter's* L'Enfant Sauvage.

FILM FUTURE

Gathering material for this, the final feature of *Film Review*, was a most rewarding and cheering task, for when the companies began to send me in their lists of films in various stages of late production, from shooting and editing to sitting on the shelf waiting for the final release dates and arrangements, I began to realise that there can't for a long time yet be any question of a shortage of product. In fact there is, for me, a certain embarrassment of riches: I could not possibly, without extending the feature to such extent that it would unbalance the rest of the volume, use anything like all the material so kindly and carefully gathered for me – which is a good point to diverge for a moment and put on record my gratitude to all the film companies, more especially to those, the majority, who enthusiastically and unsparingly give me their complete co-operation in the production of this, and every other feature of the annual.

Anyway, I hope what I have selected will give you a pretty clear idea of the celluloid riches in store for you in the months to come: certainly it has given me a renewed interest and enthusiasm in my job of watching the movies. It is only at this time next year we shall know if our enthusiasm and optimism was misplaced or not. Until then, happy moviegoing.

And a very pretty group, too: with Lee Marvin (top left on steps) at the centre of it, playing the title role in Cinema Center's *Monte Walsh*, that of a cowboy trying to cling to the old and fast vanishing way of life in the Old West.

Stuck in the mud – driver Steve McQueen in Cinema Center's *The Reivers*, which, the story of a wild weekend in 1905 Jefferson, is being made on location in Carrollton, Mississippi, and Hollywood in association with McQueen's own production company, Solar Productions.

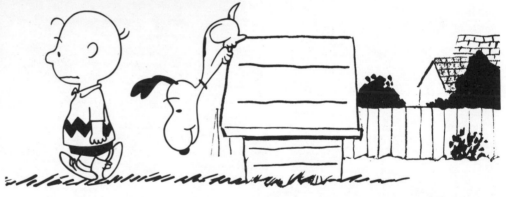

Rod Taylor, Theodore Bikel and The Body – female – in Cinema Center's *Darker Than Amber*, a contemporary adventure drama about a murder, and dope smugglers, also starring Suzy Kendall and Jane Russell.

That rarity, a feature cartoon, and it is coming from Cinema Center Films. Called *A Boy Named Charlie Brown*, it brings the famous and familiar (in America) Charles Schulz "Peanuts" characters to life, so to speak. And it's all about Charlie's efforts to win a spelling contest.

Escaped prisoners from a chain gang, Robert Shaw and Malcolm McDowell – over there on the left, in the dust – scramble up and away from the helicopter which has been assigned to hunt them both down in Cinema Center's Joseph Losey-directed *Figures in a Landscape*.

Malcolm McDowell and Nanette Newman are the co-stars in the Associated British production film *The Raging Moon*, which caused quite a stir when it was announced as being Bryan Forbes's first personally-directed film since he took over the responsibility for all the company's production plans. The story is about two young people who have to live their lives from wheelchairs.

Alec Guinness as a very solid ghost of Marley – complete with chains – and, a dim figure on his left, his mean, surviving partner Ebenezer Scrooge (played by Albert Finney) in the musical version of the Charles Dickens classic, *A Christmas Carol*, which will be presented by Cinema Center films.

Roger Moore under stress in the new Michael Relph and Basil Dearden film for Associated British, *The Man Who Haunted Himself*, which is described as a gripping psychological drama about an ordinary sort of businessman who suddenly finds himself in a maze of bizarre events and can't decide whether they are outside or, perhaps, within himself?

Pamela Franklin decides that attack is the best form of defence, so when cornered by the mysterious stranger (Sandor Eles) in a deserted French farm, she picks up a stone and smashes it into his face. It happens in Bryan Forbes's Associated British production, *And Soon the Darkness*, a thriller about two girls on holiday in France, one of whom mysteriously vanishes and is sought by her friend.

Flat Out – that's Richard Warwick, playing an officer in the Guards in the Associated British film *The Breaking of Bumbo*, which in telling the story of a young recruit takes the audience behind the façade of the most famous of British Army Regiments.

Mark Lester as the desperate little boy in *Eyewitness* who cannot convince his parents that he has seen a murder and is threatened by the killers, who see him as the only possible snag in their plans. Lionel Jeffries, as the boy's somewhat eccentric old grandfather, is the lad's only ally. This Irving Allen production for ABPC was made largely on location in Malta.

Robert Redford is the star of Paramount's *Downhill Racer*, together with Gene Hackman and Camilla Sparv: direction by Michael Ritchie.

Barbra Streisand is the star of the big new Paramount musical *On a Clear Day You Can See Forever*, with music by Alan Jay Lerner and Burton Lane. And Barbra's co-star – not in this scene – is Yves Montand.

Trying to keep their cool? Showered kissers are Julie Andrews and Rock Hudson and the scene is from Paramount's big Blake Edwards film *Darling Lili*, which was made in Dublin, Brussels, Paris and Hollywood.

Giving, by all accounts, delightful performances, co-stars Jack Lemmon and Sandy Dennis make Paramount's *The Out-of-Towners* a major comedy, built around the obvious situations of a couple of characters from out of town finding all the snags of in-town living.

"Lonesome Cowboy" new star Jon Voight and Anthony Perkins in Paramount's *Catch-22*, a comedy about the Second World War, a dream fantasy which includes Orson Welles as the brilliant General who decides that one way to win the war is to bomb the sea!

Suzy Kendall and Nigel Green in Dino de Laurentiis's Yugoslavian–Italian co-production for Paramount, *Fraulein Doktor*, directed by Alberto Lattuada.

Marlo Thomas, who makes her large-screen début in the title role in C.I.R.O.'s *Jenny*, comes to it with a very considerable American television reputation. In the film she plays a young, unmarried, pregnant girl who comes to New York to have her baby and there meets a young man trying to escape the military call-up.

Otto Preminger chose Liza Minnelli, Judy Garland's daughter who had such a big success in "Pookie", as his star for his new Paramount picture *Tell Me That You Love Me, Julie Moon*. Co-stars include Ken Howard and Robert Moore – that's him in the wheelchair.

Woody Allen plays an unusual, bumbling sort of young crook in C.I.R.O.'s *Take the Money and Run*, who always ends up back in jail, escaping each time and getting deeper and deeper into a criminal mess.

New star Raymond St. Jacques plays the leading role in C.I.R.O.'s *Change of Mind*, playing the first recipient of a brain transplant – complication being that he, a negro, gets a white man's brain!

Cocktail time in the swimming pool in the Italian-made Fox film *The Archangel*, in which Vittorio Gassman plays an inept lawyer caught up by Pamela Tiffin in a crazy murder plot – or rather, plots.

For his role in Palomar's *They Shoot Horses, Don't They?* Gig Young won the year's Oscar for the best male supporting performance. In this highly praised (in America) film about a harrowing 1932 Dance Marathon, Jane Fonda plays the lead, that of a bitter, sharp-tongued contestant who is a born loser.

The world's first black heavyweight boxing champion, Jack Jefferson, played by James Earl Jones, rejects the plea for a reconciliation from his former mistress, played by Marlene Warfield, in this scene from 20th Century-Fox's screen version of the Howard Sackler Pulitzer prize Broadway stage success *The Great White Hope*.

Domestic discord in Fox's *Move*, with Paula Prentiss as the wife trying to understand husband Elliott Gould's anti-social attitudes so that they can recapture their lost happiness.

Well, *this* one should be worth looking out for! From Fox, called *Run Shadow Run*; a scene from the surrealistic film within a film, and the girl taking it all pretty calmly is Susanne Benton.

192

Remember Fox's "Planet of the Apes"?
Well, spurred on by the terrific success of
this movie they've made a sequel. Called
Beneath the Planet of the Apes it includes a
number of the original cast and, of course,
those delightful-looking ape-men: in this
case not so delightfully applauding their
leader's decision to make war on the mutated
humans.

Barbara Perkins and Patrick O'Neal learn to
eat the Russian way – and it's very important
they do it right, for they play spies trained
by the Americans to undertake a very
dangerous mission in Fox's *The Kremlin
Letter*.

Yes, that wonderful face on the right could
only belong to the old but evergreen Jean
Gabin, here driving co-star Irina Demick to
a rendezvous in Fox's French gangster
piece, *The Sicilians*.

George C. Scott, who gave a remarkable
performance in the May-premièred Fox
film *Patton – Lust for Power* – the latter part
of the title being added for outside-
America consumption!

It is Otto's brother Ingo Preminger who is making his début as a film producer in Fox's *M★A★S★H*, a story about the Korean War seen against a background of a field hospital – within sound of the guns, but full, it appears, of unmartial happenings. Yuko Hahn watches Elliott Gould's efforts to capture the chopstick eating method.

Genevieve Gilles and Michael Crawford enjoy a game of miniature football in a French café where they stop to have a drink in Fox's *Hello-Goodbye*.

Fox's *Tora! Tora! Tora!* attempts to do for the attack on Pearl Harbour what "The Longest Day" did in presenting the invasion of Europe, and, in fact, is modelled along the same impressive celluloid lines.

Plenty of chills and thrills should be found by "horror" addicts in Anglo-Amalgamated's *The Dunwich Horror*, in which Dean Stockwell plays the very devil – literally – with pretty Sandra Dee, who is defended by a professor who realises the eerie situation in which she has become involved.

The horrid moment of long distance running-truth: British Marathon contestant Michael Crawford collapses right at the end and has the humiliation of seeing the next man stagger past him to victory in *The Games*, the Michael Winner film for Fox.

A dramatic role for Elvis Presley in Fox's *Charro!* in which he plays a "sometimes" sheriff in the post-Civil (American) War period who tries to save a town from disaster. And with him, looking equally concerned about things, Ina Balin.

Along similar chilling lines, and from the same company, comes Anglo's *The Oblong Box*, an adaptation of one of Edgar Allen Poe's creepy classics in which Britain's King of Horrors, Christopher Lee (shown with Sally Gleeson) co-stars with his American counterpart, Vincent Price.

A smoother, more sophisticated Warren Mitchell than the one familiar in that popular TV series "Till Death Us Do Part" will be seen in Granada Anglo-Amalgamated's *All The Way Up*, a comedy about a rather endearing character who is prepared to achieve the top of the heap no matter who or what may try to stop him.

Same company, same intention: this time it is *The Horror of Frankenstein*, and at least part of it is the odd character (Monster Dave Prowse) putting his nasty hands on pretty Kate O'Mara in this scene.

John Hurt is now safely established as the most popular film star in all penguinland: he used to feed them during the location shooting of *Forbush and the Penguins*, the fascinating new Associated British production which was largely made on a remote and forbidding Antarctic location.

Be careful lady – charming Dawn Addams – that smooth, wavy-haired, sophisticated character kissing your hand is Peter Cushing. That, allied to the title of the film, *The Vampire Lovers*, and the company that made it, Hammer, ought to be enough to warn anyone that peeping below all the silks and satins must somewhere be a pair of gleaming fangs!

The Aristocats is the first feature cartoon to emerge from the Disney studios in a long time, and it's all about a feline family who have to use their wits to thwart the plans of the villain who would be a great deal better off, financially, if he could engineer their demise.

What promises to be a tremendously amusing Disney feature is *It's Tough to be a Bird*, in which the cartoon character shown provides a very profusely illustrated lecture on The Bird, in history, evolution, art, music and what-have-you.

Walt Disney's Western-type *The Wild Country* (originally titled "The Newcomers") is the story of a pioneering family who in the late 1880s decide to take up farming in the wild Wyoming territory – and find it harder than they ever imagined in their wildest dreams. Dad is played by Steve Forrest, Mum by Vera Miles and the sons by Ronny and Clint Howard.

198 People who "mess about in boats" will be among those most happy to see Disney's *The Boatniks*, a comedy about amateur sailors and the havoc they cause. With Robert Morse and Stefanie Powers as co-stars.

Cecil Kellaway (shown with star Elliott Gould) always makes a film interesting, which is a pretty good recommendation for Columbia's *Getting Straight*, which also stars Candice Bergen.

Summer, sea and Gayle Hunnicut – a perfect combination in Columbia's *Fragment of Fear*.

A symbolic scene, maybe?, from Columbia's *The Buttercup Chain*, with Jane Asher and Hywel Bennett as the co-stars and obviously making the chain of the title in this scene.

Alec Guinness as King Charles I (Richard Harris plays the title role) in Columbia's big historical film *Cromwell*, which, directed by Ken Hughes and produced by Irving Allen, is due for its unveiling at a Royal Charity World prémiere in London on July 16.

International, too, is Columbia's vast
historical epic *Waterloo*, made in Russia, and
with that country's full co-operation, by
Dino de Laurentiis. Christopher Plummer –
centre – shading his eyes with his hand – who
plays Wellington and Rod Steiger (playing
Napoleon) head a very starry cast.

Certainly with an international flavour will
be Columbia's *Brief Season*, for it is being
produced by Dino de Laurentiis, directed
by Renato Castellani and co-starring
Christopher Jones and Pia Degermark.

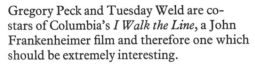

Gregory Peck and Tuesday Weld are co-stars of Columbia's *I Walk the Line*, a John Frankenheimer film and therefore one which should be extremely interesting.

Back now – and very welcome – a fully recovered Patricia Neal is star of M-G-M's *The Subject Was Roses*, a story of difficult family relationships between father, mother and son.

A similar trio relationship is explored, perhaps a shade more dramatically, in M-G-M's *My Lover, My Son*, with Donald Houston as the father, Romy Schneider as the mother and Dennis Waterman the son.

Susannah York and Peter O'Toole are the stars of M-G-M's *Brotherly Love* (at one time called "Country Dance") an adaptation of the James Kennaway novel about a noble Scot who cannot come to terms with the loss of his sister and reduction of his financial circumstances.

Anthony Quinn plays the Pope in M-G-M's *The Shoes of the Fisherman*, a story, set in the future, about the Roman Catholic State in general and one of its finer sons in particular.

Sarah Miles and Trevor Howard in M-G-M's *Ryan's Daughter*, a David Lean-directed film set in Ireland and telling a story of the familiar "troubles" of that country.

Ian Holm and Richard Attenborough in Columbia's *A Severed Head* which, directed by Dick Clement and with the late Alan Ladd's son as one of the producers, has a starry cast also including Lee Remick and Claire Bloom.

James Garner in Columbia's *A Man Called Sledge*.

Nigel Patrick plays the game in Columbia's *The Executioner* which, directed by Sam Wanamaker, has a cast which includes George Peppard, Joan Collins and Judy Geeson.

Oliver Reed with revealing photograph in Columbia's obvious entry for the year's longest title stakes: *The Lady in the Car with Glasses and a Gun*. His co-stars are Samantha Eggar and John McEnery; director and co-producer is Anatole Litvak.

Brian Keith in U.A.'s *The Mackenzie Break*, which shows the other side of the "War Escape" coin by relating the "break out" from a British P.O.W. Camp during the Second World War by a group of German U-boat commanders.

Here they are, *The Railway Children* (Gary Warren, Sally Thomsett and Jenny Agutter) in the screen adaptation of the E. Nesbitt story which is being brought to the screen by actor Lionel Jeffries (his first directing assignment; he also wrote the screenplay).

The now seldom screen-seen Marlon Brando is star of U.A.'s *Quemeda*, the name of the Caribbean island which forms the background for a bitter struggle for power by the British and the Spanish, with the sugar cane as the symbol of the prize.

The maestro himself, Federico Fellini, performs a tricky little measure to show the actor how he should do this sequence for his gargantuan *Satyricon*, which United Artists will be releasing during 1970.

Not waving red flags, maybe, but this is a group of the young stars in the Pressman-Williams production for U.A. of *The Revolutionary*, about a young man whose rebellion against his family leads him to join an anti-Establishment political group and through this to murder. Left to right: Seymour Cassel, Collin Wilcox-Horne, Jon Voight, Jennifer Salt and Robert Duvall.

U.A.'s *Kes* has made quite a lot of head-lines with its turning down by the major circuits, yet it had great success when shown for various special seasons. Latest news at press time is that its London première run at the Academy cinema may be followed by a general release. The boy whose story it is is played by David Bradley.

206

Well, it took Billy Wilder to give Sherlock Holmes a screen kiss! He gets it from grateful Genevieve Page – while a horrified Dr. Watson (Colin Blakely) looks on in Wilder's new U.A. film *The Private Life of Sherlock Holmes*, in which Robert Stephens plays the sleuth of Baker Street.

Richard Chamberlain as the composer Tchaikovsky, in the Ken Russell U.A. film based on his life story, *The Music Lovers*.

A long time coming – it was featured in this section of last year's *Film Review* – Stanley Kramer's U.A. film *The Secret of Santa Vittoria* is said to be well worth waiting for, with fine performances from a cast including Anthony Quinn and Anna Magnani.

Against a setting looking very much like a scene from "South Pacific", but in fact from U.A.'s *Master of the Islands*, which has the same Hawaiian background, Charlton Heston gets a caress from Miko Mayama.

THE IN-BETWEENS

This new, small feature, introduced last year, is an effort to bridge the difficulties presented by those big, "road-show" films which have long – sometimes very long – special runs before they get a general circuit release – if, indeed, they ever get one. While being noted here, in detail, they will in due course be recorded and illustrated in the General Release sections if they do have one at some future date.

Battle of Britain. Harry Saltzman's remarkable reconstruction of a stirring, heroic page of British history, made with some great air battle spectacle, balanced behind-the-scenes tension and general care for authenticity. A memorable movie; with plenty of stars in a large cast including Laurence Olivier, Ralph Richardson, Kenneth More. Rest of cast: Harry Andrews, Michael Caine, Trevor Howard, Curt Jürgens, Ian McShane, Nigel Patrick, Christopher Plummer, Michael Redgrave, Robert Shaw, Patrick Wymark, Susannah York, Michael Bates, Isla Blair, John Bascomb, Tom Chatto, James Cosmo, Robert Flemyng, Barry Foster, Edward Fox, W. G. Foxley, David Griffin, Jack Gwillim, Myles Hoyle, Duncan Lamont, Sarah Lawson, Mark Malicz, André Maranne, Anthony Nicholls, Nicholas Pennell, Andrzej Scibor, Jean Wladon, Wilfried Van Aacken, Karl Otto Alberty, Alexander Allerson, Dietrich Frauboes, Alf Jungermann, Peter Hager, Wolf Harnish, Reinhard Horras, Helmut Kircher, Paul Neuhaus, Malte Petzel, Manfred Reddemann, Hein Riess, Rolf Stiefel. Dir: Guy Hamilton. Pro: Harry Saltzman & S. Benjamin Fisz. Screenplay: James Kennaway & Wilfred Greatorex. (Saltzman–U.A.) Rel: Special. (T & Pan.) 131 Mins. Cert. U.

Trevor Howard, top left, looks out and down at the all-important Group Plot Room which illustrates the progress of this particular moment in *Battle of Britain*, in the remarkably faithful Harry Saltzman film reconstruction of that great chapter of British history.

Hello, Dolly! One of the brightest, liveliest, most spectacular and generally entertaining musicals in a long time; based on the stage show which in turn was based on Thornton Wilder's play about Jewish life, "The Matchmaker". With Barbra Streisand as the lady widow who fixes weddings (and just about everything else) but has a heck of a time fixing it so that wealthy, skinflint merchant Walter Matthau will ask her to be his wife! Tremendously spectacular; and oh, that haunting title number. Rest of cast: Michael Crawford, Louis Armstrong, Marianne McAndrew, E. J. Peaker, Danny Lockin, Joyce Ames, Tommy Tune, Judy Knaiz, David Hurst, Fritz Feld, Richard Collier, J. Pat O'Malley. Dir: Gene Kelly. Pro & Written: Ernest Lehman: based on the Michael Stewart stage musical which in turn was based on Thornton Wilder's play "The Matchmaker". (Chenault Pro Inc–Fox.) Rel: Special. (Todd–AO & D.) 148 Mins. Cert. U.

Paint Your Wagon. Large-scale adaptation of the stage musical with plenty of jolly colour, lively if long musical numbers and the sort of performance by Lee Marvin which lifts any film above itself and often wins the "lifter" an Oscar! Marvin plays a rumbustious character in the Californian Gold Rush days at the turn of the century who takes on Clint Eastwood as his pardner and when he buys a Mormon's young, second wife (Jean Seberg) for himself, shares her with his pal! Rest of cast: Harve Presnell, Ray Walston, Tom Ligon, Alan Dexter, William O'Connell, Ben Baker, Alan Baxter, Paula Trueman, Robert Easton, Geoffrey Norman, H. B. Haggerty, Terry Jenkins, Karl Bruck, John Mitchum, Sue Casey,

Eddie Little Sky, Harvey Parry, H. W. Gim, William Mims, Roy Jenson, Pat Hawley, The Nitty Gritty Dirt Band. Dir: Joshua Logan. Pro: Alan Jay Lerner. Screenplay: Paddy Chayefsky (Paramount.) Rel: Special. (Pan & T.) 164 Mins. Cert. A.

Lee Marvin, whose terrific performance in Paramount's large-scale Gold Rush musical *Paint Your Wagon* lifted the film several steps above itself, making it something of a happily memorable experience.

Part of the tremendously spectacular procession which is one of the high-spots in Fox's bright, lively and extremely entertaining musical *Hello, Dolly!*, starring Barbra Streisand – seen right, with boa!

The Lion in Winter. Magnificently if stagily conceived illuminated manuscript page from British history: an adaptation by the playwright himself of James Goldman's Broadway success about the so-called Winter (Christmas) Court held by England's King Henry II at the Castle of Chinon in that part of France which then belonged to him, to which are invited his long imprisoned Queen Eleanor of Aquitaine, King Philip of France and Henry's three sons, Geoffrey, Richard (the Lion Heart) and John. For twenty-four hours these five intrigue, plot, double-cross, lie and love a little as they struggle to resolve the future of the English crown. Finely wrought, beautifully photographed, wonderfully wordy and brilliantly acted by Peter O'Toole (Henry), Katharine Hepburn (Eleanor), John Castle (Geoffrey), Timothy Dalton (Philip), Anthony Hopkins (Richard). Rest of cast: Jane Merrow, Nigel Stock, Nigel Terry. Dir: Anthony Harvey. Pro: Martin Poll. Screenplay: James Goldman. (Joseph E. Levine–Avco–Embassy.) Rel: Special. (Pan & Colour.) 134 Mins. Cert. A.

The Royal Hunt of the Sun. Admirable, honest and effective screen adaptation of Peter Shaffer's fine stage play which, set against the historical background of the shameful Spanish conquest of Peru, arrays some intelligent human problems about man's conflict of conscience and his eternal religious dilemmas. With outstanding performances from Robert Shaw as the bastard, adventurer and soldier, General Pizzaro and Christopher Plummer (a most remarkable creation) as the Inca Emperor. Rest of cast: Nigel Davenport, Michael Craig, Leonard Whiting, Andrew Keir,

James Donald, William Marlowe, Percy Herbert, Alexander Davion, Sam Krauss. Dir: Irving Lerner. Pro: Eugene Frenke & Philip Yordan. Screenplay: Philip Yordan. (Rank.) Rel: Special. (T & Techniscope.) 121 Mins. Cert. U.

Peter O'Toole and Katharine Hepburn, as King Henry II and Queen Eleanor of England, whose magnificent acting in Avco–Embassy's reconstruction of a page of British history, *The Lion In Winter*, helped to make this one of the year's films of major distinction.

Michael Craig, Robert Shaw and Christopher Plummer in *The Royal Hunt of the Sun*, the Rank film of the Peter Shaffer play about the Spanish conquest of Peru which introduced dramatic comment on some of man's oldest and constant dilemmas.

REVIVALS

The Longest Day (Fox).

Alice in Wonderland (Disney).

La Femme Du Boulanger – The Baker's Wife
Marcel Pagnol's classic (not generally
re-released but revived for a special season
by Gala films).

During the year a number of films have been
reissued and generally released.
Here are the titles and dates:
The First Men in the Moon. Chas. H.
Schneer's prophetic screen version of the
even more far-seeing H. G. Wells story.
Re-Rel: Aug. 3. (Originally released in 1964
and reviewed in "Film Review" of that year.)
In Search of the Castaways. The Disney
adaptation of the Jules Verne story. Re-Rel:
May 17. (Originally released on Jan. 6,
1963 and reviewed in Film Review of
1963–64.)

The Jolson Story. Columbia's 1946
(reviewed in "Film Review" of that year)
biographical big musical about Al Jolson,
with Larry Parks playing the part. Re-Rel:
Floating.
The Longest Day. Darryl Zanuck's epic-
scaled, magnificently conceived and honestly
presented story of the Invasion of Normandy.
Re-Rel: Aug. 24. Originally released in
October, 1964, and reviewed in "Film
Review" of that date.
One Million Years B.C. Hammer's picture of
the very far distant past, one of Raquel
Welch's earlier movies. Originally released in
December, 1967. Re-Rel: Aug. 10.
One Hundred and One Dalmatians. One of
Walt Disney's most wholly delightful
feature cartoons, following the adventures of
a pair of Dalmatians as they struggle to
recover their stolen puppies. Originally
released in July, 1962. Re-Rel: Aug. 10.
20,000 Leagues Under the Sea. Walt Disney's
lavish, colourful and entertaining adaptation
to the screen of Jules Verne's classic thriller
about Captain Nemo and his underwater
craft "Nautilus". Originally released in
August, 1955 and reviewed in the "Film
Review" of that year. Re-Rel: Oct. 21.
She. Ursula Andress as Rider Haggard's
famous character, a 2,000-year-old temptress
who has learnt the secret of eternal life and
beauty. A Hammer film. Originally released
in April, 1965 and reviewed in the "Film
Review" of that year. Re-Rel: Aug. 10.
Alice in Wonderland. The Walt Disney
feature cartoon. Originally released in 1951
and reviewed at that time. Re-Rel: Dec. 21.

RELEASES OF THE YEAR IN DETAIL

Note: In the following pages certain abbreviations have been made in order to save space. The technical abbreviations are as follows: (T) Technicolor; (C CinemaScope; (Tech) Technirama; (Total) Totalscope; (M) Metrocolor; (D) Deluxe Colour; (Pan) Panavision. Company names you will find abbreviated as follows: (Anglo) Anglo-Amalgamated; (U.I.) Universal-International; (Lion) British Lion; (Fox) 20th Century-Fox; (U.A.) United Artists

1969-70

Adalen '31
Bo Widerberg's long, leisurely and poetic story of the strike in the north of Sweden in 1931, at Adalen, which brought about a confrontation of the strikers and the military in which several were killed and others injured. Also the more personal stories of several people whose lives are affected by the event. All this against a lovely background of the country in the sunshine of the Spring. Cast: *Peter Schildt, Kerstin Tidelius, Roland Hedlund, Stefan Feierbach, Martin Widerberg, Marie de Geer, Anita Björk, Olof Bergström, Jonas Bergström, Olle Björling, Pierre Lindstedt.* Dir & Screenplay: Bo Widerberg. (Svensk Filmindustri–Paramount.) First shown at Academy One, Oct., 1969. (T. & Techniscope.) 115 Mins. Cert. X.

The Adventurers
Film based on the vast Harold Robbins novel: set in South America and telling a turbulent tale of political and amorous passions in a big, spectacular, familiar way. Cast: *Bekim Fehmiu, Charles Aznavour, Alan Badel, Candice Bergen, Thommy Berggren, Delia Boccardo, Ernest Borgnine, Rossano Brazzi, Olivia de Havilland, Anna Moffo, Leigh Taylor-Young, Christian Roberts, Yorgo Voyagis, Fernando Rey, John Ireland, Jorge Martinez de Hoyos, Sydney Tafler, Yolande Donlan, Angela Scoular, Milena Vukotic, Ferdy Mayne, Jaclyn Smith, Katharine Balfour, Roberta Donatelli, Peter Graves, John Frederick, Allan Cuthbertson, Zienia Merton, Roberta Haynes, Lois Maxwell, Loris Loddi, Vanessa Lee, Michael Balfour, Katia Christina, Katiushka Lanvin, Christine Delit, Nadia Scarpitia, Helena Ronee, Randi Lind, Linda Towne, Joal Carlo, Marcus Beck, Gisela Kopel, David Canon, Jose Luis Ospina, Manuelo Serrano, Rey Vasquez, Kiki Goncalves, Juan Estelrich, Anthony Hickox, Carl Eklund.* Dir & Pro: Lewis Gilbert. Screenplay: Michael Hastings & Lewis Gilbert. (Joseph E. Levine–Paramount.) Rel: June 21. (Pan & Colour.) 171 Mins. Cert. X.

Age of Consent
Michael Powell's beautifully photographed (on location) film about a disillusioned artist who finds a nubile girl as model and through her a new purpose in life along the Great Barrier Reef. A polished performance by *James Mason* as the artist and a wonderfully shapely one by a – often fetchingly nude – newcomer, *Helen Mirren.* Rest of cast: *Jack MacGowran, Neva Carr-Glyn, Antonia Katsaros, Michael Boddy, Harold Hopkins, Slim De Grey, Max Moldrun, Frank Thring, Dora Hing, Clarissa Kaye, Judy McGrath, Lenore Katon, Diane Strachan, Roberta Grant, Lonsdale (the dog – Trained by Scotty Denholm), Prince Nial.* Dir: Michael Powell. Pro: M. Powell & J. Mason. Screenplay: Peter Yeldham from the Norman Lindsay novel. (Mason/Powell–Columbia.) Rel: Dec. 7. (T.) 98 Mins. Cert. A.

Alfred the Great
One-two, slam-bang cinematic version of a chapter of earlier English history, with young Alfred yearning for the Church but accepting the inevitability of his

kingly destiny! With several battle set-pieces, some amusing moments and a complete lack of cakes – or outstanding performances. Cast: *David Hemmings, Michael York, Prunella Ransome, Colin Blakely, Julian Glover, Ian McKellen, Alan Dobie, Peter Vaughan, Julian Chagrin, Barry Jackson, Vivien Merchant, Christopher Timothy, John Rees, Andrew Bradford, Michael Billington, Ralph Nossek, David Glaisyer, Eric Brooks, Keith Buckley, Trevor Jones, Peter Blythe.* Dir: Clive Donner. Pro: Bernard Smith. Screenplay: Ken Taylor & James R. Webb, based on the latter's story. (Bernard Smith/James R. Webb–M-G-M.) Rel: Oct. 12. (Pan & Metrocolor.) 122 Mins. Cert. A.

Alice's Restaurant
Story about a hippy community in the States, starring *Arlo Guthrie,* son of the late Woody Guthrie, as a wandering folk-rock music composer and singer. An amusing script and some fine performances contribute with good direction to make this a pop-period film not to be missed. Arlo plays himself. *Pat Quinn* appears as Alice. *Pete Seeger* also makes an appearance. Rest of cast: *James Broderick, Michael McClanathan, Geoff Outlaw, Tina Chen, Kathleen Dabney, William Obanhein, Seth Allen, Monroe Arnold, Joseph Boley, Vinnette Carroll, Sylvia Davis, Simm Landres, Eulalie Noble, Louis Beachner, MacIntyre Dixon, Rev. Dr. Pierce Middleton, Donald Marye, Shelley Plimpton, M. Emmet Walsh, Ronald Weyand, Eleanor Wilson, Simon Deckard, Thomas De Wolfe, Judge James Hannon, Graham Jarvis, John Quill, Frank Simpson.* Dir: Arthur Penn. Pro: Hillard Elkins & Joe Manduke. Screenplay: Venable Herndon & A. Penn. (U.A.) Rel: May 10. (T.) 110 Mins. Cert. X.

Angel Baby – Engelchen oder die Jungfrau von Bamberg
German, English-dubbed film about a provincial teenage Miss who goes to Munich with the idea of losing her virginity, but finds it isn't so easy, even after trolloping around a rather unprepossessing bunch of males. When it does happen at last, she goes back to her Bavarian small town boy-friend ready to give him, a virgin still, the benefit of her new status, one assumes! All rather heavily Teutonic in its humour. Cast: *Gila von Weiterhausen, Hans Clarin, Uli Koch, Dieter Augustin, Gudrun Vöge, Edgar Boelke, Michael Luther, Peter Wortmann, Christof Wackernagel.* Dir: Marran Gosov. Pro: Rob Houwer. Screenplay: Marran Gosov, Franz Geiger. (Cinecenta.) First shown at Cinecenta, Oct., 1969. (Colour.) 74 Mins. Cert. X.

As the Naked Wind from the Sea – Som Havets Nakna Vind
Typically Swedish sex film: about a young violinist and his erotic holiday with several girls. Cast: *Hans Gustafsson, Lillemor Ohlsson, Anne Nord, Barbro Hedstrom, Gio Petre, Ingrid Swedin, Barbro Hjort af Ornes, Gudrun Brost, Siw Mattson, Stephan Karlsen, Charlie Elvegard, Ann Andersson, Chris Wahlstrom, Birger Malmsten, Ulf Tistam.* Dir: Gunnar Hoglund.

Screenplay: Gustav Sandgren & Gunnar Hoglund. (Cinecenta.) Film chosen to open Cineclub 24, London. 111 Mins. No cert.

Bagnolo – Dorf zwischen schwarz und Rot
Interesting documentary about the very real rivalry for heart and mind of the inhabitants of the small Italian town of the title, where the Communists and the Christian Democratic Party each do their best to show that it is they who have the best to offer the people, and prove it by will and deed. Dir: Bruno Jori. (Academy.) First shown at Academy One, April, 1970. 62 Mins. Cert. U.

Barquero
Mexican-Western with *Lee Van Cleef* the ferryman who finds his job develops into a series of bloody confrontations with bandits. Rest of cast: *Warren Oates, Forrest Tucker, Kerwin Matthews, Mariette Hartley, Marie Gomez, Armando Silvestre, John Davis Chandler, Craig Littler, Ed Bakey, Richard Lapp, Harry Lauter, Brad Weston.* Dir: Gordon Douglas. Pro: Hal Klein. Screenplay: George Schenck & William Marks. (Schenck–U.A.) Rel: June 28. (D.) 108 Mins. Cert. X.

Beneath the Planet of the Apes
Follow-up to "The Planet of the Apes", carrying on from where the former film ended, with *Charlton Heston*'s realisation that he is in a world desolated and depopulated by The Bomb and his decision to venture out into the Forbidden Lands, a trek which leads him into new adventures. Rest of cast: *James Franciscus, Kim Hunter, Maurice Evans, Linda Harrison, Paul Richards, Victor Buono, James Gregory, Jeff Corey, Natalie Trundy, Thomas Gomez, David Watson.* Dir: Ted Post. Pro: Arthur P. Jacobs. Screenplay: Paul Dehn from the story by him and Mort Abrahams. (Apjac–Fox.) Rel: June 21. (T.) 94 Mins. Cert A.

The Best House in London
Mild little comedy with lots of confused story threads centred on the opening in London of a gorgeous Paris-style brothel – which, after a great opening night, is forced to close the following day. Cast: *David Hemmings, Joanna Pettet, George Sanders, Dany Robin, Warren Mitchell, John Bird, William Rushton, Bill Fraser, Maurice Denham, Wolfe Morris, Martita Hunt, Arnold Diamond, Hugh Burden, John De Marco, George Reynolds, Jan Holden, Mike Lennox, Arthur Howard, Clement Freud, Neal Arden, Walter Brown, Suzanne Hunt, Carol Friday, Marie Rogers, Avril Angers, Betty Marsden.* Dir: Philip Saville. Pro: Philip Breen & Kurt Unger. Screenplay: Denis Norden. (Ponti–M-G-M.) Rel: Sept. 21. (E.) 96 Mins. Cert. X.

Better a Widow – Meglio Vedova
Peter McEnery as the young British oil engineer caught between two opposing Mafia groups in Sicily but managing to survive and catch lovely young quick-widowed *Virna Lisi.* Rest of cast: *Gabriele Ferzetti, Jean Servais, Agnes Spaak, Nino Terzo, Carla Calo,*

216

Salvatore Fucile, Roy Bosier, Bruno Lauzi, Adriano
Vitale. Dir: Duccio Tessari. Screenplay: A. Baracco,
E. de Concini, B. Degas, T. Gates & D. Tessari.
(Ultra Film–Universal–Rank.) Rel: April 19. (T.)
101 Mins. Cert. A.

The Birthday Party
Harold Pinter's own screen adaptation of his play,
a wonderful outpouring of words and ambiguous
meanings. About the two mysterious strangers, a
cheery Jew and a gloomy Irishman, who arrive at
failed pianist Stanley's mean seaside lodging and
proceed to drive him off his trolley before they take
him off to . . .? Cast: *Robert Shaw, Patrick Magee,
Dandy Nichols, Sydney Tafler, Moultrie Kelsall,
Helen Fraser.* Dir: Wm. Friedkin. Pro: Max Rosenberg
& Milton Subotsky. (Palomar–Connoisseur.) First
shown at Academy Three, Feb., 1970. (T.) 124 Mins.
Cert. X.

Black God, White Devil – Deus e o Diablo na Terra do Sol
Brazilian Cinema Nuova film, directed by Glauber
Rocha, based on the master and slave relationship:
a fictional account of the history of a barren area of
Brazil where underdevelopment in the latter part of the
19th century led to an explosion of unresolved
influences. Cast: *Yona Magalhaes, Geraldo Del Rey,
Othon Bastos, Mauricis de Valle, Lidio Silva.* Dir
& Written: Glauber Rocha. Pro: Luiz Augusto
Mendes. (Luiz Augusto Mendes/Copacabana–
Connoisseur.) First shown at Times Cinema, Feb.,
1970. 110 Mins. Cert. X.

The Blood Demon–Die Schlangengrube und das Pendel
Christopher Lee creating celluloid shivers with his
performance as the ghost of Count Regula, killed 40
years ago as penalty for his murdering a dozen young
girls. Re-incarnated, he seeks complete immortality
with his 13th victim! Rest of cast: *Lex Barker, Karin
Dor, Carl Lange, Vladimir Medar, Christiane Rucker,
Dieter Eppler.* Dir: Harald Reinl. (New Realm.)
Rel: Floating. (E.) 76 Mins. Cert. X.

The Brain — Le Cerveau
Lively and mildly amusing crime farce-comedy with
David Niven as the man behind The Great Train
Robbery, now trying to pull off a similar set-up in
France, with the assistance of *Jean-Paul Belmondo* and
Bourvil, small-timers confused by the convolutions of
the big-timers as Niven sets himself up against the
Mafia. Rest of cast: *Eli Wallach, Silvia Monti,
Fernand Valois, Raymond Gerome, Jacques Balutin,
Jacques Ciron, Fernand Guiot.* Dir: Gerard Oury.
Pro: Alain Poire. Screenplay: G. Oury, Marcel
Jullian & Daniele Thompson. (Gaumont International
–Paramount.) Rel: Feb. 1. (Franscope & Colour.)
100 Mins. Cert. U.

The Bridge at Remagen
Story based on the struggle to gain control of the only
bridge left across the Rhine, at Remagen, which can
make all the difference to the quicker ending of the
war. Cast: *George Segal, Robert Vaughn, Ben Gazzara,
Bradford Dillman, E. G. Marshall, Peter Van Eyck,
Matt Clark, Fritz Ford, Tom Heaton, Bo Hopkins,
Robert Logan, Anna Gael, Paul Prokop, Steve Sandor,
Frank Webb, Hans Christian Blech, Joachim Hansen,
Gunter Meisner, Richard Munch, Heinz Reincke,
Sonja Zeimann, Vit Olmer, Rudolf Jelinek.* Dir: John
Guillermin. Pro: David L. Wolper. Screenplay:
Richard Yates & Wm. Roberts. (Wolper–U.A.) Rel:
Sept. 7. (Pan & D.) 116 Mins. Cert. A.

Buckskin
Something of a philosophical Western, with *Barry
Sullivan* as the frontiersman who realises that the West
is changing and, accepting the job of Montana
Territorial Marshal, proceeds to prove his point by .
clearing out the bad citizens of Gloryhole. Rest of cast:
*Joan Caulfield, Wendell Corey, Lon Chaney, John Russell,
Barbara Hale, Barton MacLane, Bill Williams,
Richard Arlen, Leo Gordon, Gerald Michenaud,
George Chandler, Aki Aleong, Michael Larrain,
Craig Littler, James X. Mitchell, Emile Meyer,
Robert Riordan, Le Roy Johnson, Manuela Thiess.*
Dir: Michael Moore. Pro: A. C. Lyles. Screenplay:
Michael Fisher. (Paramount.) Rel: July 20. 65 Mins.
Cert. U.

Bullet for Rommel – L'Urlo dei Giganti
An Italian–Spanish, English-dubbed film with *Jack
Palance* leading a five-man army on a special, and
specially dangerous, mission into Germany. Rest of
cast: *Alberto de Mendoza, John Gramack, Carlos
Estrada, Antonio Pica, Andrea Bosic, Mirko Ellis,
Gerard Tichy, John Douglas, Maruchi Fresno.* Dir:
Henry Mankiewicz. Pro: Luis Mendez. Screenplay:
Jose Luis Merino. (E. J. Fancey.) Rel: Floating.
101 Mins. Cert. A.

Butch Cassidy and The Sundance Kid
Rather meandering in mood, style and content, but
nevertheless very amusing and highly entertaining
Western-style story, based at least in part on history,
about a couple of young bank and train robbers who
find civilisation catching up on their trade and,
doggedly pursued, escape to Bolivia, where they
eventually pull one job too many and are surrounded
and killed by the military. Nice performances by *Paul
Newman* and *Robert Redford* in the title roles; lovely
backgrounds. Rest of cast: *Katharine Ross, Strother
Martin, Henry Jones, Jeff Corey, George Furth, Cloris
Leachman, Ted Cassidy, Kenneth Mars, Donnelly Rhodes,
Jody Gilbert, Timothy Scott, Don Keefer, Charles
Dierkop, Francisco Cordova, Nelson Olmstead, Paul
Bryar, Sam Elliott, Charles Akins, Eric Sinclair.*
Dir: George Roy Hill. Pro: John Foreman. Screenplay:
William Goldman. (Campanile–Fox.) Rel: April 5.
(D. & Pan.) 110 Mins. Cert. A.

Can Heironymus Merkin Ever Forget Mercy Humppe and Find True Happiness?
The longest-ever (well, nearly!) film title to one of the
oddest, most confused, erotic movies ever made.
Undisciplined talent bubbling over as writer-
composer-director-producer-star player *Anthony*
Newley conducts 107 minutes of what appears to be
self-examination with the help of his real, plus
fictional family, lots of films, newspaper clippings and
what-have-you! Rest of cast: *Joan Collins, Milton
Berle, George Jessel, Stubby Kaye, Bruce Forsyth,
Patricia Hayes, Victor Spinetti, Tom Stern, Connie
Kreski, Judy Cornwell, Berri Cornish, Roy Desmond,
Sally Douglas, Desmond Walter Ellis, Gilly Grant,
Isabel Hurll, Rosalind Knight, Aleta Morrison, Louis
Negin, Tara Newley, Alexander Newley, Margaret
Nolan, Julian Orchard, Ronald Radd, Ronald Rubin,
Margo Segrave, Sue Shepherd, Bernard Stone, Yolanda,
Lynda Baron, Joyce Blair, Bruce Boa, Rubin Bullivant,
Laurie Leigh, Robert Hutton, Eve Pearce, John Poore,
Muriel Young.* Dir & Pro & co-written (with Herman
Raucher), Anthony Newley. (Universal/Taralex
Corp–Rank.) Rel: Floating. (T.) 107 Mins. Cert. X.

Capricious Summer – Rozmarne Leto
A little gem of a Czech film from Jiri ("Closely
Observed Trains") Menzel, which with charm, wit
and whimsy tells the story of three old friends at a
little broken-down spa town, who each in turn try
their carnal luck with the luscious and willing young
assistant of a visiting conjurer; each in turn being
brought to the sad realisation of his limitations in that
direction. Done with taste, discretion and irony.
Grand performances by *Rudolf Hrusinsky, Vlastimil
Brodsky, Frantisek Rehak, Mila Myslikova, Jara
Drchalova* and *Jiri Menzel* himself. Dir: Jiri Menzel.
Screenplay: J. Menzel & Vaclav Nyvlt. (Contemporary.) First shown at the Paris-Pullman, Oct. 1969.
(Colour.) 75 Mins. Cert. A.

Captain Nemo and the Underwater City
A sort of sequel to the Jules Verne story; based on the
characters but with little else to do with the author.
About a bunch of assorted characters saved from a
wrecked ship by the "Nautilus" and taken to the cap-
tain's underwater city. Plenty of special effects! Cast:
*Robert Ryan, Chuck Connors, Nanette Newman,
Luciana Paluzzi, Bill Fraser, Kenneth Connor, John
Turner, Allan Cuthbertson, Christopher Hartstone,
Vincent Harding, Ralph Nosseck, Michael McGovern,
Allan Barry, Anthony Bailey, Ann Patrice, Margot
Ley, Patsy Snell.* Dir: James Hill. Pro: Bertram
Ostrer. (M-G-M.) Rel: Dec. 21. (Pan & Metrocolor.)
106 Mins. Cert. U.

Carmen, Baby.
An up-dated variation on the old operatic story, made
in Holland, with *Claude Ringer* as the young cop so
bemused by attractive prostitute Carmen – played by
Uta Levka – that he knocks off a couple of her lovers
before stabbing her! All somewhat simple! Rest of
cast: *Carl Mohner, Barbara Valentin, Walter Witz,
Christiane Rucker, Michael Munzer, Doris Arden,
Christian Federsdorf, Arthur Brass.* Dir & Pro: Radley
Metzger. Screenplay: Jesse Vogel. (Gala.) Rel:
Floating. (Colour & Scope.) 82 Mins. Cert. X.

Carry On Camping
Yet another in the very long line of Gerald Thomas–
Peter Rogers comedies, and, like its predecessors,

broad, very British, blue-veined and uproarious, with *Sidney James* and *Bernard Bresslaw* taking their girl-friends on a nudist camp-holiday to "warm them up" only to find – the first of many disasters – that it isn't that sort of place at all! Rest of cast: *Kenneth Williams, Barbara Windsor, Terry Scott, Charles Hawtrey, Hattie Jacques, Dilys Laye, Peter Butterworth, Julian Holloway, Betty Marsden, Trisha Noble, Brian Oulton, Derek Francis, Elizabeth Knight, Sandra Caron, Georgina Moon, Jennifer Pyle, Jackie Poole, Sally Kemp, Amelia Bayntun, Patricia Franklin, Michael Nightingale, George Moon, Valerie Shute, Vivien Lloyd, Lesley Duff, Anna Karen, Valerie Leon.* Dir: Gerald Thomas. Pro: Peter Rogers. Screenplay: Talbot Rothwell. (Adder–Rank.) Rel: Aug. 31. (Colour.) 88 Mins. Cert. A.

Carry On Again, Doctor
Typical addition to this everlasting – and everlastingly successful – series of broadly comic films, with a succession of blue gags interleaved in various slapstick sequences. With *Kenneth Williams* the snooty surgeon seeking the cash for his own clinic and hoping wealthy widow *Joan Sims* will supply it: a plan furthered and frustrated by young cockney medico *Jim Dale*, whose amorous inclinations are always causing chaos. Rest of cast: *Sidney James, Charles Hawtrey, Hattie Jacques, Barbara Windsor, Patsy Rowlands, Lucy Griffiths, Ann Lancaster, Faith Kent, Shakira Baksh, Frank Singuineau, Harry Locke, Georgina Simpson, Valeria Shute, Patricia Hayes.* Dir: Gerald Thomas. Pro: Peter Rogers. Screenplay: Talbot Rothwell. (Adder–Rank.) Rel: Jan. 11. (Colour.) 89 Mins. Cert. A.

Changes
A typical new new-wave film about a young American just out of college who is searching to find out what life is all about. Although he doesn't want to become a hippy, or yippy, or any other kind of hairy wonder, and doesn't really want to opt out of Society, is nevertheless unable to accept responsibility and leaves the various girls who take him under their wing directly he sees the bars of any possible spiritual prison. Cast: *Kent Lane, Michele Carey, Jack Albertson, Manuela Thiess, Marcia Strassman, Kenneth Washington, Tom Fielding, Bill Kelly.* Dir & Pro: Hall Bartlett. Screenplay: Bill E. Kelly & H. Bartlett. (Cinerama.) Rel: Floating. (Pan. & Colour.) 93 Mins. Cert. A.

Che!
Omar Sharif as the late Cuban revolutionary in a non-committed, and finally rather unsatisfactory, story about him and his dictator Fidel Castro (played by *Jack Palance*). Rest of cast: *Cesare Danova, Robert Loggia, Woody Strode, Barbara Luna, Frank Silvera, Albert Paulsen, Linda Marsh, Tom Troupe, Rudy Diaz, Perry Lopez, Abraham Sofaer, Richard Angarola, Sarita Vara, Paul Bertoya, Sid Haig, Adolph Caesar, Paul Picerni, Ray Martell.* Dir: Richard Fleischer. Pro: Sy Bartlett. Screenplay: Michael Wilson & Sy Bartlett. (Fox.) Rel: Nov. 9. (Pan & D.) 96 Mins. Cert. X.

Chicago, Chicago
Thoroughly entertaining adaptation of the Ben Hecht book "Gaily, Gaily" (the film's American title), a reminiscence-style story about a naïve young hick who comes to the big city, is robbed, taken pity on by a notorious local Madame and in her plushy bordelhouse (and on the Chicago newspaper on which she gets him a job) learns the facts of life: not only love but also of the horribly crooked politics, bribery and corruption which were rife in the city, *circa* 1910. Gently satirical, beautifully acted (especially by *Brian Keith* and promising newcomer *Beau Bridges*) and richly amusing. Rest of cast: *Melina Mercouri, George Kennedy, Hume Cronyn, Margot Kidder, Wilfrid Hyde-White, Melodie Johnson, Joan Huntington, John Randolph, Claude Bryar, Eric Shea, Merie Earle, James Christy, Charles Tyner, Harry Holcombe, Roy Poole, Clark Gordon, Peter Brocco, Maggie Oleson, Nikita Knatz.* Dir & Pro: Norman Jewison. Screenplay: Abram S. Ginnes. (Mirisch–U.A.) Rel: May 10. (D.) 107 Mins. Cert. X.

Chitty Chitty Bang Bang
Albert R. Broccoli's very lush and lavish giant-screen adaptation of Ian Fleming's fairy story about the old car rescued from the rubbish dump and scrap dealer by two children, restored to magical splendour by their inventor dad who drives it across the seas and into the air in his chase and final defeat of the wicked old kiddy-hating baron who has kidnapped his eccentric old dad. Lovely colour, good fun, lots of lilting tunes and nice performances from *Dick Van Dyke, Sally Ann Howes* (as pretty as an English summer), *Lionel Jeffries* and many others. Rest of cast: *Gert Frobe, Anna Quayle, Benny Hill, James Robertson Justice, Robert Helpmann, Heather Ripley, Adrian Hall, Barbara Windsor, Davy Kaye, Alexander Dore, Bernard Spear, Stanley Unwin, Peter Arne, Desmond Llewelyn, Victor Maddern, Arthur Mullard, Ross Parker, Totti Truman Taylor, Larry Taylor, Max Bacon.* Dir: Ken Hughes. Pro: Albert R. Broccoli. Screenplay: Roald Dahl & K. Hughes. (Broccoli–U.A.) Rel: Dec. 28. (Super-Pan & T.) 145 Mins. Cert U.

The Christmas Tree – l'Arbre de Noël
Almost outrageously sentimental but often amusing (thanks largely to *Bourvil's* lovely performance) story about a millionaire's small son who is doomed to an inevitable and early radiation death, and the last six months of his life when dad (*William Holden*) tries to give him his heart's desires – including a couple of wolves stolen by him from the Paris Zoo. Rest of cast: *Virna Lisi, Brook Fuller, Madeleine Damien, Friedrich Ledebur, Mario Feliciani.* Dir: Terence Young. Pro: Robert Dorfmann. Screenplay: Terence Young. Based on a novel by Michel Batalle. (Fox.) Rel: Floating. (Colour.) 108 Mins. Cert. U.

Cinderella – Italian Style – C'era una Volta
Quite amusing little Italian-made, English-dubbed fairy tale, with *Sophia Loren* as the rich man's idea of an ideal poor girl and *Omar Sharif* as a handsome Prince who can be beastly. Rest of cast: *Dolores Del Rio,*

Georges Wilson, Leslie French, Marina Malfatti, Anna Nogara, Rita Forzano, Rosemary Martin, Carlotta Barilli, Flear Montbelli, Anna Liotti. Dir: Francesco Rosi. Pro: Carlo Ponti. Screenplay: F. Rosi, T. Guerra, R. La Capria & G. P. Griffi. (Ponti–M-G-M.) Rel. Aug. 10. (Widescreen & T.) 103 Mins. Cert. U.

Complicated Girl – Una Ragazza Piuttosto Complicata
Italian film about a young man who lives in a world of fantasy, embraces into it the pretty girl he meets and then allows his illusions to lead him to murder. Cast: *Jean Sorel, Catherine Spaak.* Dir: Damiano Damiani. Based on the Alberto Moravia story. (Cinecenta.) First shown at Cinecenta, Nov., 1969. 94 Mins. Cert. X.

The Computer Wore Tennis Shoes
A typical Disney family comedy about a young man who, by a quirk of nature, unintentionally takes over the answers from a computer installed, by a not wholly altruistic business man, in his college: and is triggered off to reveal the fact that the fellow is engaged on beating the racing game! Cast: *Kurt Russell, Cesar Romero, Joe Flynn, William Schallert, Alan Hewitt, Richard Bakalyan, Debbie Paine, Frank Webb, Michael McGreevey, Jon Provost, Frank Welker, W. Alex Clarke, Bing Russell, Pat Harrington, Fabian Dean, Fritz Feld, Pete Renoudet, Hillyard Anderson.* Dir: Robert Butler. Pro: Bill Anderson. Screenplay: Joseph L. McEveety. (Disney.) Rel: March 29. (T.) 90 Mins. Cert. U.

The Confrontation – Fényes Szelek
Rather odd Miklós Jancsó film, his first in colour, about the idealistic communistic young students who, after the completion of the Hungarian Revolution of 1947, take education into their own hands, only to be jumped upon by the more realistic régime, who set out to show them that Communism means strict discipline. Strange for an iron curtain movie in that it can easily be read as a disillusioned revealing of the less happy angles of communistic policies. Oddly woven into this are a constant series of red songs and dances. Cast: *Lajos Balazsovits, Andrea Drahota, Andras Balint, Kati Kovacs, Andras Kozak, Benedek Toth.* Dir: Miklós Jancsó. Screenplay: Gyula Hernadi. (Mafilm, Studio 1, Budapest–Academy.) First shown at Academy One, April, 1970. (Agascope & E.) 85 Mins. Cert. A.

Contempt – Le Mépris
Jean-Luc Godard's film of the Alberto Moravia novel about the break-up of a seemingly very happy marriage. Cast: *Brigitte Bardot, Jack Palance, Michel Piccoli, Georgia Moll, Fritz Lang.* Dir & Written: Jean-Luc Godard. Pro: Carlo Ponti & Georges de Beauregard. (Contemporary.) First shown at Paris Pullman, April, 1970. (C & Colour.) 103 Mins. Cert. X.

Crescendo
Horror in the South of France where writer *Stephanie Powers* gets mixed up with a musician's

widow and her doping son. Rest of cast: *James Olson, Margaretta Scott, Jane Lapotaire, Joss Ackland, Kirsten Betts.* Dir: Alan Gibson. Pro: Michael Carreras. Screenplay: Jimmy Sangster & Alfred Shaughnessy. (Hammer–Warner–Pathe.) Rel: June 7. (T.) 95 Mins. Cert. X.

Crossplot
Roger Moore involved with model *Martha Hyer* who is involved through her aunt with the Marchers for Peace plot and the assassination of a visiting President! All very fast and furious. Rest of Cast: *Claudie Lange, Alexis Kanner, Francis Matthews, Bernard Lee, Derek Francis, Ursula Howells, Veronica Carlson, Dudley Sutton, Tim Preece, Mona Bruce, Norman Eshley, Michael Culver, Gabrielle Drake, John Lee.* Dir: Alvin Rakoff. Pro: R. S. Baker. Screenplay: Leigh Vance. (Tribune–U.A.) Rel: Dec. 14. (E.) 96 Mins. Cert. A.

A Curious Way to Love – La Morte Lafatto L'uovo
Hmm, Yes! A Chicken Farmer husband sets a nasty trap for his wife, with the aid of his mistress, who with her lover sets a trap for both of them! And so, who is it that ends up in tiny pieces as chicken feed? That's the problem the police have to face up to! Glamorous people taking part in this nasty business include *Gina Lollobrigida, Jean-Louis Trintignant, Ewa Aulin* and *Renato Romano.* Rest of cast: *Giulio Donnini, Cleofe Del Cile, Ugo Adinolfi, Aldo Bonamano, Livio Ferraro, Margherita Horowitz, Guiliano Raffaelle, Gian Carlo Sisti, Jean Sobieski, Vittorio Andre, Biagio Pelligra, Monica Millese, Conrad Anderson, Rina de Filippo, Mario Guizzardy, Barbara Pignaton, Jean Rougeuf, Ludmil Tritonov.* Dir: Giulio Questi. (Butcher's.) Rel: Floating. (E.) 101 Mins. Cert. X.

Daddy's Gone A-Hunting
Thriller about a girl pursued by her ex-lover, who has developed a mental kink because she killed his child when she left him by having an abortion. Cast: *Carol White, Paul Burke, Mala Powers, Rachel Ames, Barry Cahill, Matilda Calnan, Andrea King, Gene Lyons, Ron Masak, Dennis Patrick, James Sikking, Scott Hylands.* Dir & Pro: Mark Robson. Screenplay: Larry Cohen & Lorenzo Semple Junr. (Robson–Anglo–Warner–Pathe.) Rel: Nov. 2. (T.) 108 Mins. Cert. X.

The Damned – La Caduta degli Dei
Powerful, fascinating, overlong and basically brilliant story about a German steel family, individually depraved and effete, whose struggle for power when the old head of them is murdered, is as ruthless and bloody as the greater struggle for power going on in the country as the Nazis finally take over. With *Dirk Bogarde* quite outstanding as the Hamlet-like outsider as ruthless as any as he struggles towards the chair at the head of the long table. Rest of cast: *Ingrid Thulin, Helmut Griem, Helmut Berger, Renaud Verley, Umberto Orsini, Rene Kolldehoff, Albrecht Schönhals, Nora Ricci, Irina Wanka, Valentina Ricci, Karen Mittendorf,*

Florinda Bolkan, Charlotte Rampling. Dir: Luchino Visconti. Pro: Alfredo Levy & Ever Haggiag. Screenplay: Nicola Badalucco, Enrico Medioli & L. Visconti. (Warner–Pathe.) Rel: Floating. (T.) 153 Mins. Cert. X.

The Dance of Death
Straightforward screening, without more than a minute or two's concession to the changed medium, of the National Theatre Company's production of the grim and great August Strindberg play, with *Laurence Olivier* giving one of the finest performances of his career as the man chained inescapably to a woman with an intense and deep love–hate relationship which makes their life together impossible, but also makes it impossible to part. Rest of cast: *Geraldine McEwan, Robert Lang, Janina Faye, Carolyn Jones, Maggie Riley, Jeanne Watts, Malcolm Reynolds, Peter Penry-Jones.* Dir: David Giles. Pro: John Brabourne. (Paramount.) Rel: Floating. (T.) 149 Mins. Cert. A.

David Copperfield
Rather slow and pedestrian version of the Charles Dickens classic, but enlivened by some brilliant cameos of characterisation, such as *Ralph Richardson's* superb Mr. Micawber, *Laurence Olivier's* horrid Mr. Creakle and *Ron Moody's* truly slimy Uriah. Rest of cast: *Richard Attenborough, Cyril Cusack, Edith Evans, Pamela Franklin, Susan Hampshire, Wendy Hiller, Robin Phillips, Michael Redgrave, Emlyn Williams, Sinead Cusack, James Donald, James Hayter, Megs Jenkins, Anna Massey, Andrew McCulloch, Nicholas Pennell, Corin Redgrave, Isobel Black, Liam Redmond, Donald Layne-Smith, Christopher Moran, Jeffrey Chandler, Kim Craik, Helen Cotterill, Alistair Mackenzie.* Dir: Delbert Mann. Pro: Frederick Brogger. Screenplay: Jack Pulman. (Omnibus/Biography–Fox.) Rel: Jan. 4. (T.) 118 Mins. Cert. U.

Day of Anger
German-Italian Western about a young man who, taken under the wing of a notorious gunman learns to hate his business when he realises the bestiality of his mentor's methods. Cast: *Lee Van Cleef, Giuliano Gemma, Walter Rilla, Christa Linder, Ennio Balbo, Lukas Ammann, Andrea Bosic, Pepe Calvo, Giorgio Gargiullo, Anna Orso, Hans Otto Alberty, Nino Nini, Virgilia Gazzolo, Eleonora Morana, Benito Stefanelli.* Dir: Tonino Valerii. Pro: Alfonso Sansone & Errico Chroscicky. Screenplay: T. Valerii, E. Gastaldi & R. Genta. (Anglo–EMI–Warner–Pathe.) Rel: May 31. (T. Techniscope.) 78 Mins. Cert. X.

Dayton's Devils
Leslie Nielsen leading a carefully selected and meticulously trained gang, including *Rory Calhoun* and *Lainie Kazan*, in a martially original and timed plan to steal some 2½ millions of dollars from an American Air Force Base – at first daringly successful but then horribly disastrous. Rest of cast: *Hans Gudegast, Barry Sadler, Pat Renella, Georg Stanford Brown, Rigg Kennedy.* Dir: Jack Shea. Pro: R. W. Stabler. Screenplay: Fred De Gorter. (British Lion.) Rel: Oct. 19. (E.) 89 Mins. Cert. A.

Death of a Gunfighter
Richard Widmark as the old-style Marshal who won't resign his job, either by request, or threat, or physical attack, and in the end has to be shot down by the community he has defended so ably for so long because there's just no alternative way of getting him out of office! Rest of cast: *Lena Horne, John Saxon, Michael McGreevey, Darleen Carr, Carroll O'Connor, Mercer Harris, Kent Smith, Larry Gates, Morgan Woodward, James O'Hara, Harry Carey, Jacqueline Scott, Dub Taylor, Jimmy Lydon.* Dir: Allen Smithee (i.e. Robert Totlen, Don Siegel.) Pro: Richard E. Lyons. Screenplay: Joseph Cavelli. (Universal–Rank.) Rel: Oct. 26. (T.) 94 Mins. Cert A.

The Deserter and the Nomads – Zbehovia a Pontnici
A rather odd little Czech–Italian production which in condemning the futility of war and violence – describing itself as an "allegoric motion picture poem"– manages to show quite a bit of both in its three parts, "The Deserter", "Sunday" and "The Nomads": the first the story of a gipsy deserter in World War One, the second a Russian soldier – Slovak peasant confrontation in the Second World War and the third a glimpse of atomic bombed future. Cast: *Gezja Ferenc, Helena Grodova, Stefan Ladizinsky, August Kuban, Jana Stehnova, Alexandra Sekulova, Albert Pagac, Vasek Kovarik, Frantisek Peto.* Dir: Juraj Jakubisko. Pro: Moris Ergas. Screenplay: Ladislao Tazky. (Columbia.) First shown at Cameo Poly, May, 1970. (Colour.) 102 Mins. Cert. X.

The Devil's 8
Christopher George as the tough Federal agent sent to smash up a corrupt organisation which is using the business of "moonshine" manufacture to gain power in one of America's southern states. Rest of cast: *Fabian, Ralph Meeker, Tom Nardini, Leslie Parrish, Ross Hagen, Larry Bishop, Cliff Osmond, Robert Doqui, Ron Rifkin, Baynes Barron, Joseph Turkel, Lada Edmund, Jr., Marjorie Dayne.* Dir & Pro: Burt Topper. Screenplay: J. G. White, W. Huyck & J. Milius, from a Larry Gordon story. (American International/Anglo–Warner–Pathe.) Rel: Aug. 17. (D.) 98 Mins. Cert. A.

Diamonds for Breakfast
Loosely constructed little comedy about an ex-Grand Duke of Russia, now keeping a boutique in Hampstead, who allows the shades of his ancestors to persuade him to recruit a bevy of useful beauties and rob the crown jewels of all the Russians – conveniently being shown for some shady Soviet reason at an English stately home. Cast: *Marcello Mastroianni, Rita Tushingham, Elaine Taylor, Maggie Blye, Francisca Tu, The Karlins, Warren Mitchell, Nora Nicholson, Bryan Pringle, Leonard Rossiter, Bill Fraser, David Horn, Ann Blake, Ian Trigger, Charles Lloyd Pack.* Dir: Christopher Morahan. Pro: Carlo Ponti – Pierre Rouve. Screenplay: P. Rouve, Ronald Harwood – N. F. Simpson. (Ponti–Paramount.) Rel: Dec. 7. (E.) 102 Mins. Cert. A. This film had a premiere run in Nov. 1968, and was featured in "The Neglected Ones" feature in the last volume.

Diamond Rush – Le Paria
Franco–Spanish, English-dubbed film about a gangster who, having successfully held up the Tangier–Antwerp express, escapes to the mountains with his loot, there being sheltered by a woman and a child who give him a new meaning to his life, which he sacrifices for them when he is cornered and attacked by his ex-mates, his mistress and the cops. Cast: *Jean Marais, Marie-Jose Nat, Horst Frank, Nieves Navarro* etc. Dir: Claude Carliez. Pro: Helene Dassonville. (Ceres–Carlton Continental–Santo Alcocer–Rank.) Rel. Feb. 15. (E.) 105 Mins. Cert A.

Did You Hear the One About the Travelling Saleslady?
Minor American backwoods farce-comedy about the misadventures of a lady saleswoman and crazy inventor who between them keep Kansas's Primrose Junction in continual uproar. Cast: *Phyllis Diller, Bob Denver, Joe Flynn, Paul Reed, Jeannette Nolan, Eileen Wesson, Bob Hastings, George Neise, Anita Eubank, David Hartman, Kelly Thordsen.* Dir: Don Weis. Pro: Si Rose. Screenplay: John Fenton Murray. (Universal–Rank.) Rel: Aug. 31, (re-released on Jan. 11, 1970.) (T.) 74 Mins. Cert. U.

Doctor Zhivago
Mammoth (3¼ hour plus interval) David Lean-directed adaptation (made in 1965) of the Pasternak story set prior to and during the Russian Revolution. Wonderfully photographed, superbly visual, with many of the scenes and some whole sequences memorable; but most of the characters – with the exception of *Rod Steiger*, who is magnificent – are never brought alive and the result is a cold, sparkling but hard gem of a film, extremely rewarding to watch. Rest of cast: *Omar Sharif, Julie Christie, Geraldine Chaplin, Alec Guinness, Tom Courtenay, Siobhan McKenna, Ralph Richardson, Rita Tushingham, Jeffrey Rockland, Tarek Sharif, Bernard Kay, Klaus Kinski, Gerard Tichy, Noel Willman, Geoffrey Keen, Adrienne Corri, Jack MacGowran, Mark Eden, Erik Chitty, Roger Maxwell, Wolf Frees, Gwen Nelson, Lucy Westmore, Lili Murati, Peter Madden.* Dir: David Lean. Pro: Carlo Ponti. Screenplay: Robt. Bolt. (M-G-M.) Rel: Special. (70 mm Panavision & Metrocolor.)

Don't Look Back
Cinéma Vérité movie about Pop star *Bob Dylan*, with various other Pop People making appearances, including *Joan Baez.* Dir: D. A. Pennebaker. First shown at ICA Cinema, Aug. 1969. 95 Mins.

Doppelgänger
Gerry and Sylvia Anderson of "Thunderbird" TV and large screen puppetry fame, turn to live-action for a similar-storied science-fiction fantasy about the century-hence discovery of a new planet which is exactly the same in every way (even to the individual people) to earth – except that it's the other way round! Cast: *Ian Hendry, Roy Thinnes, Patrick Wymark, Lynn Loring, Loni von Friedl, Herbert Lom, George Sewell, Franco Derosa, Edward Bishop.* Dir: Robert Parrish. Pro: Ernest Holding. (The Andersons–Universal–Rank.) Rel: Oct. 26. (T.) 101 Mins. Cert. A.

Duet for Cannibals – Duett für Kannibaler
Sombre Swedish psychological sex drama about a man drawn with his girl-friend into an obscure "game" engineered by his employer and, perhaps, his wife: a quartet dance which can be seen either as art or artifice. Cast: *Adriana Asti, Lars Ekborg, Gosta Ekman, Agneta Ekmanner.* Dir: Susan Sontag. (Contemporary.) First shown at Paris-Pullman, Nov., 1969. 106 Mins. Cert. X.

A Dream of Kings
Anthony Quinn in a made-to-fit role of the Chicago Greek, a womaniser and gambler, who failing all other means of getting his ailing son to Greece and the healing sunshine, cheats and is beaten-up. And so his wife, seeing she cannot convince him of the fantasy of his ideas, herself raises the money and sends son and father off. Rest of cast: *Irene Papas, Inger Stevens, Sam Levene, Val Avery, Tamara Daykarhanova, Peter Mamakos, James Dobson, Zvee Scooler, Bill Walker, H. B. Haggerty, Alan Reed Sr., Radames Pera, Theoharis Lemonopoulos, Stasa Damascus, Katherine Theodore, James Fortunes, Ernest Sarracino, Renata Vanni, Chris Marks, Sandra Damato, Effie Columbus, Peter Kogeones.* Dir: Daniel Mann. Pro: Jules Schermer. Screenplay: Harry Mark Petrakis & Ian Hunter. (Warner–Pathe.) Rel: February. (T.) 110 Mins. Cert. X.

Easy Rider
Peter Fonda's off-beat movie, about a trip across America made by him and his hippy pal on motor-bikes and their experiences with some of the pleasant, and far less pleasant aspects of the current American scene. Superbly visual. Cast: *Peter Fonda, Dennis Hopper, Antonio Mendoza, Phil Spector, Mac Mashourian, Warren Finnerty, Tita Colorado, Luke Askew, Jack Nicholson.* Dir: Dennis Hopper. Pro: Peter Fonda. Screenplay: Peter Fonda, Dennis Hopper, Terry Southern. (Pando–Raybert/Columbia.) Rel: March 1. (T.) 95 Mins. Cert. X.

Emma Hamilton – Lady Hamilton – zwischen Schmach und Liebe
Richard Johnson as the blind-eyed hero of Trafalgar rescuing Emma, a Queen, and his country with equal nonchalance in an unabashed melodramatic page of fictionalised history; with lovely colour, amusing lines (!) and (making all worthwhile) a largely undressed – and quite divine – *Michele Mercier*, who makes her Lady H. a cross between Nell Gwynne and Eliza Dolittle. Rest of Cast: *John Mills, Harald Leipnitz, Boy Gobert, Gabriella Giorgelli, Venantino Venantini, Dieter Borsche, Mario Pisu, Howard Ross, Gisela Uhlen, Mirko Ellis, Lorenzo Terzon, Gigi Ballista, Robert Hundar, Nadja Tiller.* Dir: Christian-Jaque. Pro: Wolf C. Hartwig. Screenplay: Jameson Brewer, Werner P. Zibaso & Christian-Jaque, based on the Alexandre Dumas story. (Rank.) Rel: Nov. 30. (T. & Pan.) 96 Mins. Cert. X.

Entertaining Mr. Sloane
Very finely acted screen adaptation of the (dirty) black and sick Joe Orton stage comedy(!) about a brother and sister who both take a sensual fancy to the young killer named in the title, fight over him and finally, holding over him the threat of exposure of the murder of their old father, make a vile pact to share him between them, having him for six months each! Cast: *Beryl Reid, Harry Andrews, Peter McEnery, Alan Webb.* Dir: Douglas Hickox. Pro: Douglas Kentish. Screenplay: Clive Exton. (Anglo–Warner–Pathe.) Rel: May 31. (T.) 94 Mins. Cert. X.

Erotic Urge – Trois Filles vers le Soleil
A story about three girls who set off to hitch-hike to St. Tropez, each finding romance of some sort along the way. Cast: *Jacqueline Vandal, Sabine Sun, Catherine Monnet, Jean Barney, Jean-Pierre Moutier, Jean-Louis Tristan, Maurice Teynac.* Dir: Roger Baumont. Pro: G. Glass. Screenplay: R. Baumont, Philippe Le Franc & Claude Mulot. (S.F.) First shown at Jacey, Piccadilly, Sept., 1969. (E.) 81 Mins. Cert. X.

Erotique – Traquenards Erotiques
Anna Gael as the girl who becomes mixed-up with thugs and white slavers and is only saved from them at the end by the poet who loves her and follows her to Paris when he fears she is in danger. Rest of Cast: *Hans Meyer, Roland Lesaffre, Claude Charney, Robert Lombard, Anne Renate, Dominique Erlanger, Charles Dalin, Jean Droze.* Dir: Jean-Francois Davy. Pro: Joel Lifschutz. Screenplay: Michel Levine, J. F. Davy. (Miracle.) First shown at Jacey Tatler, Oct. 1969. (E.) 85 Mins. Cert. X.

Every Home Should Have One
Satirical comedy largely aimed at the world of TV advertising, with *Marty Feldman* making his large-screen star début as a naïve copywriter almost accidentally selected to lead a big campaign to put 'sex into porridge'. Rest of cast: *Shelley Berman, Judy Cornwell, Julie Ege, Patrick Cargill, Jack Watson, Patience Collier, Penelope Keith, Dinsdale Landen, Annabel Leventon, John McKelvey, Moray Watson, Sarah Badel, Michael Bates, Roland Curram, Dave Dee, Hy Hazell, David Hutcheson, Judy Huxtable, John Wells, Harold Innocent, Maggie Jones, Frances de la Tour, Ellis Dale, Charles Lewsen, Vicki Hodge, Erika Bergman.* Dir: Jim Clark. Pro: Ned Sherrin. Screenplay: M. Feldman, Barry Took & Denis Norden. (British Lion.) Rel: May 3. (E.) 94 Mins. Cert. X.

Everything for Sale – Nszystko Na Sprzedaz
Andrzej ("Ashes and Diamonds") Wajda's rather strange and complicated tribute to the star he made famous, the late Zbigniew Cybulski. It is in the form of an intricate film about making a film in which the star never turns up, having been killed by falling under a train – as, indeed, Cybulski was. The fact and fiction are fused and the result if not particularly successful is always provocative, intellectually exciting and worth watching. Cast: *Andrzej Lapicki, Beata Tyszkiewicz, Elzbieta Czyzewska, Daniel Olbrychski, Witold Holtz, Malgorzata Potocka, Bogumil Kobiela, Elzbieta*

Kepinska, Irena Laskowska, Tadeusz Kalinowski, Wieslaw Dymny, Wojciech Solarz, Josef Fuks, Witold Dederko, Andrzej Kostenko. Dir & Written: Andrzej Wajda. (Contemporary.) First shown at Academy Two, late June, 1969. (Colour.) 105 Mins. Cert. A.

Eye of the Cat
Macabre little thriller, injected with with-it erotic touches, about a horrible plot cooked up by a pretty but nasty little beauty-shop assistant (*Gayle Hunnicutt*, most effective) who persuades the two young nephews of a wealthy old invalid (*Eleanor Parker*) to murder her and steal her money. Rest of cast: *Michael Sarrazin, Tim Henry, Laurence Naismith, Jennifer Leak, Linden Chiles, Mark Herron, Annabelle Garth*. Dir: David Lowell Rich. Pro: Bernard Schwartz, Philip Hazelton. Screenplay: Joseph Stefano. (Universal–Rank.) Rel: Sept. 14. (Colour.) 102 Mins. Cert. X.

The Faceless Monster – Amanti d'Oltretomsa
Horrible happenings in the old castle where a brilliant, crazy scientist having experimented with the electric regeneration of blood, uses his wife's (who together with lover he kills) to make young and beautiful his old assistant! Cast: *Barbara Steele, Paul Miller, Helga Line, Lawrence Clift*. Dir: Allan Grunewald. (New Realm.) Rel: Floating. 73 Mins. Cert. X.

The Fat and the Lean – Le Gros et le Maigre
16-minute Roman Polanski film about the Master and Slave relationship, a bitter fable, made in France in 1961. Described by Polanski as "the story of a fat man, a thin man, and a goat, or how difficult it is to escape one's destiny". Cast: *Roman Polanski, Andre Katelbach*. Dir. Polanski. Pro: Claude Joudioux. Screenplay: Polanski & Jean-Pierre Rousseau. (A.P.E.C. Dist.–New Cinema Presentations.) First shown at Times Cinema, Feb. 1970.

Find a Place to Die – Joe, Cercati un Posto per Monre
Italian Western: ruthless tracking down of a golden fortune by various unpleasant characters including the mine-owner's wife who ends up with a gun-runner as two of the few survivors. Cast: *Jeffrey Hunter, Pascale Petit, Giovanni Pallavicino, Daniela Giordano, Reza Fazeli, Adolfo Lastretti, Piero Lulli*. Dir: Anthony Ascott. Pro: Hugo Fregonese. Screenplay: Ralph Grave. (Miracle.) Rel: July 20. (E.) 90 Mins. Cert. X.

A Fine Pair – Ruba al prossimo tuo
They are *Claudia Cardinale* and *Rock Hudson*, the former rather unconvincingly tricking the latter, a New York cop, into helping her further her jewel-thieving plans in Austria. All very complicated, with the two main participants trying to switch their sides of the legal fence. Rest of cast: *Tomas Milian, Leon Askin, Ellen Corby, Walter Giller, Guido Alberti, Peter Dane*. Dir: Francesco Maselli. Pro: Leo L. Fuchs. Screenplay: F. Maselli, L. Montagnana, L. Gelbart & V. C. Leone. (Cristaldi/Warner–Pathe.) Rel: Nov. 30. 89 Mins. Cert. A.

Finnegans Wake
Imaginative and spirited attempt by Mary Ellen Bute to do the impossible and transfer to celluloid some pages from James Joyce, breathing fresh life into the difficult masterpiece by way of the superb locations, in Southern Ireland generally and along the River Liffey in particular, photographed beautifully by her husband Ted Nemeth. Cast: *Martin J. Kelly, Jane Reilly, Peter Haskell, Page Johnson, John V. Kelleher, Maura Pryor, Ray Flanagan, Jo Jo Slavin*. Dir & Pro: Mary Ellen Bute. Screenplay: Mary Ellen Bute & Mary Manning, upon whose stage play it is based. (Contemporary.) First shown at Academy, Dec., 1969) 90 Mins. Cert. A.

The Five Man Army – Un Esacito di 5 Uomini
Italian-made, English-speaking, American directed film set in Mexico in 1914 and telling a story about an attack by a quintet of "specialists" of one kind or another on a military train carrying $500,000 in gold, which four want for themselves and the fifth, the leader (*Peter Graves*) wants for The Revolution. Rest of cast: *James Daly, Bud Spencer, Tetsuro Tamba, Nino Castelnuovo, Daniela Giordano, Claudio Gora, Annabella Andreoli, Carlo Alighiero, Jack Stuart, Marc Lawrence, Jose Torres, Marino Mase*. Dir: Don Taylor. Pro: Italo Zingarelli. Screenplay: Dario Argento & Marc Richards. (M-G-M.) Rel: Jan. 18. 105 Mins. Cert. A.

The Fixer
A long, absorbing and entirely honourable adaptation by John Frankenheimer of the Bernard Malamud novel set in pre-Revolutionary Russia, where in order to attempt to divert the people's hatred of the aristocrats the government pin a murder on a Jewish handyman who, degraded and tortured, doggedly refuses to admit to a crime he has not committed. A very honest and admirable movie, one of the few American movies ever to attempt to match philosophical debate to historical truth. Fine performances by *Alan Bates* as "The Fixer" and *Dirk Bogarde* as his lawyer. Rest of cast: *Georgia Brown, Jack Gilford, Hugh Griffith, Elizabeth Hartman, Ian Holm, David Warner, Carol White*. Dir: John Frankenheimer. Pro: Edward Lewis. Screenplay: Dalton Trumbo (J. Frankenheimer–Edward Lewis–M-G-M.) Rel: Floating. (Metrocolor.) 130 Mins. Cert. X.

Flareup
Raquel Welch as the fugitive fleeing from an insane killer with three murders to his credit and her name next on the list. Rest of cast: *James Stacy, Luke Askew, Don Chastain, Ron Rifkin, Jeane Byron, Kay Peters, Pat Delany, Sandra Giles, Joe Billings, Carol-Jean Thompson, Mary Wilcox, Carl Byrd, Steve Conte, Tom Fadden, Michael Rougas, David Moses, Will J. White, Doug Rowe, Gordon Jump, Ike Williams*. Dir: James Neilson. Pro: Leon Fromkess. Screenplay: Mark Rodgers. (GMF Picture Corp.–M-G-M.) Rel: Jan. 18. 90 Mins. Cert. A.

Flesh
Andy Warhol's Underground production about a young American hustler's day, trying to raise $200

for his wife's girl-friend's abortion which in the end turns out to be a false alarm. Dir: Paul Morissey. Pro: Warhol. (Vaughan-Rogosier.) First shown at The Open Space, Jan., 1970.

Footprints on the Moon – Apollo 11
The filmed record of Apollo 11, including a great deal of the footage of the material taken by Astronauts Neil Armstrong, Michael Collins and Edwin Aldrin. Dir: Bill Gibson. Pro: Barry Coe. Narration written by Robt. S. Scott; spoken by Dr. Wernher Von Braun. (Fox.) Rel: Floating. (T.) 95 Mins. Cert. U.

Fort Yuma Gold – Per Pocchi Dollari Ancora
Italian–French–Spanish made, English dubbed Western set at the end of the American Civil War and concerning a crooked Confederate Major who plans to carry on the war a little longer for personal – reasons by attacking the Confederate-held Fort and pinching their million golden dollars. Cast: *Montgomery Wood, Dan Vadis, Jose Calvo, Angel Del Pozo, Sophie Daumier, Jacques Sernas*. Dir: C. J. Paget. Pro: Edmondo Amati. Screenplay: A. Finocchi, M. Capriccioli, etc. (Gala.) Rel: July 20. (T.) 100 Mins. Cert. X.

48 Hours of Love
The plan of a young Swedish architect to test out his fiancee before marrying her leads them to her old boy-friend (and his wife) in France and a rapidly increasingly complicated quartet relationship and tension which ends in disaster. Cast: *Sven Bertil Taube, Thelma Ramstrom, Francis Lemonnier, Bull Ogier, Jean-Pierre Monelle*. Dir: Cecil Saint-Laurent. Pro: Georges de Beauregard. (S.F. Film Distributors.) Rel: Floating. (E.) 90 Mins. Cert. X.

Funny Girl
Barbra Streisand repeating her stage triumph as the really Funny Girl of the title – in fact the routine theatrical success story was based on the life of famous American comedienne and Ziegfeld star Fanny Brice. With *Omar Sharif* playing the gambling hubbie who loses, gambles on a shady deal and goes to jail; coming out to confirm his final parting with his spouse. Rest of cast: *Kay Medford, Anne Francis, Walter Pidgeon, Lee Allen, Mae Questel, Gerald Mohr, Frank Faylen, Mittie Lawrence, Gertrude Flynn, Penny Santon, John Harmon*. The Ziegfeld Girls in the spectacular scene from the Follies played by: *Thordis Brandt, Bettina Brenna, Virginia Ann Ford, Alena Johnston, Karen Lee, Mary Jane Mangler, Inga Neilsen, Sharon Vaughn*. Dir: William Wyler. Music: Jules Styne. Lyrics: Bob Merrill. Screenplay: Isobel Lennart, based on her musical stage play. Pro: Ray Stark. (Columbia.) Rel: Jan. 25. (T & Pan.) 147 Mins. plus interval, overture etc. Cert. U.

Futtocks End
British comedy set in the decaying country mansion of the title, where tradition is maintained and chaos reigns – especially when an odd assortment of guests arrive to spend a traditional British country-house weekend there. Cast: *Michael Hordern, Ronnie Barker*,

Roger Livesey, Julian Orchard, Kika Markham, Mary Merrall, Hilary Pritchard, Peggy Ann Clifford, Richard O' Sullivan, Jennifer Cox, Suzanne Togni, Sammie Winmill, Barry Gosney, Ernest Jennings, Kim Kee Lee, Aubrey Woods. Dir & Pro: Bob Kellett. Screenplay: Ronnie Barker. (David Paradine–Lion.) Rel: May 3. 49 Mins. Cert. A.

Gappa – The Triphibian Monster – Dai kyoju Gappa

A Japanese chiller-diller set on a remote tropical island where an expedition pinches a baby monster right out of the egg and takes it back to Japan – to be followed by the furious parents, who set to wiping out Tokyo! (Border.) Rel: Oct. 5. (E.) 81 Mins. Cert. X.

The Gendarme of St. Tropez – Le Gendarme de Saint-Tropez

The triumph of the village Gendarme made sergeant of St. Tropez, when he recovers a stolen painting and with the help of his daughter's teenage friends, captures the crooks. And he's played by *Louis de Funes*. Rest of cast: *Genevieve Grad, Daniel Cauchy, Maria Pacome, Patrice Laffont, France Rumilly, Michel Galabru, Claude Pieplu, Madeleine Delavaivre, Fernand Sardou, Christian Marin, Jean Lefebvre*. Dir & Screenplay, with Jacques Vilfrid and Richard Balducci: Jean Girault. (Miracle.) Rel: Nov. 9. 79 Mins. Cert. U. This film was included as a "floating release" in last year's annual'.

Gendarme in New York – Le Gendarme à New York

Second in the "Gendarme" series (first was "Gendarme of St. Tropez") and funnier than the first: *Louis de Funes*, representing France at the International Police Congress in New York finds his daughter has stowed away in order to accompany him and then has the job of getting her secretly home so that his superiors don't find out. Rest of cast: *Genevieve Grad, Alan Scott, Jean Lefebvre, Michel Galabru, Christian Marin, Grosso & Modo*. Dir: Jean Girault. Screenplay: J. Girault & Jacques Vilfrid. (Societe Nouvelle de Cinematographie–Miracle.) Rel: Nov. 9. 84 Mins. Cert. U.

Gentle Love – Tu Seras Terriblement Gentille

Quiet and slim little French film about a photographer tired of life in Lyons who goes to Paris to make his fortune, drifts away from his left-behind wife who eventually herself finds fame and fortune as a top fashion model. And then, just as she is about to go to New York, the husband turns up again and they discover they can't after all live apart. All very glossy. Cast: *Karen Blanguernon, Leslie Bedos, Frederic de Pasquale, Victor Lanoux, Jean Moussy, Rene Goliard, Jean-Paul Moulinot, Tessa Sanfers, Tony Kinna, Madeleine Lambert*. Dir: Dirk Sanders. Pro: Rene Thevenet. Screenplay: D. Sanders, Paul Soreze. (Cinecenta.) Rel: Floating. 94 Mins. Cert. U.

The Girls – Flickorna

Mai Zetterling's not always convincing cry of protest about the status of women in today's world; shown in a story about three actresses in a travelling production of "Lysistrata" whose own personal problems become mixed up with those of the characters in the play. An intriguing if not entirely successful blend of fantasy and fact, realism and imagination. Cast: *Bibi Andersson, Harriet Andersson, Gunnel Lindblom, Gunnar Bjornstrand, Erland Josephson, Ake Lindstrom, Frank Sundstrom, Stig Engstrom*. Dir: Mai Zetterling. Screenplay: Mai Zetterling & David Hughes. (Contemporary.) First shown at Paris-Pullman, Jan., 1970. 100 Mins. Cert. X.

The Girl Who Knew Too Much

The girl in question being lovely Chinese maiden *Nancy Kwan*, only one of the many involved, both directly and indirectly, lovely and very much less lovely, in a Red plot to take over the big Crime Syndicate Inc. and so disrupt American commercial life from the inside! Rest of cast: *Adam West, Nehemiah Persoff, Buddy Greco, Robert Alda, Patricia Smith, David Brian, Weaver Levy, John Napier, Mark Roberts, Steve Peck, Diane Van Valin, Chick Chandler, Lisa Todd*. Dir: Francis D. Lyon. Pro: Earl Lyon. (United Pictures Corp./Commonwealth United Entertainment–Monarch.) Rel: July 27. (Colour.) 79 Mins. Cert. U.

Gold is Where You Find It

Irish comedy about a gold mine that isn't – until it gushes oil! And all because a poor-boy-made-good (in the U.S.) returns home to Shanbally for a visit and brings a pocket full of gold nuggets as souvenirs. Cast: *Eddie Byrne, Dermot Kelly, Sam Kydd, Pat McAnally, Barry Keegan, Barbara Berkely, P. G. Stephens, Patrick Jordan, Michael Jannie, Middleton Woods*. Dir: Francis Searle. (Monarch.) Rel: Aug. 3. (E.) 27 Mins. Cert. U.

The Good Guys and the Bad Guys

An unusually amusing Western which manages at the same time to guy the old traditions of the genre and yet retain a serious balance to the story: about a conscientious town marshal (of Progress!) who is sacked but continues with his job of bringing in a gang of outlaws and finally achieves it, with the help of an old enemy, in a very fast and funny chase climax. Cast: *Robert Mitchum, George Kennedy, David Carradine, Martin Balsam, Tina Louise, Douglas V. Fowley, Lois Nettleton, John Davis Chandler, John Carradine, Marie Windsor, Dick Peabody, Kathleen Freeman, Jimmy Murphy, Garrett Lewis, Nick Dennis*. Dir: Burt Kennedy. Pro & Screenplay: R. M. Cohen & D. Shyrack. (Robert Goldstein–Warner–Pathe.) Rel: Nov. 23. (T & Pan.) 90 Mins. Cert. A.

Goodbye, Columbus

Delightful, light comedy about a boy who meets girl, wins girl, and then parts from her when circumstances get too much for both of them. The background, which makes the movie such good, quiet fun, is the truly observed portrait of American Jewish family life. Nice performances from newcomers *Richard Benjamin* and *Ali MacGraw*. Rest of cast: *Jack Klugman,*

Nan Martin, Michael Meyers, Lori Shelle, Royce Wallace, Sylvie Strauss, Kay Cummings, Michael Nurie, Betty Greyson, Monroe Arnold, Elaine Swain, Richard Wexler, Rubin Schaefer, Bill Derringer, Mari Gorman, Gail Ommerle. Dir: Larry Peerce. Pro: Stanley R. Jaffe. Screenplay: Arnold Schulman. (Paramount.) Rel: Sept. 28. (T.) 102 Mins. Cert. X.

Goodbye, Mr. Chips

Musical re-make of one of the great old sentimental cinema successes; based on the James Hilton best-seller about a public schoolmaster, a dry young stick, who wins affection only when he has met the girl of his life and married her. Still plenty of heart-tugs, with *Peter O'Toole* giving an outstanding performance as Chips (the old Donat part) and *Petula Clark* (in the old Greer Garson role). Rest of cast: *Sir Michael Redgrave, George Baker, Michael Bryant, Jack Hedley, Sian Phillips, Alison Leggatt, Clinton Greyn, Michael Culver, Barbara Couper, Elspeth March, Clive Morton, John Gugolka, Michael Ridgeway, Craig Marriott, Elspet Gray, Jeremy Lloyd, Jack May, Leo Britt, Royston Tickner, Patricia Hayes*. Dir: Herbert Ross. Pro: Arthur P. Jacobs. Screenplay: Terence Rattigan. (Apjac–M-G-M.) Rel: April 5. (Pan & Metrocolor.) 151 Mins. Cert. U.

Goto, L'Ile d'Amour – Goto, Island of Love

Highly individual French film made by young Polish director Walerian Borowczyk: a turgid tale set on a small and completely isolated island where the community live a poor and savage existence and where a little weasel of a man, surviving one of the periodical fights to the death between criminals, climbs from the lowly position of Keeper of the Dogs and Killer of the Flies to that of Governor–King by the simple expedients of murder and lies. Cast: *Pierre Brasseur, Ligia Branice, Jean-Pierre Andreani, Guy Saint-Jean, Ginette Leclerc, Rene Dary, Fernand Bercher, Raoul Darblay, Hubert Lassiat, Michel Thomass*. Dir & Screenplay: Walerian Borowczyk. (Contemporary.) First shown at Paris-Pullman, Oct., 1969. 93 Mins. Cert. X.

The Great Train Robbery – Die Gentlemen bitten zur kasse

German-made, English dubbed, careful if strangely unexciting, documentary-style reconstruction of THE famous British crime! Cast: *Horst Tappert, Hans Cossy, Gunther Neutze, Karl Heinz Hess, Hans Reiser, Rolf Nagel, Harry Engel, Wolfran Schaerf, Gunther Tabor, Franz Mosthav, Wolfried Lier, Kurt Conradi, Horst Beck, Paul Edwin Roth, Kai Fischer, Siegfried Lowitz, Lothar Grutzner, Dirk Dautzenberg, Albert Hoerrman*. Dir: John Olden & Claus Peter Witt. Pro: Egon Monk. Screenplay & Story: Henry Kolarz. (NDR–Gala.) First shown at the Berkeley, Aug., 1969. 97 Mins. Cert. U.

The Green Slime

Japanese–American co-effort; science-fiction about a little piece of green slime brought back from outer space which multiplies intself into a terrifyingly fast-increasing legion of horrific monsters! Cast: *Robert*

Horton, Richard Jaeckel, Luciana Paluzzi, Bud Widom, Ted Gunther, Robert Dunham, David Yorston, William Ross, Gary Randolf, Richard Hylland. Dir: Kinji Fukasaku. Pro: Ivan Reiner & W. M. Manley. Screenplay: Chas. Sinclair, Wm. Finger, Tom Rowe. (Southern Cross Films–M-G-M.) Rel: Sept. 21. (Toeicolour.) 90 Mins. Cert. X.

Guns in the Heather
Youthful adventure in Oirland where an American and an Irish boy become mixed-up with a plot by the Americans to smuggle out of the country a defecting Iron Curtain nuclear physicist professor. Cast: *Glenn Corbett, Alfred Burke, Kurt Russell, Patrick Dawson, Patrick Barr, Hugh McDermott, Patrick Westwood, Eddie Byrne, Godfrey Quigley, Kevin Stoney, Shay Gorman, Niall Toibin, Ernst Walder, Robert Bernal, Vincent Dowling, John Horton, J. G. Devlin, Nicola Davies, Gerry Alexander, Eamon Morrissey, Declan Mulholland, Mary Larkin, Paul Farrell.* Dir: Robt. Butler. Pro: Ron Miller. Screenplay: Herman Groves. (Disney.) Rel: July 27. 90 Mins. Cert. U.

Guns of the Magnificent Seven
Third of the "Seven" Mexican-Westerns with *George Kennedy* and *James Whitmore* as the new leaders of the septet of gunmen defending the interests of the poor, downtrodden peasants. Only three eventually survive the jailbreak and ambush of the Federales. Rest of cast: *Monte Markham, Bernie Casey, Joe Don Baker, Scott Thomas, Reni Santoni, Michael Ansara, Wende Wagner, Frank Silvera, Fernando Rey.* Dir: Paul Wendkos. Pro: Vincent M. Fennelly. Screenplay: Herman Hoffman. (U.A.) Rel: Floating. (Colour.) 106 Mins. Cert. A.

The Gypsy Moths
Somewhat routine story about lost marital love, stuffy, routine life in a Kansas small town, and the advent and impact of a group of daredevil sky-divers, who put on a show which ends in tragedy. Enlivened by some magnificent sequences in the air, where the cameras amazingly follow the delayed-action parachutists as they tumble, dance and perform their spectacular tricks while plunging to earth at 100-plus m.p.h. Cast: *Burt Lancaster, Deborah Kerr, Gene Hackman, Scott Wilson, William Windom, Bonnie Bedilia, Sheree North, Carl Reindel, Ford Rainey, John Napier.* Dir: John Frankenheimer. Pro: Hal Landers & Bobby Roberts. Screenplay: Wm. Hanley. (Frankenheimer/Lewis–M-G-M.) Rel. Nov. 16. (Metrocolor.) 106 Mins. Cert. A.

Hamlet
Straightforward transference to celluloid of the Round House theatrical production, considerably photographed in close-up and medium shot. Cast: *Nicol Williamson, Anthony Hopkins, Judy Parfitt, Mark Dignam, Marianne Faithfull, Michael Pennington, Gordon Jackson, Ben Aris, Clive Graham, Peter Gale, John Carney, John Trenaman, Robin Chadwick, Richard Everett, Roger Livesey, John Railton, Roger Lloyd-Pack, Michael Elphick, Bill Jarvis, Ian Collier, Jennifer Tudor, Anjelica Huston, Mark Griffith.*

Dir: Tony Richardson. Pro: Neil Hartley. (Woodfall-Columbia.) Rel: Floating. (T.) 117 Mins. Cert. U.

Happening in White
Remarkably photographed film of snow and water sports, with *Gunther Sachs* achieving extremely fine effects by novel methods. Among those taking part: *Tom Leroy, Harmann Gollner, Sonja Pfersdorf, Gunther Matzdorf, Luggi Leitner, Artur Furrer, Nino Bibbia.* Pro: Gunther Sachs. (S.F. Film Distributors.) Rel: April 5. 47 Mins. Cert. U.

Happy Deathday
A straightforward filming of the M.R.A. play by Peter Howard: about a dying man and his family's varying reactions to the news. Cast: *Cyril Luckham, Harry Baird, Clement McCallin, Yvonne Antrobus, Bryan Coleman, Harriette Johns, John Comer.* Dir: Henry Cass. Pro: Louis Fleming & Donald Loughman. (MRA Productions.) First shown at Westminster Theatre, Feb., 1970. (T.) 89 Mins. Cert. A.

The Happy Ending
Jean Simmons in the role that earned her an Academy award nomination: as a young wife whose marriage goes unaccountably wrong, starts drinking and sinks into attempted suicide before finally making an attempt to get back into life. Rest of cast: *John Forsythe, Shirley Jones, Lloyd Bridges, Teresa Wright, Dick Shawn, Nanette Fabray, Robert Darin, Tina Louise, Kathy Fields, Karen Steele, Gail Hensley, Eve Brent, William O'Connell, Barry Cahill, Miriam Blake.* Dir, Pro & Written: Richard Brooks. (United Artists.) Rel: June 7. (Pan & T.) 112 Mins. Cert. X.

Hard Contract
James Coburn as a professional American killer who on his first trip to Europe (with a list of people to "remove") finds *Lee Remick* at Spain's Torremolinos and quickly discovers she has penetrated his callous, armoured shell, with obvious and finally pretty deadly result. Rest of cast: *Lilli Palmer, Burgess Meredith, Patrick Magee, Sterling Hayden, Claude Dauphin, Helen Cherry, Karen Black, Sabine Sun.* Dir & Screenplay: S. Lee Pogostin. Pro: Marvin Schwartz. (Schwartz–Fox.) Rel: Nov. 16. (Pan & D.) 106 Mins. Cert. X.

The Heart is a Lonely Hunter
Expertly wrung (!), beautifully acted, superior kind of tear-jerker with *Alan Arkin* as a deaf-mute who unwittingly wins friends everywhere but goes to his sad suicide's grave unaware that the girl he loves and who once resented him now returns his passion. Rest of cast: *Laurinda Barrett, Stacy Keach, Jr., Chuck McCann, Biff McGuire, Percy Rodriguez, Cicely Tyson, Sondra Locke, Jackie Marlowe, Johnny Popwell, Wayne Smith, Peter Mamakos, John O'Leary, Hubert Harper, Sherri Vise.* Dir: Robt. Ellis Miller. Pro: T. C. Ryan & Marc Merson. Screenplay: T. C. Ryan. (Warner–Seven Arts.) Rel: Floating. (T.) 123 Mins. Cert. A.

Heart of a Mother – Serdtze Materi
Outstanding Russian film by Mark Donskoi (who directed the Gorki trilogy) about the youth of Lenin, between his 14th (1884) and 23rd (1893) years: superbly creating the feeli : of a time and place, and a warm family relationship. A minor classic. Cast *Elena Fadeyeva, Danili Sagal, Rodion Nakhapetov, Gennady Thertov, Nina Menshikova, Nina Vikovskaya.* Dir: Mark Donskoi. Screenplay: Zoya Voshresenskaya & Irina Donskaya. (Contemporary.) First shown at the Paris Pullman, March, 1970. (Scope.) 100 Mins. Cert. U.

Heaven With a Gun
Pardoned *Glenn Ford*, now a trouble-shooter sent to hot spots to peacefully keep the peace comes up against plenty of problems when faced with the Cattlemen–Sheepmen feud at Vinegaroon, which is just at the verge of open war. Rest of cast: *Carolyn Jones, Barbara Hershey, John Anderson, David Carradine, J. D. Cannon, Noah Beery.* Dir: Lee H. Katzin. Pro: Frank & Maurice King. Screenplay: Richard Carr. (King Bros.–M-G-M.) Rel: July 6. (Pan & Metrocolor.) 98 Mins. Cert. X.

Hell is Empty
Jess Conrad as the weak young American caught up with some foreign gangsters and left holding the figurative baby – a charge of murdering one of the guards at the plant they break into. Rest of cast: *Martine Carol, Anthony Steel, James Robertson Justice, Shirley-Anne Field.* Dir: John Ainsworth. Pro: Mike Eland. (Rank.) Rel: Aug. 31. Re-released on Jan. 11, 1970. (E.) 90 Mins. Cert. A.

Hell's Angels '69
Two wealthy brothers, crooks, plan to rob the famous "Caesar's Palace" gambling joint in Las Vegas using a gang of leather-clad motor-cycle thugs as a cover. Cast: *Tom Stern, Jeremy Slate, Conny Van Dyke, Steve Sandor, J. D. Spradlin, Sonny Barger, Terry the Tramp and the original Oakland Hell's Angels.* Dir: Lee Madden. Pro: Tom Stern. Screenplay: Don Tait. (Anglo–Warner–Pathe.) Rel: Feb. 8. (T.) 98 Mins. Cert. X.

The Honeymoon Killers
A semi-realist account of a particularly nasty-flavoured murder story: about a fat nurse who teams up with a young Spaniard and becomes the less scrupulous member of a team which preys on lonely widows, killing them by poison, hammer or gun! Based on the actual New York Lonely Hearts Killers case in the early 1950's and, intentional or not, pretty good propaganda for the retention of the death sentence. Cast: *Shirley Stoler, Tony LoBianco, Mary Jane Higby, Doris Roberts, Kip McArdle, Marilyn Chris, Donna Duckworth, Barbara Cason, Ann Harris, Mary Breen, Elsa Raven, Mary Engel, Guy Sorel, Mike Haley, Diane Asselin, Col. William Adams.* Dir & Written: Leonard Kastle. Pro: Warren Steibel. (CIRO) Rel: Floating. 106 Mins. Cert. X.

Hostile Witness
Screen adaptation of the Jack Roffrey stage play about a Q.C. who finds himself accused of murder and in court fighting a losing battle against the evidence that is gradually piled up against him, piled up until he himself begins to wonder if he is, after all, guilty but insane . . . and then the truth begins to dawn. *Ray Milland, Sylvia Syms, Felix Aylmer, Raymond Huntley, Geoffrey Lumsden, Norman Barrs, Percy Marmont, Dulcie Bowman, Ewan Roberts, Richard Hurndall, Ronald Leigh-Hunt, Sandra Fehr, Edward Waddy, Maggie McGrath, Ballard Berkeley.* Dir: Ray Milland. Pro: David E. Rose. Screenplay: Jack Roffey. (U.A.) Rel: June 28. (T.) 101 Mins. Cert. U.

How to Commit Marriage
Bob Hope gets with it in an occasionally amusing, slimly farcical, sparsely wise-cracked story about parents who hide their own divorce plans when they are confronted by their young daughter's announcement that she's getting married. Taking the somewhat heavy-handed mickey out of Pop People, Indian Mystique Cults and other facets of the Permissive Society. Nice, though, to see *Jane Wyman* back – as Bob's wife. Rest of cast: *Jackie Gleason, Maureen Arthur, Leslie Nielsen, Paul Stewart, Prof. Irwin Corey, Tina Louise, Tim Matthieson, Joanna Cameron,* "*The Comfortable Chair*" *Group,* and *Mildred,* the scene-stealing chimp. Dir: Norman Panama. Pro: Bill Lawrence. (Ex Pro: Bob Hope himself.) Ben Starr & Michael Kanin. (CIRO.) Rel: Dec. 14. (T.) 98 Mins. Cert. A.

I Love You, Alice B. Toklas
Generally mild, black-spotted occasionally hilarious comedy which tells a story of a Jewish lawyer practising in Los Angeles who ditches his wife-to-be at the altar and goes to live with a pretty little flower-child (pretty little screen newcomer *Leigh Taylor-Young*) until the ways of her layabout hippie pals send him back to civilisation – and another at-the-altar change of mind! Rest of cast: *Peter Sellers, Jo Van Fleet, Joyce Van Patten, David Arkin, Herbert Edelman, Salem Ludwig, Louis Gottlieb, Grady Sutton, Janet Clark, William Bramley, Jorge Moreno.* Dir: Hy Averback. Pro: Chas. Maguire. Screenplay: Paul Mazursky & Larry Tucker – the film's executive producers. (Warner–Pathe.) Rel: July 13. (T.) 93 Mins. Cert. X.

Ice Station Zebra
Very large-scale, spectacular, exciting and technically first-rate giant-screen melodrama about a race to the North Pole by an American atomic-powered sub. and Russian paratroops, each after a satelite-shed canister which lands near the Arctic British Weather Station, the contents of the canister being capable of completely changing the balance of power. Terrific first half with the cruise beneath the ice-cap; slightly less but still very tense second half with the actual confrontation at the sabotaged camp. All vastly entertaining, with good performances, quite neat script. Cast: *Rock Hudson, Ernest Borgnine, Patrick McGoohan, Jim Brown, Tony Bill, Gerald S. O'Loughlin, Alf Kjellin, Murray Rose, Ted Hartley, Ron Masak,*

Joseph Bernard, Michael Mikler, Sherwood Price, Lee Stanley, Jonathan Lippe. Dir: John Sturges. Pro: Martin Ransohoff – John Calley. Screenplay: Harry Julian Fink. (Cinerama–Super Panavision–Metrocolor.) (Filmways–M-G-M.) Rel: Nov. 9. 145 Mins. Cert. U.

The Illustrated Man
Bizarre little fantasy about a man so tattooed that there is only one clear spot on his body – and if you look at that too long you find yourself in the future! And the tattooed man goes on searching for the seductive woman who persuaded him to make the pictures – promising to kill her when he catches up with her. Cast: *Rod Steiger, Claire Bloom, Robert Drivas, Don Dubbins, Jason Evers, Tim Weldon, Christie Matchett.* Dir: Jack Smight. Pro: H. B. Kreitsek, Ted Mann. Screenplay: H. B. Kreitsek, based on stories by Ray Bradbury. (SKM–Warner–Seven Arts.) Rel: Floating. (Pan & T.) 103 Mins. Cert. X.

Innocence Unprotected – Nevinost Bez Zastite
Very odd little Jugoslav film which uses another film, of the home movie type made clandestinely during the war by an acrobat and strong man; the story of an outrageous melodrama of the old, silent-days type. The whole thing is irrelevant, untidy and uneven but fascinating nevertheless and that largely because of its unpretentiousness. With a cast headed by *Dragoljub Aleksic.* Dir: Dusan Makavejev. (Hunter.) First shown at Cameo Poly, Aug., 1969. (Part colour.) 78 Mins. Cert. U.

The Insatiables – Gli Insaziabile
Italian-made, English-speaking, Hollywood-set murder mystery in which a local newspaper reporter investigates the apparent killing of a pal by a local giant business corporation and comes up with some surprising answers as to both killed and killer. Cast: *Dorothy Malone, Robert Hoffmann, Frank Wolff, John Ireland, Luciana Paluzzi, Roger Fritz, Romina Power.* Dir: Alberto de Martino. Pro: Edmondo Amati. Screenplay: Alberto de Martino, V. Flamini. (Cinecenta.) First shown at Cinecenta, Jan., 1970. (Colour.) 102 Mins. Cert. X.

Isadora
Large, lavish but not entirely successful attempt to catch something of the life and art of famous non-conventional dancer Isadora Duncan, with *Vanessa Redgrave* in the leading role. Rest of cast: *James Fox, Jason Robards, Ivan Tchenko, John Fraser, Bessie Love, Cynthia Harris, Libby Glenn, Tony Vogel, Wallas Eaton, John Quentin, Nicholas Pennell, Ronnie Gilbert, Christian Duvalex, Margaret Courtenay, Arthur White, Iza Teller, Vladimir Leskovar, John Warner, Ina De La Haye, John Brandon, Lucinda Chambers, Simon Lutton Davies, Alan Gifford.* Dir: Karel Reisz. Pro: Robt. & Raymond Hakim. Screenplay: Melvyn Bragg & Clive Exton, based on "My Life" by I. Duncan & "Isadora Duncan, An Intimate Portrait" by Sewell Stokes. (Universal–Rank.) Rel: Floating. (T.) 138 Mins. Cert. A.

The Italian Job
A jokey comedy-thriller with *Michael Caine* as the Cockney crook small-timer who comes out of jail and takes up the big-time robbery plan laid down by Italian pal when the latter is wiped out by the Mafia – who take a very dim view of foreigners pinching millions of Fiat-bound Chinese gold. And it's all done for laughs. Rest of cast: *Noël Coward, Benny Hill, Raf Vallone, Tony Beckley, Rossano Brazzi, Maggie Blye, Irene Handl, John Le Mesurier, Fred Emney, John Clive, Graham Payn, Michael Standing, Stanley Caine, Barry Cox, Harry Baird, George Innes, John Forgeham, Robert Powell, Derek Ware, Frank Jarvis, David Salamone, Richard Essame, Mario Volgoi, Renato Romano, Robert Rietty, Timothy Bateson, Arnold Diamond, Simon Dee, Alistair Hunter, Louis Mansi.* Dir: Peter Collinson. Pro: Michael Deeley. Screenplay: Troy Kennedy Martin. (Paramount.) Rel: July 27. (Pan.) 100 Mins. Cert. U.

Joanna
Really beautifully photographed but otherwise unexciting story of the girl of the title, a pretty but rather stupid little baby-voiced girl who comes up from Frome, sleeps around and becomes involved with a negro murderer, whose baby she cheerfully goes off to have back in daddy's house at Frome. A pretty unflattering (intentional or not) picture of today's bright and permissive young things. Cast: *Genevieve Waite, Christian Doermer, Calvin Lockhart, Donald Sutherland, Glenna Forster-Jones, David Scheuer, Marda Vanne, Geoffrey Morris, Michele Cooke, Manning Wilson, Clifton Jones, Dan Caulfield, Michael Chow, Anthony Ainley, Jane Bradbury, Fiona Lewis, Jayne Sofiano, Elizabeth MacLennan, Richard Hurndall, Annette Robertson, Jenny Hanley, John Gulliver, Brenda Kempner, Peter Porteous.* Dir & Written: Michael Sarne. Pro: M. S. Laughlin. (Fox.) Rel: March 15. (Pan & D.) 113 Mins. Cert. X.

John and Mary
Young and exciting British director Peter Yates shows that as well as brilliant thrillers ("Bullitt") he can be equally at ease with intimacy on the screen in this smooth, amusing and sympathetic relating of a with-it, permissive romance which develops from a casual night of intimacy between tidy little flat-owner *Dustin Hoffman* and the girl (*Mia Farrow*) that he picks up. Rest of cast: *Michael Tolan, Sunny Griffin, Stanley Beck, Tyne Daly, Alix Elias, Julie Garfield, Marvin Lichterman, Marian Mercer, Susan Taylor, Olympia Dukakis, Carl Parker, Richard Clarke, Cleavon Little, Marilyn Chris, Alexander Cort, Kristoffer Tabori.* Dir: Peter Yates. Pro: Ben Kadish. Screenplay: John Mortimer. (Debrod Pro.–Fox.) Rel: March 15. (Pan & D.) 92 Mins. Cert. X.

Johnny Cash! The Man, His World, His Music
Documentary originally made for American TV about this popular singing star; at work, at home and at play. Dir: R. Elfstrom. Pro: Arthur and Evelyn Barron. (Crispin.) Rel: Floating. (Colour.) 94 Mins. Cert. U.

224

Justine
Interesting, but in the end unsuccessful, attempt to condense Lawrence Durrell's famous "Alexandria Quartet" of novels into one movie; the result being confusing and obtuse, especially to anyone not familiar with the stories. Cast: *Anouk Aimée, Dirk Bogarde, Robert Forster, Anna Karina, Philippe Noiret, Michael York, John Vernon, Jack Albertson, Cliff Gorman, George Baker, Elaine Church, Michael Constantine, Marcel Dalio, Michael Dunn, Barry Morse.* Dir: George Cukor. Pro: Pandro S. Berman. Screenplay: Lawrence B. Marcus. (Fox.) Rel: Sept. 28. (Colour.) 116 Mins. Cert. X.

Killer on a Horse
Western set in a small frontier town called Hard Times, which is terrorised by a gunman who rides in, kills, burns and otherwise destroys it; and how, when it is eventually rebuilt and repopulated the gunman rides in again, to find hate and death awaiting him. Cast: *Henry Fonda, Janice Rule, Keenan Wynn, Janis Paige, John Anderson, Warren Oates, Fay Spain, Edgar Buchanan, Aldo Ray, Denver Pyle, Michael Shea, Arlene Golonka, Lon Chaney, Royal Duno, Alan Baxter, Paul Birch, Dan Ferrone, Paul Fix, Elisha Cook, Kalen Liu, Ann McCrea, Bob Terhune, Ron Burke.* Dir: Burt Kennedy. Pro: Max E. Youngstein & David Karr. Screenplay: Burt Kennedy. (M-G-M.) Rel: April 12. (Metrocolor.) 78 Mins. Cert. X.

Killer! – Que La Bête Meure
Claude Chabrol's completely unobtrusively brilliant suspense story, based on the Nicholas Blake novel "The Beast Must Die", about a man, a widower whose only small son is killed by a hit-and-run driver and, when the police fail to find a clue, devotes his life to tracking the man responsible down with the cold determination to kill him. He does find the man, he does attempt the crime . . . and then . . .? A fine performance by *Michel Duchaussoy,* as the man caught in his own web. Also *Caroline Cellier, Jean Yanne, Anouk Farjac, Marc di Napoli, Maurice Pialat, Guy Morley, Lorraine Rainer, Louise Chevalier, Dominique Zardi, Stephan di Napoli Raymond, Michel Charrel, France Girard, Bernard Papineau, Robert Rondo, Jacques Masson, George Charrier, Jean Louis Maury.* Dir: Claude Chabrol. Pro: Andre Genoves. Screenplay: Paul Gegauff. (Cinecenta.) First shown at Cinecenta and Gala Royal cinemas, April, 1970. (Colour.) 110 Mins. Cert. A.

King of the Grizzlies
One of the Disney real-life adventures: about a Cree Indian who saves a grizzly bear cub from death and, when on the several occasions he comes across the animal each time it seems to remember and spare him. Cast: *John Yesno, Chris Wiggins, Hugh Webster, Jack Van Evera* and *Wahb,* the Grizzly King. Dir: Ron Kelly. Pro: Winston Hibler. Screenplay: Jack Speirs. (Disney.) Rel: May 17. (T.) 93 Mins. Cert. U.

Krakatoa – East of Java
Honest, spectacular, action drama, climaxed with a horrific, terrifying reconstruction of the great Krakatoa eruption of 1883, and preceded by any number of story threads, such as a diver with broken lungs taking his last plunge, convict mutiny and taking over of the ship, the diving bell that gets trapped below the seas and the balloon which gets trapped above them, searching for the sunken treasure galleon and so on. Some nice performances. Cast: *Maximilian Schell, Diane Baker, Brian Keith, Barbara Werle, John Leyton, Rossano Brazzi, Sal Mineo, J. D. Cannon, Jacqui Chan, Marc Lawrence, Geoffrey Holder, Sumi Haru, Victoria Young, Midori Arimoto, Niall MacGinnis, Alan Hoskins, Robert Hall, Peter Kowalski, Joseph Hann.* Dir: Bernard Kowalski. Pro: Wm. R. Forman. Screenplay: Clifford Gould & Bernard Gordon. (Cinerama.) Rel: March 22. (T & Widescreen.) 137 Mins. Cert. A.

Kill Them All And Come Back Alone – Ammazzali Tutti e Torno Solo
Italian–Western which starts off on a fairly light note but gets heavier and gorier and more brutal as it dashes its hectic, unconvincing if lively way along a story about a struggle for Union gold which the Confederates – and everyone else – are anxious to lay their hands on. Cast: *Chuck Connors, Frank Wolff, Franco Citti, Leo Anchoriz, Ken Wood, Hercules Cortes, Alberto dell'Acqua.* Dir: Enzo G. Castellari. Pro: Edmondo Amati. (Fida Cinematografica–Centauro/Universal–Rank.) Rel: Nov. 30. (T & Techniscope.) 98 Mins. Cert. X.

La Chamade – Heartbeat
The film of the Françoise Sagan novel with its familiar theme about a young girl and a middle-aged man. *Catherine Deneuve* plays the lush-living, comfort-loving mistress of a sophisticated, wealthy businessman (*Michel Piccoli*) who drifts off for a while to live with a poor young publisher's reader, but finally realises that she cannot do without luxury, so returns to her old lover. A leisurely tale, with the considerable polish on the surface hiding the noveletty heart. Rest of cast: *Roger Van Hool, Irene Tunc, Jacques Sereys, Philippine Pascal.* Dir: Alain Cavalier. Screenplay: F. Sagan & A. Cavalier. (Cavalier–U.A.) First shown at Cameo Victoria, Jan. 1970. (D.) 95 Mins. Cert. X.

The Last Grenade
Old-fashioned-style adventure thriller, based on the John Sherlock novel "The Ordeal of Major Grigsby", about the grim determination of the Major to get revenge on another soldier of fortune who in the Congo war double-crossed him and all but wiped out the Major's guerilla band: a vengeance trail that leads to Hong Kong, a General's wife and a string of defeats before posthumous victory. Cast: *Stanley Baker, Alex Cord, Honor Blackman, Richard Attenborough, Rafer Johnson, Andrew Keir, Ray Brooks, Julian Glover, John Thaw, Philip Latham, Neil Wilson, Gerald Sim, A. J. Brown, Pamela Stanley, Kenji Takaki, Paul Dawkins.* Dir: Gordon Flemyng. Pro: Josef Shaftel. Screenplay: Kenneth Ware. (CIRO.) Rel: May 3. (Colour.) 93 Mins. Cert. A.

L'Astragale – The Ankle
That's French for ankle bone and escaping *Marlene Jobert* breaks it when she drops over the jail wall and so meets *Horst Buchholz,* another jailbird, and begins a passionate love affair with him which leads, inevitably, to a sad ending. Rest of cast: *Magali Noel, Claude Genia, Georges Geret, Jean-Pierre Moulin, Gisele Hauchecorne, Claude Marcault, Raoul Delfosse, Jurgen Draeger, Brigitte Grothum, Nicole Pescheux, Martine Ferriere, Michel Robin, Raymond Meunier, Eugene Berthier.* Dir & Dialogue: Guy Casaril. Pro: Pierre Braunberger. (Braunberger–Wachsberger/Columbia.) First shown at Curzon, Aug., 1969. (E.) 102 Mins. Cert. X.

La Femme Infidele – The Unfaithful Wife
Beautifully polished, expert Claude Chabrol film which tells the story of a husband whose happy marriage is threatened when he finds his wife has a lover. On the spur of the moment he kills the lover, and the wife hides from the police the evidence she finds of his guilt. Under the theme of the interactions between appearance and reality, deception and truth lies a vastly subtle and complex examination of the whole basis of masculine–feminine relationship. A brilliant film, beautifully acted. Cast: *Stephane Audran, Michel Bouquet, Maurice Ronet, Serge Bento, Michel Duchaussoy, Guy Marly, Stephane Di Napoli.* Dir & Written: C. Chabrol. Pro: Georges Casati. (Les Films La Boetie, Paris/Cinegai, Rome–Gala.) First shown at Continentale, mid-June, 1969. (E.) 98 Mins. Cert. A.

La Taranta
19-minute film made by Gianfranco Mingozzi in 1961: a documentary made during an ethnographic exploration in the provinces of Salerno, a record of the last examples of the mysterious tarantism rites. Screenplay: Ernesto de Martino. Pro: Franco Finzi de Barbora. (Pantheon–Connoisseur.) First shown at Times Cinema, Feb. 1970.

Laughter in the Dark
Rather odd, initially comedy adaptation of Vladimir Nabokov's highly melodramatic story about a rich man whose fascination for a tarty little baggage (a cinema usherette) leads him to degradation, social ruin and, eventually, blindness. Duped as such by the girl and her lover, he turns his gun on her – ironically to kill himself! Cast: *Nicol Williamson, Anna Karina, Jean-Claude Drouot, Peter Bowles, Sian Phillips, Sebastian Breaks, Kate O'Toole, Edward Gardner, Helen Booth, Sheila Burrell, Willoughby Goddard, Basil Dignam, John Atkinson, Donald Bissett, John Golightly, Mavis Villiers, Allison Blair, Diana Harris, Celia Brook.* Dir: Tony Richardson. Pro: Neil Hartley. Screenplay: Edward Bond. (Woodfall–U.A.) Rel: Floating. (D.) 104 Mins. Cert. X.

La Voie Lactée – The Milky Way
Luis Bunuel's film in which he returns to baiting the holies: something like an anthology of heresies, it follows the footsteps of two pilgrims (or tramps?) as they wander their way from Paris towards Spain and meet en route such events as a boy with a strange,

commanding presence and stigmatic hands, the Marquis de Sade and even Christ himself, with his disciples. Cast: *Paul Frankeur, Laurent Terzieff, Alain Cuny, Edith Scob, Bernard Verley, François Maistre, Claude Cerval, Muni, Jean Piat, Denis Manuel, Daniel Pilon, Claudio Brook, Julien Guiomar, Marcel Peres, Delphine Seyrig, Julien Bertheau, Elen Bahl, Michel Piccoli, Michel Etcheverry, Agnes Capri, Pierre Clementi, Georges Marchal.* Dir: Luis Bunuel. (Planet.) First shown at Cameo Poly and Classic (Baker St.) cinemas, Oct., 1969. (E.) 98 Mins. Cert. A.

Land Raiders
Telly Savalas as the bully-big boss of a small Western town trying to force the redskins off their land and fighting them, and his more reasonable young brother *George Maharis,* to the death. Rest of cast: *Arlene Dahl, Janet Landgard, Jocelyn Lane, George Coulouris, Guy Rolfe, Phil Brown, Marcella St. Amant, Paul Picerni, Robert Carricart, Gustavo Rojo, Fernan Dorey, Ben Tatar, John Clark, Charles Stahlnaker, Susan Harvey.* Dir: Nathan Juran. Pro: Chas. H. Schneer. Screenplay: Ken Pettus. (Schneer–Columbia.) Rel: Dec. 7. (T.) 101 Mins. Cert. A.

The Last Shot You Hear
Somewhat complicated marital murder thriller with a wife's lover planning to kill her husband, a plan discovered by the victim's secretary, who uses her knowledge as a threat by which she takes the lover for herself . . . but the dark doings don't end there! Cast: *Hugh Marlowe, Zena Walker, Patricia Haines, William Dysart, Thorley Walters, Joan Young, Lionel Murton, Helen Horton, John Nettleton, John Wentworth, Alistair Williamson, Daphne Barker, Lynley Laurence, Julian Holloway, James Mellor, Ian Hamilton, Shaun Curry, Stephen Moore, Job Stewart, Janet Kelly.* Dir: Gordon Hessler. Pro: Jack Parsons. Screenplay: Tim Shields, from the William Fairchild play "The Sound of Murder". (Lippert–Fox.) Rel: March 15. 91 Mins. Cert. X.

Last Summer
Quite outstanding little film about a group of three rich teenagers spending their holidays by the seaside and the cruel and tragic situation which arises when another girl appears on the scene. A portrait in frightening depth of rich American teenagers – and, perhaps, any modern teenagers. Cast: *Barbara Hershey, Richard Thomas, Bruce Davison, Cathy Burns, Ernesto Gonzalez, Peter Turgeon, Lou Gary, Andrew Krance, Wayne Mayer.* Dir: Frank Perry. Pro: Alfred Crown, Sidney Beckerman. Screenplay: Eleanor Perry, based on the Evan Hunter novel. (Warner–Pathe.) Rel: Floating. 97 Mins. Cert. X.

The Lawyer
Tightly directed, expertly scripted and convincingly acted story of a murder in a small, rich, pretty primitive Cow Town in the Middle West of the U.S., where a young and dedicated, if hard-shelled young lawyer, fights local police – and jury – prejudice in defence of his doctor client, accused of the crime. Some superb

courtroom sequences. *Barry Newman* quite outstanding as the sharp young lawyer, but matched by *Harold Gould's* outstanding performance as the old, artful prosecuting attorney. Rest of cast: *Diana Muldaur, Robert Colbert, Kathleen Crowley, Warren Kemmerling, Booth Colman, Ken Swofford, E. J. Andre, William Sylvester, Jeff Thompson, Tom Harvey, Ivor Barry, Melendy Britt, John Himes, Ralph Thomas, Mary Wilcox, Gene O'Donnell, Walter Matthews, Ray Ballard, James McEachin, Robert L. Poyner.* Dir: Sidney J. Furie. Pro: Brad Dexter. Screenplay: S. J. Furie and Harold Buchman. (Paramount.) Rel: March 8. (Colour.) 120 Mins. Cert. X.

Le Gai Savoir
Jean-Luc Godard's odd little excursion into education. With *Jean-Pierre Laud, Juliet Bertho.* Dir: Jean-Luc Godard. (Kestrel.) First shown at ICA Cinema, July, 1969. (Colour.) 91 Mins.

Legend of the Witches
A film exploration of one of the oldest Pagan religions – witchcraft. Its birth, persecution, persistency and revival in today's world. Dir: Malcolm Leigh. (Border Films.) Rel: Floating. 87 Mins. Cert. X.

Let It Be
A film about the Beatles, jointly and individually working, recording, talking and taking it easy at home. Including a number of their hit tunes. Dir: Michael Lindsay-Hogg. Pro: Neil Aspinall. (Apple–U.A.) Rel: June 28. (Colour.) 81 Mins. Cert. U.

Life Love Death – La Vie, L'Amour, La Mort
Claude Lelouch's cool, documentary-style, technically fascinating relation, without involvement or passion, of the facts, based on a news story, of the following, apprehension, trial and judicial decapitation of a sex multi-murderer: a film which switches suddenly at the end into the anti-death penalty propaganda as the harrowing final scenes at the guillotine are enacted. Cast: *Amidou, Caroline Cellier, Janine Magnan, Marcel Bozzuffi, Lisette Bersy, Albert Naud, Jean-Pierre Sloan, Nathalie Durrand, Sylvia Saurel, Denyse Roland, Claudia Morin, Catherine Samie, Rita Maiden, Pierre Collet, Albert Rajau, Jacques Henry, Jean-Marc Allegre, Colette Taconnat, Jean Collomb, Robert Hossein, Annie Girardot, El Cordobes.* Dir: Claude Lelouch. Pro: Alexandre Mnouchkine. Screenplay: C. Lelouch & Pierre Uytterhoeven. (U.A.) First shown at Cameo-Poly Feb., 1970. (D.) 116 Mins. Cert. X.

The Looking Glass War
Another of John Le Carré's anti-Bond-image spy stories; about a couple of MI5 old-timers, nostalgic for the great days of World War Two, more or less wistfully creating an international threat in order to go cloak-and-daggering again; sending a half-crazy, ill-trained young Polish defector to his death in East Germany on a dubious mission which ends in disaster. Cast: *Christopher Jones, Pia Degermark, Ralph Richardson, Anthony Hopkins, Paul Rogers, Susan George, Ray McAnally, Robert Urquhart, Maxine*

Audley, Anna Massey, Frederick Jaeger, Paul Maxwell, Timothy West, Vivien Pickles, Peter Swanwick, Cyril Shaps, Michael Robbins, Guy Deghy, David Scheur, John Franklin, Linda Hedger, Nicholas Stewart. Dir: Frank R. Pierson. Pro: John Box. Screenplay: F. R. Pierson based on the John Le Carré novel. (Frankovich–Columbia.) Rel: Feb. 8. (T & Pan.) 107 Mins. Cert. A.

The Looters – Estouffade à la Caráibe
Franco–Italian produced, English-dubbed adventure melo with *Frederick Stafford* as the reformed safe-cracker lured by pretty *Jean Seberg* into helping her father get the gold from a safe on a Caribbean island which is in the throes of a revolution. Rest of cast: *Mario Pisu, Maria Rosa Rodriguez, Serge Gainsbourg, Paul Crauchet, Fernand Bellan, Vittorio Sanipoli, Cesar Torres, Marco Guglielmi.* Dir: Jacques Besnard. Pro: Andre Hunebelle. Screenplay: Pierre Foucaud. (Border Films.) Rel: Floating. (Colour Franscope.) 102 Mins. Cert. A.

The Lost Man
"Odd Man Out"-ish story about a rebel against society – he's black in this case – who takes part in a robbery which goes badly wrong and leads to him murdering a guard, for which he is trailed, wounded and finally cornered and dies with the white girl who hides and befriends him. Cast: *Sidney Poitier, Joanna Shimkus, Al Freeman, Jr., Michael Tolan, Leon Bibb, Richard Dysart, David Steinberg, Beverly Todd, Paul Winfield, Bernie Hamilton, Richard Anthony Williams, Dolph Sweet, Arnold Williams, Virginia Capers, Vonetta McGee, Frank Marth, Maxine Stuart, George Tyne, Paulene Myers, Lee Weaver, Morris Erby, Doug Johnson, Lincoln Kilpatrick.* Dir & Screenplay: Robert Alan Aurthur. Pro: Edward Muhl & Melville Tucker. (Universal–Rank.) Rel: April 19. (T & Pan.) 110 Mins. Cert. A.

The Love God?
Comedy about a bird-watching magazine owner who is conned by a pornographer into turning his publication into a girlie periodical along "Playboy" lines and then begins to find that he enjoys his new career. Cast: *Don Knotts, Anne Francis, Edmond O'Brien, James Gregory, Maureen Arthur, Maggie Peterson, Jesslyn Fax, Jacques Aubuchon, Marjorie Bennett, Jim Boles, Ruth McDevitt, Roy Stuart, Herbert Voland, James Westerfield, Bob Hastings, Larry McCormick, Robert P. Lieb, Willis Bouchey, Herbie Faye, Johnny Seven, Joseph Perry, Jim Begg, Carla Borelli, Nancy Bonniwell, Shelly Davis, A'Leshia Lee, Terri Harper, B. S. Pully.* Dir & Written: Nat Hiken. Pro: E. J. Montagne. (Universal–Rank.) Rel: April 26. (T.) 103 Mins. Cert. A.

Love is a Splendid Illusion
About a man who trying to build up his interior decorating business is tempted by the pretty women he meets and nearly allows his philandering to bring disaster to both business and family. Cast: *Simon Brent, Andree Flamand, Lisa Collings, Anna Matisse,*

226 *Mark Kingston.* Dir: Tom Clegg. Pro: Bachoo Sen. (Schulman.) First shown at Cameo-Royal, Jan. 1970. (Colour.) 80 Mins. Cert. X.

Les Astronauts
Amusing and original animated featurette about a man who invents his own peculiar spacecraft and has some very strange adventures indeed. Dir: Walerian Borowczyk, in collaboration with Chris Marker. (Contemporary.) First shown at Paris-Pullman, Oct. 1969. 14 Mins. Cert. U.

Les Jeunes Loups – The Young Wolves
Marcel Carne tackles the "problems" of the generation after his own in a story about light relationships and lighter behaviour among a group of young people which he views with objectivity but without the great art of his pre-war period. Cast: *Haydée Politoff, Christian Hay, Yves Beneyton, Roland Lesaffre, Serge Leeman, Elisabeth Teissier.* Dir: Marcel Carne. Pro: Vera Belmont & Rene Pigneres. Screenplay: Marcel Carne & Claude Accursi. (Classics.) First shown at Cameo-Poly, Sept., 1969. 111 Mins. Cert. X.

The Libertine – La Matriarca
Italian piece of erotica which still knows when to draw the pornographic line and, anyway, retains enough sense of humour to keep a neatly-judged balance. A sort of twisted, up-dated, Freudian-influenced version of "The Taming of the Shrew" with *Catherine Spaak* as the young widow who, finding out that her late and unlamented hubbie has been keeping a private nest for "birds" – including her best friend – decides to taste sex anywhere, anyhow and from anyone – but is finally tamed, bedded and wedded by weary doctor *Jean-Louis Trintignant.* Rest of cast: *Fabienne Dali, Frank Wolff, Paolo Stoppa, Philippe Leroy.* Dir: Pasquale Festa Campanile. Screenplay: Nicolo Ferrari & Ottavio Jemma. (Cinecenta.) First shown at Cinecenta and Gala Royal, Aug., 1969. (E.) 84 Mins. Cert. X.

The Love Bug
Delightful Disney comedy about a little German car – the "Bug" of the title – which has a mind very much of its own and helps its previously unfortunate driver-racer to win the cups and defeat the machinations of his nasty rival – hilariously played by smooth *David Tomlinson.* Rest of cast: *Dean Jones, Michele Lee, Buddy Hackett, Joe Flynn, Benson Fong, Joe E. Ross, Barry Kelley, Iris Adrian, Ned Glass, Robert Foulk, Gil Lamb, Nicole Jaffe, Wally Boag, Russ Caldwell, Max Balchowsky, P. L. Renoudet, Brian Fong, Alan Fordney, Stan Duke, Gary Owens, Chick Hearn, Pedro Gonzalez-Gonzalez, Andy Granatelli.* Dir: Robert Stevenson. Pro: Bill Walsh. Screenplay: Bill Walsh & Don DaGradi. (Disney.) Rel: July 27. (T.) 107 Mins. Cert. U.

Ma Nuit chez Maud – My Night with Maud
Delicate, witty and artistic little French film about a night of repression – and talk – for Maud (*Françoise Fabian*) when the snow maroons strict Catholic *Jean-Louis Trintignant* in her apartment. Rest of cast: *Marie-Christine Barrault, Antoine Vitez, Léonide Kogan, Anne*

Dubot, Guy Léger. Dir & Screenplay: Eric Rohmer. Pro: Pierre Cottreill. (Academy–Connoisseur.) Rel: Floating. 113 Mins. Cert. A.

Mackenna's Gold
Carl Foreman Western with a more or less routine story set against some magnificent (and magnificently photographed) natural backgrounds. *Gregory Peck* as the man who has memorised a map of a golden canyon and is captured by bandit *Omar Sharif* and forced into leading him to it, together with a mixed bag of goodies and baddies, an expedition that's always only a few steps ahead of the Apaches (who claim the gold as theirs) and the good old U.S. Cavalry (who would like to get hold of the bandit). Rest of cast: *Telly Savalas, Camilla Sparv, Keenan Wynn, Julie Newmar, Ted Cassidy, Lee J. Cobb, Raymond Massey, Burgess Meredith, Anthony Quayle, Edward G. Robinson, Eli Wallach, Eduardo Ciannelli, Dick Peabody, Rudy Diaz, Robert Phillips, Shelley Morrison, J. Robert Porter, John Garfield Jr., Pepe Callahan, Madeleine Taylor Holmes, Duke Hobbie, Victor Jory.* Dir: J. Lee Thompson. Pro: Carl Foreman & Dimitri Tiomkin. Screenplay: C. Foreman – based on the Will Henry novel. (Foreman–Columbia.) Rel: July 20. (T & Pan.) 136 Mins. Cert. A.

The Mad Room
Murder thriller with *Stella Stevens* as the paid companion to a wealthy widow who is brutally murdered. By her? Or by the two unbalanced teenagers just out of a mental hospital? Or . . . ? Rest of cast: *Shelley Winters, Skip Ward, Carol Cole, Severn Darden, Beverly Garland, Michael Burns, Barbara Sammeth, Jenifer Bishop, Gloria Manon, Lloyd Haynes, Lou Kane.* Dir: Bernard Girard. Pro: Norman Maurer. Screenplay: B. Girard & A. Z. Martin, based on a screenplay by Garrett Fort & Reginald Denham based on the play "Ladies in Retirement". (Maurer–Columbia.) Rel: Dec. 7. (T.) 93 Mins. Cert. X.

The Magic Christian
Somewhat loose adaptation of the novel of the same title by Terry Southern; an odd sort of satire which goes out to get its laughs from such episodes as the millionaire–sadist practical joker of the title tipping a case full of fivers into a tank of animal urine and blood and then advertising free money! Cast: *Peter Sellers, Ringo Starr, Isabel Jeans, Caroline Blakiston, Wilfrid Hyde White, Richard Attenborough, Leonard Frey, Laurence Harvey, Christopher Lee, Spike Milligan, Roman Polanski, Raquel Welch, Tom Boyle, Terence Alexander, Peter Bayliss, Joan Benham, Patrick Gargill, Graham Chapman, John Cleese, Clive Dunn, Freddie Earlle, Fred Emney, Kenneth Fortescue, Peter Graves, Patrick Holt, David Hutcheson, Hattie Jacques, John Le Mesurier, Jeremy Lloyd, David Lodge, Victor Maddern, Ferdy Mayne, Guy Middleton, Peter Myers, Dennis Price, Robert Raglan, Graham Stark, Leon Thau, Frank Thornton, Michael Trubshawe, Edward Underdown, Michael Aspel, Michael Barratt, Harry Carpenter, W. Barrington Dalby, John Snagge, Alan Whicker, Yul Brynner.* Dir: Joseph McGrath. Pro: Denis O'Dell. Screenplay: Terry Southern,

J. McGrath & Peter Sellers. (Commonwealth United.) Rel: March 15. (T.) 95 Mins. Cert. A.

The Man With the Golden Mask
Italian period melodrama set in 16th-century Italy – the time of the bloody Borgias. Cast: *Jean Sorel, Lisa Gastoni, Edmund Purdom.* Dir: Sergio Corbucci. Pro: Joseph Fryd. (M-G-M.) Rel: June 14. (E.) 86 Mins. Cert. X.

Marlowe
James Garner, as Raymond Chandler's famous private-eye, accepts *Sharon Farrell's* assignment to find her brother and soon discovers that this is only a part of a much deeper and dirtier mystery which embraces dope, blackmail and murder . . . toughly sorting it all to come up with a – surprise? – solution. And it's all fast and furious and very well done. Rest of cast: *Gayle Hunnicutt, Carroll O'Connor, Rita Moreno, William Daniels, H. M. Wynant, Roger Newman, Jackie Coogan, Nate Esformes, Christopher Cary, Read Morgan, George Tyne, Corinne Camacho, Kenneth Tobey, Paul Stevens.* Dir: Paul Bogart. Pro: Gabriel Katzka & Sidney Beckerman. Screenplay: Stirling Silliphant. (M-G-M.) Rel: Nov. 16. (Metrocolor.) 95 Mins. Cert. A.

Marooned
A good old-style (deriving from pre-Pearl White days) suspense thriller set against a terrifyingly topical, ultra-modern background: the story of a trio of astronauts marooned in outer space in their spaceship when the machine's retro-rockets refuse to fire, and the struggle of *Gregory Peck* and his ground crew to rescue them – in spite of a hurricane – before their oxygen runs out. Cast: *Richard Crenna, David Janssen, James Franciscus, Gene Hackman, Lee Grant, Nancy Kovack, Mariette Hartley, Scott Brady, Craig Huebing, John Carter, George Gaynes, Tom Stewart, Frank Marth, Duke Hobbie, Dennis Robertson, George Smith, Vincent van Lynn, Walter Brooke, Mauritz Hugo, Bill Couch, Mary-Linda Rapelye.* Dir: John Sturges. Pro: M. J. Frankovich. Screenplay: Mayo Simon, based on a Martin Caidin novel. (Francovich/Sturges–Columbia.) Rel: April 12. (Colour & Pan.) 133 Mins. Cert. U.

Matchless
Highly complicated, restless spy thriller which has the dual distinction of having been directed by Alberto Lattuada and having as its main character a man whose useful asset is that he can when in a tight corner become invisible! Cast: *Patrick O'Neal, Ira von Furstenberg, Donald Pleasence, Henry Silva, Nicoletta Machiavelli, Howard St. John, Sorrell Booke, Tiziano Cortini, Giulio Donnini, Andy Ho, Elizabeth Wu, M. Mishiku, Jacques Herlin.* Dir: Alberto Lattuada. Pro: Ermanno Donati & Luigi Carpentieri. Screenplay: Dean Craig, L. Malerba, Jack Pulman & A. Lattuada. (U.A.) Rel: June 7. (T.) 104 Mins. Cert. A.

Mayerling
Lavish and lush romantic tragedy based on the true story of the fatal-ending affair between the Austrian Archduke Rudolf and little Maria Vetsera (*Omar*

Sharif and *Catherine Deneuve*), when, faced with disgrace because of his dabbling in the Hungarian revolt and the refusal of the Emperor to countenance a divorce, he took Maria to Mayerling, his shooting lodge, shot her and then committed suicide. Superbly photographed against authentic Austrian backgrounds, extremely well played in many cases, but never as moving as it should be. Rest of cast: *James Mason, Ava Gardner, James Robertson Justice, Genevieve Page, Andréa Parisy, Ivan Desny, Maurice Teynac, Mony Dalmés, Moustache, Fabienne Dali, Roger Pigaut, Bernard Lajarrige, Véronique Vendell, Jacques Berthier, Charles Millot, Lyne Chardonnet, Jacqueline Lavielle, Roger Lumont, Jean-Michel Rouzière, Irène von Meyendorff, Ylia Chagall, Jacques Toulouse, Jacques Ciron, Jean-Claude Bercq, Alain Saury*. Dir: Terence Young. Pro: Robert Dorfmann. Screenplay: Terence Young, based on the Claude Anet novel, and the Michael Arnold book. (Assoc. British–Warner–Pathe.) Rel: October 5. (T. & Pan. 70 mm.) 141 Mins. Cert. A. (This film was included as a "Floating Release" in last year's annual.)

Me, Natalie
Wonderfully winning little movie about a pleasantly human teenager with a complex about her lack of beauty: her growing up to more assured womanhood, first against a warmly realistic Jewish family life in the Bronx and then against her "freedom" in her flat in Greenwich Village. A lovely performance by *Patty Duke*, with sterling support from a rich cast that includes *Salome Jens, Nancy Marchand, Martin Balsam, Phil Sterling* and *Elsa Lanchester*. Rest of cast: *James Farentino, Deborah Winters, Ronald Hale, Bob Balaban, Matthew Cowles, Ann Thomas, Al Pacino, Catherine Burns, Robyn Morgan, Dan Keyes, Peter Turgeon, Milt Kamen, Ross Charap, Dortha Duckworth, Milo Boulton, Dennis Allen, Robert Frink, Melinda Blachley*. Dir: Fred Coe. Pro: Stanley Shapiro. Screenplay: A. Martin Zweiback. (Shapiro–Cinema Center–Warner–Pathe.) Rel: Nov. 30. (T.) 111 Mins. Cert. X.

Medium Cool
Fictional story set against a completely authentic background of the riots in Chicago in the summer of 1968: a film about political, sporting and personal violence, with the camera, and therefore the spectator, totally involved, leaving him with a terrifying picture as to what the future could hold. Cast: *Robert Forster, Verna Bloom, Peter Bonerz, Marianna Hill, Harold Blankenship, Sid McCoy, Christine Bergstrom, Robert McAndrew, William Sickinger, Beverly Younger, Marrian Walters, Edward Croke, Sandra Ann Roberts, Doug Kimball, Peter Boyle, Georgia Todda, Charles Geary*. Dir: Haskell Wexler. Pro: Tully Friedman. Screenplay: H. Wexler. (Paramount.) Rel: Floating. 111 Mins. Cert. X.

Memories of Underdevelopment – Memorias del Subdesarrollo
One of the rare Cuban films to be seen in this country, written and directed by Tomas Guitierrez Alea: with a surprising honesty and lack of blatant propa-

ganda, it somewhat leisurely examines the case of a young man of the old regime who stays on when his wife and parents emigrate to America, and tries to come to terms with the Revolution, without any final success, however. Cast: *Sergio Corrieri, Daisy Granados, Eslinda Nunez, Beatriz Ponchora*. Dir & Written: T. G. Alea. (Contemporary.) 104 Mins. Cert. X.

Michael and Helga – Helga und Michael
Follow-up to the very successful German sex film, "Helga"; this one examines the sexual problems of the young marrieds. Cast: *Ruth Gassman, Felix Franchy*. Dir: Erich F. Bender. Pro: Dr. Roland Cammerer. Rel: Floating. 85 Mins. Cert. X.

Michael Kohlhaas – Michael Kohlhaas – der Rebell
David Warner as a rather glum hero involved in a story of injustice and rebellion in 16th-century Germany. Rest of cast: *Anna Karina, Anita Pallenberg, Relia Basic, Michael Gothard, Anton Diffring, Inigo Jackson, Anthony May, Tim Ray, Vaclav Lohninsky, Iwan Palluch, Emanuel Schmied, Thomas Holtzmann, Kurt Meisel, Peter Weiss, Maurice Warner, Mikulas Ladizinsky, Keith Richards, Gregor Von Rezzori, Nada Kotrosova, Hanna Axmann, Zdenek Kryzanek*. Dir: Volker Schlondorff. Pro: Jerry Bick. Screenplay: Edward Bond, Clement Biddle-Wood, V. Schlöndorff. (Gershwin and Kastner–Columbia.) Rel: Dec. 7. (T.) 95 Mins. Cert. X.

Midnight Cowboy
A story of sleazy life in New York and the two oddly assorted characters who team up in their desperate need of friendship in a world of decadence. A film enlivened by two outstanding performances, by newcomer *Jon Voight*, who is sure he can make a good life selling himself for sex, and *Dustin Hoffman* as the shabby cynic. Rest of cast: *Sylvia Miles, John McGiver, Brenda Vaccaro, Barnard Hughes, Ruth White, Jennifer Salt, Gil Rankin, Gary Owens, T. Tom Marlow, George Eppersen, Al Scott, Linda Davis, J. T. Masters, Arlene Reeder, Georgann Johnson, Jonathan Kramer, Anthony Holland, Bob Balaban, Jan Tice, Paul Benjamin, Peter Scalia, Vito Siracusa, Peter Zamaglias, Arthur Anderson, Tina Scala, Alma Felix, Richard Clarke, Ann Thomas, Viva, Gastone Rossilli, Joan Murphy, Al Stetson*. Dir: John Schlesinger. Pro: Jerome Hellman. Screenplay: Waldo Salt. (Hellman/Schlesinger–U.A.) Rel: Feb. 1. (D.) 113 Mins. Cert. X.

Mission Batangas
Dennis Weaver as the opportunistic American flyer who becomes mixed up in the war in the Philippines in 1942 and finds himself, to his astonishment, falling in love with a missionary's daughter (*Vera Miles*) and prepared to take a gamble with his life to strike a blow for the U.S. against the Japs. Rest of cast: *Keith Larsen, Pol Salcedo, Helen Thompson, Vic Diaz, Bruno Punzalan, Fred Galang, Tony Dungan, Ernesto La Guardia*. Dir & Pro: Keith Larsen. Screenplay: Lew Antonio. (Grand National.) Rel: Sept. 14. (T.) 82 Mins. Cert. A.

Model Shop
Gary Lockwood as the draftee whose one night of love with "Model Shop" (where males come to take sexy pictures) employee *Anouk Aimée* gives them both a new and brighter outlook on life. Rest of cast: *Alexandra Hay, Carol Cole, Severn Darden, Tom Fielding, Neil Elliot, Jacqueline Miller, Anne Randall, Duke Hobbie, Craig Littler, Hilarie Thompson, Jeanne Sorel, Jon Lawson*. Dir, Pro. & Written: Jacques Demy. (Columbia.) Rel: Feb. 22. (T.) 92 Mins. Cert. X.

The Molly Maguires
Richard Harris as the undercover agent sent by the mine-owners to infiltrate and betray a group of highly militant, Irish immigrant, anthracite coal-miners who in 1870 in Pennsylvania used every possible violent means to attempt to improve both wages and conditions. Rest of cast: *Sean Connery, Samantha Eggar, Frank Finlay, Anthony Zerbe, Bethel Leslie, Art Lund, Anthony Costello*. Dir: Martin Ritt. Pro: M. Ritt & Walter Bernstein. Screenplay: W. Bernstein, based on the A. H. Lewis book. (Paramount.) Rel: May 24. (Pan & Colour.) 125 Mins. Cert. A.

More
Story about a young German who meets and falls in love with an American girl in Paris, only to find that she is deeply enmeshed in drugs and into which world he is drawn towards the final tragedy at the end of their strange holiday in Ibiza. Cast: *Mimsy Farmer, Klaus Grunberg, Heinz Engelmann, Michel Chanderli, Louise Wink, Henry Wolf, Georges Montant*. Dir: Barbet Schroeder. Pro: Dave Lewis, Charles Lachman. Screenplay: B. Schroeder & Paul Gegauff. (Tigon.) Rel: Floating. (Colour.) 116 Mins. Cert. X.

Monte Carlo or Bust
Lively, large-scale comedy about a – highly fictional – Monte Carlo Rally in the twenties, with a lot of amusing people taking part: *Terry-Thomas*, for instance, as the utter, utter cad stooping to every cheating means to defeat rival driver *Tony Curtis* and so win the wager and the latter's half of the car factory they jointly own; *Gert Frobe* as the jail-breaker trying to smuggle a fortune in his spare tyre; *Walter Chiari* as the gallant Roman cop who, winning, hands the cup to doctor – yes, doctor – *Mireille Darc*.With wonderful introduction drawn by Ronald Searle and sung by *Jimmy Durante*. Grand family fun. Rest of cast: *Bourvil, Lando Buzzanca, Peter Cook, Marie Dubois, Susan Hampshire, Jack Hawkins, Nicoletta Machiavelli, Dudley Moore, Peer Schmidt, Eric Sykes, Jacques Duby, Hattie Jacques, Derren Nesbitt, Nicholas Phipps, William Rushton, Michael Trubshawe, Richard Wattis, Walter Williams*. Dir & Pro: Ken Annakin. Screenplay: Jack Davies & Ken Annakin. (Paramount.) Rel: August 3. (Pan & T.) 125 Mins. Cert. U.

Moon Zero Two
Another science-fiction thriller about life on the moon a decade ahead: *James Olson* as a veteran astronaut who now has his own odd jobs business, which brings him the assignment of searching for a vanished moon

miner, which in turn produces a great deal of stellar skulduggery. Rest of cast: *Catherin von Schell, Warren Mitchell, Adrienne Corri, Ori Levy, Dudley Foster, Bernard Bresslaw, Neil McCallum, Joby Blanshard, Michael Ripper, Robert Tayman, Sam Kydd, The "Gojos".* Dir: Roy Ward Baker. Pro & Screenplay: Michael Carreras. (Hammer/Warner–Pathe.) Rel: Oct. 26. (T.) 100 Mins. Cert. U.

The Most Dangerous Man in the World

Gregory Peck as the Nobel prize-winning scientist co-opted by Mr. President to go deep into Red China with the mission of finding out about, and getting back to the U.S., the secret of a newly discovered enzyme which will grow wheat and suchlike as easily above the snowline of the Himalayas as in the deserts of Africa and jungles of India! And goes knowing he may never come back: but not knowing that he has in the transmitter he carries in his head a handy little bomb which can be set off by remote radio control when it is considered that as a matter of policy he should be removed! Exciting climax with the bomb ticking, the Reds chasing, the Russians waiting, and *Peck* struggling to cross the mined, wired border. Rest of cast: *Anne Heywood, Arthur Hill, Alan Dobie, Conrad Yama, Zienia Merton, Ori Levy, Eric Young, Burt Kwouk, Alan White, Keye Luke, Francisca Tu, Mai Ling, Janet Key, Gordon Sterne, Robert Lee, Helen Horton, Keith Bonnard, Cecil Cheng, Lawrence Herder, Simon Cain, Anthony Chinn, Edward Cast.* Dir: J. Lee Thompson. Pro: Mort Abrahams. Screenplay: Ben Maddow, from Jay Richard Kennedy's novel "The Chairman" – which during its making was the film's title. (Apjac–Fox.) Rel: July 3. (Pan & D.) 99 Mins. Cert. A.

Mrs. Brown, You've Got a Lovely Daughter

A film made largely to exploit the charm of *Herman and His Hermits* pop group, with a story centred on *Herman's* racing greyhound, which wins the races, is lost, and then turns up again while the lad is learning some home truths about life and romance. Cast: *Peter Noone, Karl Green, Keith Hopwood, Derek Leckenby, Barry Whitwam, Stanley Holloway, Mona Washbourne, Lance Percival, Marjorie Rhodes, Sheila White, Sarah Caldwell, Hugh Futcher, Drewe Henley, Avis Bunnage, John Sharp, Nat Jackley, Billy Milton, Dermot Kelly, Tom Kempinski, Lynda Baron, Joan Hickson, Iris Sadler, Pamela Cundell, Paul Farrell, Michele Cook, James Myers, Margery Manners.* Dir: Saul Swimmer. Pro: Allen Klein. Screenplay: Thaddeus Vane. (Klein–M-G-M.) Rel: Aug. 10. (Pan & Metrocolor.) 95 Mins. Cert. U. (This film was included as one of "The Neglected Ones" in the feature with that title in last year's annual.)

The Movement Movement

Half-hour (all but 4 minutes) interest film about the work, ideas and aims of a group of Kinetic artists working in Paris. Dir & Photographed: Bruce Parsons. Narration: George Thomson. Pro: Derrick Knight in assoc. with Guy Neyrac. (Knight Films.) Rel: Floating. 26 Mins. Cert. U.

My Dog, the Thief

About an American helicopter traffic reporter who finds new popularity when a huge St. Bernard dog stows away with him. Landed with the creature, his headaches are topped by the discovery that the animal is a kleptomaniac! But, of course, it all works out amusingly happy in the end! Cast: *Dwayne Hickman, Mary Ann Mobley, Elsa Lanchester, Joe Flynn, Roger C. Carmel, Mickey Shaughnessy, John Van Dreelen, Charles Lane, Jim Begg, Vaughn Taylor.* Dir: Robt. Stevenson. Pro: Ron Miller. Screenplay & Story: Wm. Raynor, Myles Wilder & Gordon Buford. (Disney.) Rel: Mar. 29. (T.) 80 Mins. Cert. U.

The Naked Kiss

A five-years-banned (in G.B.) Samuel Fuller film about a Korean war hero who back home is soon revealed as a child violater and otherwise unpleasant character. Cast: *Constance Towers, Anthony Eisley, Michael Dante, Virginia Grey, Patsy Kelly, Betty Bronson, Marie Devereux, Karen Conrad.* Dir: S. Fuller. (Amanda.) 93 Mins. Shown with LCC Cert. X at Times Cinema, April 1970.

The Name of the Game is Kill !

Jack Lord as a wandering Hungarian refugee who, picked up by a pretty girl along an Arizonan desert highway, becomes, through her, involved with a strange family and a lot of odd events that take place in their gas station in a ghost town further along the way. Rest of cast: *Susan Strasberg, Collin Wilcox, Tisha Sterling, Mort Mills, Marc Desmond, T. C. Jones.* Dir: Gunnar Hellstrom. Pro: R. J. Todd. Screenplay: Gary Crutcher. (American International/Anglo–Warner–Pathe.) Rel: Nov. 2. (E.) 83 Mins. Cert. X.

Navajo Joe

Italian–Spanish Western with a desperate, bloody story of the slow and steady decimation of a band of white outlaws, led by a particularly horrid character called The Bastard (*Aldo Sanbrell*), by a wily and vengeful Apache, Joe (*Burt Reynolds*). Rest of cast: *Nicoletta Machiavelli, Tanya Lopert, Fernando Rey, Franca Polesello, Lucia Modugno, Pierre Cressoy, Nino Imparato, Alvaro De Luna, Valeria Sabel, Mario Lanfranchi, Lucio Rosato, Simon Arriaga, Chris Huerta, Angel Ortiz, Fianni Di Stolfo, Angel Alvarez.* Dir: Sergio Corbucci. Pro: Ermanno Donati & Luigi Carpentieri. Screenplay: Dean Craig & Fernando Di Leo. (Dino de Laurentiis–U.A.) Rel: May 10. (T & Techniscope.) 89 Mins. Cert. X.

Night of the Outrages – La Nuit la plus chaude

Adventure of two stripper girls who are held captive for some long hours by an armed – and ailing – desperado who is searching for enough money to escape abroad to organise a defence to the charge that he has murdered his wife. Cast: *Philippe Lemaire, Dona Michelle, Chantal Deberg, Agnes Ball.* Dir: Max Pecas. (S.F. Film Distributors.) First shown at the Jacey Tatler, Jan., 1970. (E.) 84 Mins. Cert. X.

A Nice Girl Like Me

Barbara Ferris as Candida, the nice young innocent –

but fertile! – charmer whose several lovers leave their mark upon her, and is finally persuaded by *Harry Andrews* to take him as the legally noted father of all her future brood. Rest of cast: *Dame Gladys Cooper, Bill Hinnant, James Villiers, Joyce Carey, Christopher Guinee, Fabia Drake, Irene Prador, Eric Chitty, Totti Truman Taylor, John Serret, Tom Gill, Ann Lancaster, Shelagh Wilcox, Sue Whitman, Douglas Wilmer, Carol Gillies, Barbara Keogh, Robert Sidaway, Beryl Cook, Sidney Johnson, Bartlett Mullens, John Clive, Sylvia Tysick, Sarah Golding, Cunitia Knight, Christine Dingle, Sorrel Breunig, Terry Duggan, Alistair Hunter, Miriam Margolyes, Carmen Carpoldi, Bill Clancy, Elisabeth Gordon, David Armour, Nichola Cowper, Rebecca Bridge, Angela Jones, Kate Harman.* Dir: Desmond Davis. Pro: Roy Millichip. Screenplay: Anne Piper & Desmond Davis. (Partisan–Avco Embassy.) Nov. 23. (Colour.) 91 Mins. Cert. A.

The Nine Ages of Nakedness

Harrison Marks' "Spectacular" in which he lies on the pretty psychiatrist's couch and talks about his family's experiences with lovely women in nine episodes starting with The Stone Age and ending with The Computer Age – and all nicely excusing a parade of "150 topless international beauties" – and if ever there was a misnomer that's it! Cast includes: *Max Wall, Max Bacon, Big Bruno Elrington, June Palmer, Julian Orchard, Oliver McGreavey, Cardew Robinson, Rita Webb, Harrison Marks.* Dir, Pro. & Written: H. Marks. (Nat Miller.) Rel: Floating. (E.) 95 Mins. Cert. X.

99 Women – 99 Mujeres

They're all incarcerated in a Spanish fortress jail on an island off the Panamanian coast, where a sadistic female governor drives them to rebellion. Cast: *Maria Schell, Luciana Paluzzi, Mercedes McCambridge, Herbert Lom.* Dir: Jess Franco. Pro: Alan Towers. Screenplay: Peter Welbeck, Carlo Fadda, Millo Cuccia, Jésus Franco. (Commonwealth United.) Rel: Floating. (Colour.) 70 Mins. Cert. X.

No Room to Die – Una Lunga Fila di Croci

Tough Italian-Western set along the Mexican border and telling a story about the confrontation between a group of outlaws, a crooked banker who uses them and two bounty hunters. Cast: *Anthony Steffen, William Berger, Nicoletta Machiavelli, Mario Brega.* Dir: Sergio Garrone. Pro: Gabriele Crisanti. (Miracle.) Rel: May 3. (E.) 88 Mins. Cert. A.

Oh Dad, Poor Dad, Mamma's Hung You in the Closet And I'm Feelin' So Sad

Completely unexplainable, macabre black comedy with tasteless trimmings, about a mother who keeps her 25-year-old mentally retarded son in isolation and takes her stuffed husband everywhere she goes in a coffin trailer, hanging him in the closet when she stays at a hotel! When the son murders the plump and playful little trollop who aspires to steal his virginity, and mother's rich, rolling-eyed old suitor dies, they join the – stuffed – family and another trailer is added to the coffinade! Cast: *Rosalind Russell, Robert Morse, Barbara Harris, Hugh Griffith, Jonathan Winters,*

Lionel Jeffries, Cyril Delavanti, Hiram Sherman. Dir: Richard Quine. Pro: Ray Stark & Stanley Rubin. Screenplay: Ian Bernard, based on A. L. Kopit's stage play. (Seven Arts/Stark–Paramount.) Rel: Floating. (T.) 86 Mins. Cert. X.

Oh! What a Lovely War
Richard Attenborough's (his first film direction, following his previous successes as actor and producer) brilliant, magnificent transcription of the satirical stage musical; bristling with ideas, full of imagination, stylish, and triumphantly human. Centred on Brighton Pier, but venturing from there to the scenes of conflict and its aftermath, punctuated by the "Tommy" songs of 1914–18, it manages to convey without resource to blood, thunder or even bitterness, the empty, useless waste and the stupidity that lie at the back of the first so-called Great War – a succession of memorable scenes ending with one almost unbearably moving one. A great film. Cast: *Ralph Richardson, Meriel Forbes, Wensley Pithey, Ruth Kettlewell, Ian Holm, John Gielgud, Kenneth More, John Clements, Paul Daneman, Joe Melia, Jack Hawkins, John Hussey, Kim Smith, Mary Wimbush, Paul Shelley, Wendy Allnutt, John Rae, Kathleen Wileman, Corin Redgrave, Malcolm McFee, Colin Farrell, Maurice Roëves, Angela Thorne, John Mills, Julia Wright, Jean-Pierre Cassel, Penny Allen, Maggie Smith, David Lodge, Michael Redgrave, Laurence Olivier, Peter Gilmore, Derek Newark, Richard Howard, John Trigger, Ron Pember, Juliet Mills, Nanette Newman, Susannah York, Dirk Bogarde, Norman Jones, Andrew Robertson, Ben Howard, Angus Lennie, Brian Tipping, Christian Doermer, Tony Vogel, Paul Hansard, John Woodnutt, Tony Thawnton, Cecil Parker, Zeph Gladstone, Stanley McGeagh, Stanley Lebor, Robert Flemyng, Thorley Walters, Norman Shelley, Isabel Dean, Guy Middleton, Natasha Parry, Cecilia Darby, Phyllis Calvert, Raymond S. Edwards, Freddie Ascott, Edward Fox, Geoffrey Davies, Christian Thorogood, Paddy Joyce, John Dunhill, John Owens, P. G. Stephens, Vanessa Redgrave, Clifford Mollison, Dorothy Reynolds, Harry Locke, George Ghent, Michael Bates, Charles Farrell, Pia Colombo, Vincent Ball, Anthony Ainley, Gerald Sim, Maurice Arthur, Arthur White, Christopher Cabot, Fanny Carby, Marianne Stone, Christine Noonan, Charlotte Attenborough.* Dir: Richard Attenborough. Pro: Brian Duffy & Richard Attenborough. (Accord–Paramount.) Rel: Sept. 7. (T.) 144 Mins. Cert. A.

The Olympics in Mexico – Olimpiada en Mexico
An all but two-hour visual report on the 1968 Olympic Games in Mexico; a selection of the 1,500,000 feet of colour film taken there by more than 80 cameramen. Dir: Alberto Isaac. Pro: Federico Amerigo. (Columbia.) Rel: Floating. (T & Techniscope.) 116 Mins. Cert. U.

Once There Was a War – Der Var Engang en Krig
Completely captivating and beautifully contrived, deceptively simple little Danish film which in casual, episodic and humorous mood figuratively flips through the pages of the family album, concentrating on the young man who comes to manhood during the German Occupation, though the war is far away, only occasion-ally impinging on the narrative. Never a false note: and beautifully acted, too. Cast: *Ole Busck, Yvonne Ingdal, Kjeld Jacobsen, Astrid Villaume, Katja Miehe Renard, Birgit Madsen, Jan Hansen, Christian Gottschalk, Karen Marie Lowert, Gregers Ussing, Birgit Bruel, Jorgen Beck, Elsa Kourani, Henry Skjaer, Holger Perfort, Jens Pedersen.* Dir: Palle Kjaerulff–Schmidt. Pro: Bo Christensen. Screenplay: Klaus Rifbjerg. (Nordisk–Contemporary.) First shown at Paris Pullman, June, 1969, 94 Mins. Cert. X.

Once Upon a Time in the West – l'era una Volta il West
Though Italian-written, produced and directed, a long, leisurely, stylish Western in the classical mould, telling a violent, brutal story about a deadly struggle for a parcel of land across which the railroad must run. With *Claudia Cardinale* the widowed owner; *Henry Fonda* the very bad baddie, "Frank", who'll shoot any-one to get it for his crippled railroad owning boss; *Jason Robards*, the less bad baddie and *Charles Bronson*, as the mournful, harmonica-playing Indian gunman who has been searching long for Frank and now that he has caught up with him plays him like a fish towards the final showdown in the sun-drenched dust. All quite cruel and brutal – but quite, quite magnificent. Rest of cast: *Frank Wolff, Gabriele Ferzetti, Keenan Wynn, Paola Stoppa, Marco Zuanelli, Lionel Stander, Jack Elam, John Frederick, Woody Strode, Enzio Santianello.* Dir: Sergio Leone. Pro: Fulvio Morsella. Screenplay: Sergio Leone, Sergio Donati. (Rafran/San Marco–Paramount.) Rel: Aug. 31. (T & Techniscope.) 144 Mins. Cert. A.

On Her Majesty's Secret Service
Latest in the Bond line and one of the most thoroughly exciting and entertaining yet; moving at terrific speed and packed with incident all the way along its two-and-a-half-hours, during which new 007 *George Lazenby* coolly battles with British phlegm against the machinations of would-be world-dominating Spectre chief *Telly Savalas*. Wonderful snow scenes, great chases, lovely photography – and Avengeress *Diana Rigg*. Rest of cast: *Ilse Steppat, Gabriele Ferzetti, Yuri Borienko, Bernard Horsfall, George Baker, Bernard Lee, Lois Maxwell, Desmond Llewelyn, Angela Scoular, Catherina Von Schell, Dani Sheridan, Julie Ege, Joanna Lumley, Mona Chong, Anoushka Hempel, Ingrit Back, Jenny Hanley, Zara, Sylvana Henriques, Helena Ronee, Geoffrey Cheshire, Irvin Allen, Terry Mountain, James Bree, Virginia North, Brian Worth, Norman McGlen, Dudley Jones, John Crewdson, Josef Vasa, Les Crawford, George Cooper, Reg Harding, Richard Graydon, Bill Morgan, Robert Rietty, Elliott Sullivan, Bessie Love, Steve Plytas.* Dir: Peter Hunt. Pro: Harry Saltzman & Albert R. Broccoli. Screenplay: Richard Maibaum. (Saltzman/Broccoli–U.A.) Rel: March 1. (Pan & T.) 140 Mins. Cert. A.

The Only Game in Town
The not-so-smooth romance of Las Vegas showgirl Fran and compulsive, unsuccessful gambler Joe – roles played by *Elizabeth Taylor* and *Warren Beatty*.

Rest of cast: *Charles Braswell, Hank Henry, Olga Valery.* Dir: George Stevens. Pro: Fred Kohlmar. Screenplay: Frank D. Gilroy – based on his own play. (Stevens/Kohlmar–Fox.) Rel: May 31. (D.) 113 Mins. Cert. A.

Paddy
About the growing-up of young *Des Cave*, who attracts the ladies and enjoys their attentions, even when it leads to him losing his job and, finally, all sense of respon-sibility. Rest of cast: *Milo O'Shea, Dearbhla Molloy, Judy Cornwell, Donal Le Blanc, Lillian Rappel, Desmond Perry, Maire O'Donnell, Vincent Smith, Ita Darcy, Desmond Ellis, Dominic Roche, Clive Geraghty, Alec Doran, Mary Larkin, Pat Layde, John Kavanagh, John Molloy, William Foley, Brendan Dunne, Mary Jo Kennedy, Mark Mulholland, Maureen Toal, Peggy Cass, Danny Cummings.* Dir: Daniel Haller. Pro: Tamara Asseyev. Screenplay (based on the novel "Goodbye to the Hill"): Lee Dunne. (Fox.) Rel: Feb. 1. (Colour.) 87 Mins. Cert. X.

The Pale Faced Girl
Short feature film about a Dublin Saturday Night and how Mick's pick-up – at the local dance – proves a rare one: and a bitter-sweet experience he'll not forget in spite of all the other girls he'll be picking up in the Saturdays to come. Cast: *Fidelma Murphy, Kevin McHugh, Tony Rohr, Patrick Duggan, George O'Gorman, Lee Dunne, Sheelagh Cullen, Clare Shenton, Laurie Leigh, Sally Kemp.* Dir & Pro: Francis Searle. (Planet.) Rel: May 31. (E.) 27 Mins. Cert. A.

Paranoia – Orgasmo
Carroll Baker as a lovely young widow who becomes the victim of a turgid plot engineered by her American lover and her crooked manager, hoping to drive her to what will look like a self-administered death. But though they do horribly succeed, the wages of sin are still . . . well, very unpleasant. Rest of cast: *Lou Castel, Colette Descombes, Tino Carraro, Lilla Brignone.* Dir: Umberto Lenzi. Pro: Salvatore Alabiso. Screen-play: Ugo Moretti, Umberto Lenzi. (Commonwealth United.) First shown at Gala Royal, Nov., 1969. (E.) 89 Mins. Cert. X.

The Peace Game – Gladiatorerna
Peter Watkins' follow-up of his sensational "The War Game", which, set at some time in the future, follows the events of one of the war games then arranged between nations to satisfy their aggressive instincts. Cast: *Arthur Pentelow, Kenneth Lo, Fredrick Danner, Bjorn Franzen, Hans Bendrik, Christer Gynge, Daniel Harle, Jurgen Schling, Hans Berger, Stefan Dillan, Rosario Gianetti, Chandrakant Desai, Tim Yum, Ugo Chiari, Jeremy Child, Richard Friday, Roy Scammell, Eberhard Fehmers, Nguyen, Erich Stering, Jean-Pierre Delamour, J. Z. Kennedy, Terry Whitmore, To Van Minh, Michael Cheuk, Taras Lee, Eng Chee Gan, Heng Ko Lei, Henry Chan, Pik-Sen Lim, Louis Cheng, Sik-Yng Waung, Bill Fay.* Dir: Peter Watkins. Pro: Bo Jonsson. Screenplay: P. Watkins & Nicholas Gosling. (Gala.) Rel: Floating. (E.) 91 Mins. Cert. X.

Picture to Post
Behind the scenes in the new stamp business; how a stamp is designed, printed and produced, a new and foreign currency earning business for the U.K. (M-G-M.) Rel: Oct. 12. (Widescreen & T.) 24 Mins. Cert. U.

Pigsty – Porcile
Pier Paolo Pasolini's cinematic enigma, in which he tells two stories, one set in the 17th century, the other in post-war Germany, and juxtaposes sequences from each without any apparent pattern. The first story is about a young man who, having killed a soldier, eats him and subsequently sets up a small cannibal community, all of which end up as food for the wild dogs; the second tale concerns the son of a German industrialist who loves pigs and prefers them to women! Puzzling, horrifying and superbly photographed against artistically impressive backgrounds. Cast: *Pierre Clementi, Franco Citti, Alberto Lionello, Margarita Lozano, Jean-Pierre Leaud, Anne Wiazemsky, Ugo Tognazzi, Marco Ferreri, Ninetto Davoli.* Dir & Written: Pier Paolo Pasolini. Pro: Gian Vittorio Baldi. (Eagle.) First shown at Cameo-Poly, Jan., 1970. (Colour.) 93 Mins. Cert. X.

The Pipeliners
Documentary about the bringing of natural gas to Persia; the laying of (British-made) pipes along 316 kilometres of mountainous terrain. (Rank.) Rel: May 24. (E.) 30 Mins. Cert. U.

A Place for Lovers – Amanti
Strangely old-fashion cinematic weepie with *Faye Dunaway* as the American girl fleeing from a fatal illness death sentence to a lovely, lonely Mansion near Venice, where she telephones casual accoster *Marcello Mastroianni* and enjoys with him for a few vivid days a passionate love affair interlude before her inevitable return to America and death. Rest of cast: *Caroline Mortimer, Karin Engh.* Dir: Vittorio de Sica. Pro: Carlo Ponti & Arthur Cohn. Screenplay: Julian Halevy, Peter Baldwin, Ennio de Concini, Tonino Guerra, Cesare Zavattini. (M-G-M.) Rel: July 6. (Metrocolor.) 88 Mins. Cert. X.

Popi
Alan Arkin as the optimistic Puerto Rican widower who tries to bring up his two small sons so that they will eventually escape from their slum surroundings, but when he finally achieves his aim finds to his pained surprise that they prefer to return to their old noisy, dirty, crowded surroundings. Rest of cast: *Miguel Alejandro, Ruben Figueroa, Rita Moreno, Joan Tompkins, Arny Freeman, Anthony Holland, John Harkins, Barbara Dana, Antonia Rey, Arnold Soboloff, Victor Junquera, Gladys Velez.* Dir: Arthur Hiller. Pro: H. B. Leonard. Screenplay: Tina & Lester Pine. (H. B. Leonard–U.A.) Rel: May 10. (D.) 98 Mins. Cert. A.

Pretty Poison
Tuesday Weld as the pretty, superficially sweet, 17-year-old girl who becomes the evil motive force in the life of restless dreamer *Anthony Perkins*, and with him embarks on a career of pyrotechnic sabotage and murder. Pretty people, indeed! Rest of cast: *Beverly Garland, John Randolph, Dick O'Neill, Clarice Blackburn, Joseph Bova, George Ryan's Winslow High-Steppers.* Dir: Noel Black. Pro: Marshal Backlar & Noel Black. Screenplay: Lorenzo Semple, Jr., based on a Stephen Geller novel. (Fox.) Rel: Floating. (D.) 89 Mins. Cert. X.

A Prince for Wales
Documentary about the life and destiny of the young Prince, who emerges complete victor from his interview with *David Frost. Donald Houston* reads the commentary. Dir & Pro: Martin D. Harris. (Rank.) Rel: July 4. (Colour.) 52 Mins. Cert. U.

The Prime of Miss Jean Brodie
Delightfully conventional, non-gimmicky adaptation of the Jay Presson Allen play of the Muriel Spark novel about a forty-one-year-old Edinburgh teacher at the Marcia Blaine School for Girls who revels in her lasting influence on her pupils as she teaches them to face up to the future rather than push academic studies into them: and how her egotism about her unconventionality in her self-styled "prime" is suddenly pricked as one of her own girls lays the information which allows the headmistress to sack her and suddenly leave her just another spinster, now past her prime! Wonderfully amusing; most entertaining; beautifully acted, especially by *Maggie Smith* (Miss Brodie) and *Pamela Franklin* (her nemesis). Rest of cast: *Robert Stephens, Gordon Jackson, Celia Johnson, Diane Grayson, Jane Carr, Shirley Steedman, Lavinia Lang, Antoinette Biggerstaff, Margo Cunningham, Isla Cameron, Rona Anderson, Ann Way, Molly Weir, Helena Gloag, John Dunbar, Heather Seymour, Lesley Patterson.* Dir: Ronald Neame. Pro: Robt. Fryer. Screenplay: Jay Presson Allen. (Fox.) Rel: Sept. 21. (D.) 116 Mins. Cert. X.

The Producers
Amusing, zany comedy based on the stage play about an unsuccessful theatrical producer who is persuaded by his accountant that he can make more money out of real flopperoos. But though he has the world's worst director, he can't make it – it's all so bad that it becomes the comedy hit of the year. Cast: *Zero Mostel, Gene Wilder, Kenneth Mars, Estelle Winwood, Renee Taylor, Christopher Hewett, Lee Meredith, Andreas Voutsinas, Dick Shawn.* Dir & Screenplay: Mel Brooks. Pro: Sidney Glazier. (Avco Embassy.) Rel: Floating. (Colour.) 88 Mins. Cert. A

A Professional Gun – Il Mercenario
Italian-made story set along the Mexican–American border early this century, telling of a strange teaming of a fervent young revolutionary (*Tony Musante*) and a cool, disillusioned gunman (*Franco Nero*) and their joint struggle against all the rich reactionaries. Rest of cast: *Jack Palance, Giovanna Ralli, Eduardo Fajardo, Bruno Corazzari, Franco Giacobini, Vicente Roca, Jose Riesgo, Fernando Villens, Juan Cazalilla, Guillermo Mendez, Jose Zalde.* Dir: Sergio Corbucci.

Pro: Alberto Grimaldi. Screenplay: Luciano Vincenzoni, Sergio Spina, Sergio Corbucci. (U.A.) Rel: Dec. 14. (T.) 105 Mins. Cert. A.

Prologue
Canadian film about two young hippy-type people, one aggressively for peace, one passively for the same thing. Posing the question, should one get on with living and let the world get on with it, or should you take an active part in demonstrations, etc. Cast: *John Robbe, Gary Rader, Peter Cullen, Victor Knight, Frank Edwards, Elaine Malus, Christopher Cordeaux, Henry Gamer, Robert Girolami, Abbie Hoffman, Magnus Flynn, Caroline Cordeaux, Howard Perry, Daniel Cordeaux, Tanya Mackay, Bruce Mackay, Renee Hebert, John Wildman, Fred Smith, Terence Ross.* Dir: Robin Spry. Screenplay: Sherwood Forest. (National Film Board of Canada – Contemporary.) Rel: Floating. 87 Mins. Cert. X.

A Promise of Bed
Triple-filmlet feature about three men and their luck with the girls: imagined and real. Cast: *Victor Spinetti, Vanessa Howard, Dennis Waterman, Vanda Hudson, John Bird.* Dir: Derek Ford. (Miracle.) Rel: Floating. 83 Mins. Cert. X.

Punch-up in Istanbul
Italian crime melodrama about a couple of car-dealer pals who win a fortune on the races, lose it when one double-crosses the other and flees to Istanbul where he loses it to a crooked nighterie owner and his gang. And the rest of the lark is the efforts of the reunited-in-adversity pals to get their cash back from the crooks. Cast includes *Yves Gabrielli, Ugo Pagliai, Alfredo Zammi, Michel Constantin, Jean-François Poron, Anny Duperey, Pierre Richard.* Dir: Francis Rigaud. (Schulman.) First shown at Cameo-Moulin, Dec. 1969. (E & Panoramique.) Cert. X.

The Queer . . . The Erotic – L'Altra Faccia del Peccato
Interest film about odd erotica around the world; such as the open Festival of Love celebrated by the Africans; the shame of Berlin girls for being virgin, leading them to go hunting boys in packs; and Hamburg's 136-roomed Love Palace; etc. (Border.) Rel: Floating. (E.) 91 Mins. Cert. X.

Rampage at Apache Wells – Der Ölprinz
Stewart Granger (as Old Surehand again) and *Pierre Brice* (as his blood brother and sidekick Winnetou) take a wagon train to peace at Lake Shelly, after defeating the wiles and warring of the Oil Prince and the Fingers Gang and the Redskins stirred up into action by the crooks. Rest of cast: *Macha Meril, Harald Leipnitz, Mario Girotti, Antje Weisgerber, Walter Barnes, Gerhard Frickhoffer, Vladimir Leib, Slobodan Dimitrijevic, Dusan Janicijevic, Davor Antolic, Veljko Maricic, Ilija Ivezic, Zvonimir Crnko, Petar Petrovic, Slobodan Vedernjak, Branko Supek, Marinco Cosic, Paddy Fox, Heinz Erhardt.* Dir: Harald Philipp. Pro: Horst Wendlandt. Based on a Karl May novel. Screenplay: Fred Denger & Harald Philipp. (Columbia.) Rel: Feb. 8. (T & C.) 90 Mins. Cert. U.

Rascal
Lovely Disney film about a small boy who spends a glorious summer (in 1918) in the central Wisconsin woodlands with his faithful pet dog and the tamed racoon of the title. A film of great visual beauty and charm. Cast: *Steve Forrest, Bill Mumy, Pamela Toll, Elsa Lanchester, Henry Jones, Bettye Ackerman, Jonathan Daly, John Fiedler, Richard Erdman, Herbert Anderson, Robert Emhardt, Steve Carlson* and *Walter Pidgeon* as the Voice of Sterling North. Dir: Norman Tokar. Pro: James Algar. Screenplay: Harold Swanton, based on the Sterling North book. (Disney.) Rel: Dec. 21. (T.) 85 Mins. Cert. U.

The Reckoning
Story of a Liverpool–Irish lad who, with the iron of hate in his soul (he hates the English; hates the classes other than his own; hates, one gathers, himself just a little!) who climbs to the top of the London business pile with complete ruthlessness (for instance, immediately sacking – as "unreliable!" – the sad little secretary who in bed passes him the information which allows him to unseat the big boss and take over his job) but shows a softer side when his "Da'" dies and he almost reluctantly follows the local code and clobbers (and kills, one wonders?) the ton-up lad who was responsible for the old man's final heart attack: getting away with that, one presumes, as with everything else, to go on his triumphant, hard-drinking, bitter way. A superb performance by *Nicol Williamson* in the leading role. Rest of cast: *Rachel Roberts, Paul Rogers, Zena Walker, Ann Bell, Gwen Nelson, Christine Hargreaves, Tom Kempinski, J. G. Devlin, John Normington, Peter Sallis, Godfrey Quigley, John Malcolm, Desmond Perry.* Dir: Jack Gold. Pro: Ronald Shedlo. Screenplay: John McGrath, based on the Patrick Hall novel, "The Harp That Once". (Shedlo–Columbia.) Rel: Feb. 22. 111 Mins. Cert. X.

Revenge in El Paso – Quattro dell' Ave Maria
Italian–Western, less sadistic than some and telling, with some humour, its tale of three bad men who, after being against each other, team up to jointly ride off with the money they've all been after. Cast: *Eli Wallach, Terence Hill, Bud Spencer, Brock Peters, Kevin McCarthy, Steffen Zacharias, Livio Lorenzon, Tiffany Hoyveld, Remo Capitani.* Dir: Giuseppe Colizzi. Pro & Screenplay: Bino Cicogna & G. Colizzi. (Paramount.) Rel: Dec. 7. (Colour.) 103 Mins. Cert. A.

Rhubarb
Silent-techniqued, goonish comedy in which for all the film's 37 minutes the only word spoken, and repeated, and repeated, *and repeated*, is that of the title! Largely it takes place on the golf-course, and "it" is a crazy succession of comedy gags and incidents. Cast: *Harry Secombe, Eric Sykes, Jimmy Edwards, Hattie Jacques, Gordon Rollings, Johnny Speight, Ann Lancaster, Sheree Winton, Kenneth Connor, Graham Stark, Anastasia Penington.* Dir & Written: Eric Sykes. Pro: Jon Penington. (Anglo–Avalon–EMI.) Rel: March 29. (Colour.) 37 Mins. Cert. U.

Ride a Northbound Horse
Disney film about a young loner's adventures in the West; about the horse he gains and loses and, after quite a lot of adventure, regains for good. Cast: *Michael Shea, Carroll O'Connor, Ben Johnson, Andy Devine, Edith Atwater, Jack Elam, Dub Taylor, Harry Carey Jr.* Dir: Robert Totten. Pro: Ron Miller. Screenplay: Herman Groves, based on the Richard Wormser novel. (Disney.) Rel: Aug. 10. (T.) 79 Mins. Cert. U.

Ring of Bright Water
Wholly delightful screen adaptation of the famous Gavin Maxwell book of the same title: about the author's adventures with his pet otters in a little cottage on a lonely, lovely part of the Scottish Highlands coast. Wonderfully photographed, easily acted, free from any sentimentality; one of the most completely captivating pictures of its year. Cast: *Bill Travers, Virginia McKenna, Peter Jeffrey, Roddy McMillan, Jameson Clark, Jean Taylor-Smith, Helena Gloag, W. H. D. Joss, Archie Duncan, Kevin Collins, John Young, James Gibson, Michael O'Halloran, Philip McCall, Christopher Benjamin, Philippa Gail, June Ellis, Bill Horsley, Tommy Godfrey.* Dir: Jack Couffer. Pro: Joseph Strick. Screenplay: Jack Couffer & Bill Travers. (Palomar–Rank.) Rel: Aug. 17. (T.) 107 Mins. Cert. U.

The Road to Katmandu
The story of a pretty hopeless, useless bunch of characters in general and a young student called Olivier in particular, as forced to leave Paris after the riots, he makes his way to Nepal, only to find disillusion, pessimism and final realisation. Cast: *Renaud Verley, Jane Birkin, Serge Gainsbourg, Elsa Martinelli, David O'Brien, Pascale Audret, Arlene Dahl.* Dir: Andre Cayatte. Pro: Ulrich Pickardt. (Franco-London Films–Cinecenta.) First shown at Cinecenta, London, May, 1970. (E.) 100 Mins. Cert. X.

A Run on Gold
Fred Astaire as a frustrated British Secret Service agent who persuades his American teacher friend, with whom he plays a "war game" by correspondence, to join him and his attractive girl-friend, *Anne Heywood,* in a meticulously detailed plan to steal 15,000,000-dollars-worth of gold! And it is all light, very light, fun! Rest of cast: *Richard Crenna, Roddy McDowall, Ralph Richardson, Cesar Romero, Adolfo Celi, Maurice Denham, John Le Mesurier, Aldo Bufi Landi, Fred Astaire, Jr., Jacques Sernas, Karl Otto Alberty, George Hartman, Caroline De Fonseca, Stanley Baugh, Bruce Beeby, Robert Henderson.* Dir: Alf Kjelln. Pro: Raymond Stross. Screenplay: J. D. Buchanan, R. Austin & Berne Giler, based on the story by Mr. Giler. (Stross–MPI–Cinerama.) Rel: Dec. 14. (Colour.) 104 Mins. Cert. A.

Run Wild, Run Free
The story of a friendship that develops between a nervously dumb little boy who lives on Dartmoor (where the whole film was beautifully filmed) and The White Colt (which was the film's original title,

and that of the original novel by David Rook). Simple, sentimental and quite charming, with a sensitive performance by *Mark* ("Oliver") *Lester* as the boy and a fine one by *John Mills* as the only one who tries to understand him. Rest of cast: *Gordon Jackson, Sylvia Syms, Bernard Miles, Fiona Fullerton.* Dir: Richard C. Sarafisn. Pro: Andrew Donally. (Irving Allen–Columbia.) Rel: Aug. 3. (Colour.) 98 Mins. Cert. U.

The Sadist – Träfracken
Swedish sex shocker about a nasty doctor – *Gunnar Bjornstrand* – who runs a clinic and uses it as a cover for his nastiness, which includes being more than unpleasant to pretty *Essy Persson.* Rest of cast: *Catrine Westerlund, Margaretha Krook, Allan Edwall, Heinz Hopf, Ulla Sjöblom, Elsa Prawitz, Ake Fridell, Gösta Prüzelius, Peter Lingren, Kristina Lingren, Christina Carlwind.* Dir: Marianne Greenwood. Pro: Inge Ivarson. Screenplay: Lars Magnus Lindgren. (Border Films.) Rel: Floating. 85 Mins. Cert. X.

Scream and Scream Again
A topical spine-tingler with three famous scream-makers heading the cast: *Vincent Price, Christopher Lee* and *Peter Cushing.* It all starts when the police find two murdered girls that have been sucked dry of blood beginning a trail that leads them to a horrid organic transplant plot. Rest of cast: *Alfred Marks, Christopher Matthews, Judy Huxtable, Anthony Newlands, Kenneth Benda, Marshall Jones, Uta Levka, Yutte Stensgaard, Julian Holloway, Judy Bloom, Peter Sallis, Clifford Earl, Nigel Lambert, Michael Gothard.* Dir: Gordon Hessler. Pro: L. M. Heyward. (M. J. Rosenberg & M. Subotsky/Warner–Pathe.) Rel: Feb. 8. (E.) 95 Mins. Cert. X.

The Seagull
Sidney Lumet's almost reverent and certainly highly effective screen transcription of the famous Chekhov play about lost ambitions and frustrated loves, with some distinguished players providing gems of performances. Cast: *James Mason, Simone Signoret, Vanessa Redgrave, David Warner, Harry Andrews, Ronald Radd, Eileen Herlie, Kathleen Widdoes, Denholm Elliott, Alfred Lynch, Frej Lindquist, Karen Miller.* Dir & Pro: S. Lumet. Translated and adapted: Moura Budberg. (Warner–Pathe.) Rel: Floating. (T.) 141 Mins. Cert. A.

Secret Ceremony
Interesting, baroque, static and very slim-storied Joseph Losey film about a rich dolly off her trolley who follows a tired prostitute, calls her "mummy" and takes her home – which is lush enough to make the lady of leisure accept the role without a great deal of fuss. It all ends in suicide and murder. With a fantastic décor, a wandering camera, Losey tries to weave a spell – and with his dexterity all but succeeds. But the cardboard characters, their suspect psychology, make it pretty hard-going for him – and us! But still one of the films most worth seeing. Cast: *Elizabeth Taylor, Mia Farrow, Robert Mitchum, Pamela Brown, Peggy*

Ashcroft. Dir: Joseph Losey. Pro: John Heyman & Norman Priggen. Screenplay: Geo. Tabori. (Universal–Rank.) Rel: Floating. (T.) 109 Mins. Cert. X.

Secrets of Sex
A collection of long and short incidents, stories, and comic interludes centred on sex in which the female emerges as more or less the villainess of the piece! Cast: *Valentine Dyall* (narrator), *Richard Schulman, Janet Spearman, Dorothy Grumbar, Anthony Rowlands, Norma Eden, George Herbert, Kenneth Benda, Yvonne Quenet, Reid Anderson, Sylvia Delamere, Cathy Howard, Mike Briton, Maria Frost, Peter Carlisle, Steve Preston, Graham Burrows, Mike Patten, Raymond George, Karrie Lambert, Joyce Leigh Crossley, Nicola Austine, Elliott Stein, Sue Bond, Laurelle Streeter, Bob E. Raymond, John Hale, Peter Carlisle, Marilyn Head, Ken Norris*. Dir & Pro: Antony Balch. Screenplay: Martin Locke, John Eliot, Maureen Owen, Elliott Stein, A. Balch. (Balch.) Rel: Floating. (E.) 82 Mins. Cert. X.

Sex is a Pleasure – Die Tolldreister Geschichten des Honoré de Balzac
German film which sets out to prove the point of the title with its story of a sexually simmering group brought together in a sumptuous chateau where Balzac appears to be the recommended reading! Cast: *Joachim Hansen, Francy Fair, Katharina Alt, Walter Buschhoff, Michaela May, Edwige Fenech, Ivan Nesbitt, Sieghardt Rupp, Angelica Ott*. Dir: Josef Zachar. Pro: Erich Tomek. Screenplay: Dr. Kurt Nachmann. (New Realm.) First shown at Jacey Tatler, Jan., 1970. (E.) 77 Mins. Cert. X.

Sexual Partnership – Oswart kolle: das Wunder der Liebe – Sexuelle Partner – Schaft
Mild little German "sex education" piece, staidly following the case of two ill-assorted young people who meet, marry, row and part, all because of the need for patience and understanding. Cast: *Petra Perry, Michael Maien*. Dir: Alexis Neve. Pro: Karin Wecker-Jacobsen. (Crispin.) First shown at Cinephone, Jan., 1970. (Colour.) 96 Mins. Cert. X.

Sexy Susan Sins Again – Fran Wirtin hat auch einen Grafen
This time when she leads the women of the town in a mass striptease in order to defeat the plot to kill Napoleon – himself disarmed by such a delicious display! *Terry Torday* as the petite Susan. Rest of cast: *Jeffrey Hunter, Pascale Petit, Jacques Herlin, Femi Benussi, Daniela Giordano, Edwige Fenech, Gustav Knuth, Harald Leipnitz, Hannelore Auer, Heinrich Schweiger, Ralf Wolter, Erich Padalewski, Anke Syring, Franz Muxeneder, Rosemary Lindt, Judith Dornys, Annemarie Szilvassy, Bela Emyei, Reza Fazelli, Carlo della Piane, Guido Von Salis, Eva Vadnai, Georg Maday*. Dir: François Legrand. Pro: Carl Szokoll. (Miracle.) First shown at Jacey Tatler, Oct., 1969. (E & Scope.) 93 Mins. Cert. X.

The Sergeant
A strong, bravura performance by dominating *Rod Steiger* as a World War Two hero and long-time professional soldier, who is sent to France in 1952 as Top Sergeant to a company weakly officered and without discipline. And there his character is revealed as his increasing liking for a private uncovers his latent homosexuality; a passion which leads to his downfall and suicide as the whole thing comes out into the open and he is dismissed by the very officer he despises. Also memorable, director John Flynn's perfect atmosphere, of France in its misty, icy winter mantle, and the camp in its lonely discomfort. Rest of cast: *John Phillip Law, Ludmila Mikael, Frank Latimore, Elliott Sullivan, Ronald Rubin, Philip Roye, Jerry Brower, "Memphis Slim"*. Dir: John Flynn. Pro: Richard Goldstone. Screenplay: Dennis Murphy, from his own novel of the same title. (Wise/Warner–Seven Arts.) Rel: July 13. (T.) 108 Mins. Cert. X.

She and He – L'Assoluto Naturale
Laurence Harvey's turgid little film about the male and female relationship. Cast: *Laurence Harvey, Slyva Koscina, Isa Miranda, Felicity Mason, Isabella Cini, Nella Tessieri-Frediani, Amalia Carrara, Franca Sciuto, Guido Mannari, Giogio Tavaroli, Vanni Castellaris*. Dir: Paolo Pietrangeli. Pro: L. Harvey. Screenplay: O. Jemma & V. Schizaldi. (Cinecenta.) Rel: Floating. 86 Mins. Cert. X.

Shock Corridor
Five-years-banned (in Britain) Samuel Fuller film about a reporter who in order to get a true story about conditions in a mental hospital has himself taken in there as a patient! Cast: *Peter Breck, Constance Towers, Gene Evans, James Best, Hari Rhodes, Larry Tucker, William Zuckert, Philip Ahn*. Dir: S. Fuller. (Amanda.) 101 Mins. Shown with LCC Cert. X at Times Cinema, April, 1970.

Silence and Cry – Csend és Kiáltás
Third in Miklós Jancsó's visually almost hypnotic, highly individual, stylistic films based on the same theme, of the way that war and revolution dehumanise and degrade (previous films: "The Round-Up", "Red and the White"). This one deals with the brutally repressive period that followed the defeat of the Communist revolution by the Admiral Horthy regime, with the gendarmerie killing off the fugitives, sleeping with the women and bullying the men. All this seen against the vast Hungarian plains, with the few poor farms: the dog barking and the wind soughing, an unforgettable, uncomfortable and superbly realised picture. Cast: *Andras Kozak, Zoltan Latinovits, Jozsef Medaras, Mari Torocsik, Andrea Drahota*. (Mafilm Studio 4–Academy.) First shown at the Academy One, June, 1969. 79 Mins. Cert. A.

The Sinners – La Piscine
Cool, competent story of a murder and the way it changes – or doesn't change! – those most closely involved. Seen against a wonderfully sparkling and sunny French Riviera background. *Alain Delon* and *Romy Schneider* as the lovers, *Maurice Ronet* as the

interloper and *Jane Birkin* as his teenaged daughter. Rest of cast: *Paul Crauchet*. Dir: Jacques Deray. Pro: Gerard Beytout. Screenplay: Jean-Emmanuel Conil. (SNC/Tritone Filmindustria–Cinecenta.) First shown at Cinecenta, London, Oct., 1969. (E.) 108 Mins. Cert. X.

The Sisters – Le Sorelle
A psychological drama about two sisters whose closeness is allied to the domination of the one by the other, and when this relationship is temporarily weakened by the marriage of one, the other fights to recapture her position, resorting even to murder. Cast: *Nathalie Delon, Susan Strasberg, Massimo Girotti, Giancarlo Giannini*. Dir: Roberto Malenotti. Pro: Enzo Boetani. Screenplay: Brunello Rondi & R. Malenotti. (Cinecenta.) First shown at Cinecenta, London, May, 1970. (T.) 112 Mins. Cert. X.

Situation Hopeless – But Not Serious
Alec Guinness as the German shop assistant who hides a couple of shot-down American pilots in his boss's cellar – and becomes so pleased with the situation that he keeps them there long after the war has ended! And still not aware of the truth when released, the two fugitives struggle through a prospering, and they think victorious, Germany towards the imagined safety of the Swiss border. Rest of cast: *Michael Connors, Robert Redford, Anita Hoefer, Mady Rahl, Paul Dahlke, Frank Wolff, John Briley, Elisabeth Von Molo*. Dir. & Pro: Gottfried Reinhardt. Screenplay: Silvia Reinhardt, based on Robert Shaw's novel "The Hiding Place". (Paramount.) Rel: Floating. 98 Mins. Cert. A.

The Sixth of July – Shestoe Iulya
Russian reconstruction of another period in the life of Lenin; the few days at the beginning of July, 1918, when the Bolsheviks' and the Left Socialist-Revolutionaries' struggle for power came to a climax. Cast: *Yuri Kayurov, A. Demidova, V. Tatosov, V. Lanovoi*. Dir: Yuli Karasik. Screenplay: Mikhail Shatrov. (Contemporary.) First shown at Paris Pullman, April, 1970.

Slaves
Stephen Boyd as a villainous ex-slave trader now running a plantation; with a mistress who nurses a hatred against him for separating her from her husband, and some slaves who plan to make a break for freedom. Rest of cast: *Dionne Warwick, Ossie Davis, Marilyn Clark, Gale Sondergaard, Shepperd Strudwick, Nancy Coleman, Julius Harris, David Huddleston, Eva Jessye, Barbara Ann Teer, James Heath, Adline King, Oscar Paul Jones, Robert Kya-Hill*. Dir: H. J. Biberman. Pro: P. Langner. Screenplay: H. J. Biberman, J. O. Killen & Aida Sherman. (Warner–Pathe.) Rel: Floating (E.) 105 Mins. Cert. X.

The Smashing Bird I Used to Know
The sad story of a lovely young girl who bears a guilt complex, accusing herself of causing her father's death when at the age of nine she panicked on a merry-go-round, and the way that this leads her at least

indirectly to murder and final tragedy. Cast: *Madeline Hinde, Renee Asherson, Dennis Waterman, Patrick Mower, Faith Brook, Janina Faye, David Lodge, Maureen Lipman, Derek Fowlds, Colette O'Neil, Megs Jenkins, Cleo Sylvestre, Valerie Wallace, Lesley Down, Michele Cook, Tania, Carol Rachell, Cherith Mellor, Cynthia Lund, Douglas Fisher, Sheila Steafel, Valerie Van Ost, Helen Christie, Joanna David, Heller Torren.* Dir: Robert Hartford-Davis. Pro: Peter Newbrook. Screenplay: John Peacock. (Titan International–Grand National.) Rel: Sept. 14. (E.) 95 Mins. Cert. X.

Spring and Port Wine
A delightfully warm and human screen adaptation of Bill Naughton's warm and beautifully observed North Country family comedy about a cotton mill engineer who acts like a benevolent dictator towards his family until the fried herring his youngest daughter refuses to eat sparks off the revolt which only near-tragedy brings him and them to a new and more understanding relationship. Extremely well acted by all concerned with *James Mason* (Dad), *Diana Coupland* (Mum), *Adrienne Posta* (neighbour) and *Rodney Bewes* (son) among the top scorers! Rest of cast: *Susan George, Hannah Gordon, Len Jones, Keith Buckley, Avril Elgar, Frank Windsor, Ken Parry, Bernard Bresslaw, Arthur Lowe, Marjorie Rhodes, Joe Greig, Christopher Timothy, Eddie Robertson, Sandra Downes, Maria Mantella, George Nutkins, Reg Green, Jack Howarth, Brian Mosley, Bryan Pringle, John Sharp.* Dir: Peter Hammond. Pro: Michael Medwin. Screenplay: Bill Naughton. (T.) Rel: Mar. 29. (T.) 101 Mins. Cert. A.

Staircase
Charles Dyer's own screen adaptation of his stage play, with *Rex Harrison* and *Richard Burton* (a wryly amusing touch if ever there was one!) playing a couple of homosexuals who find that while their life together can be unpleasant, without each other it becomes impossible. Stagey dialogue and settings; wonderful performances; a mixture of cruelty, humour (of a kind) and pathos. Rest of cast: *Cathleen Nesbitt, Beatrix Lehmann, Stephen Lewis, Neil Wilson, Gordon Heath, Avril Angers, Shelagh Fraser, Gwen Nelson, Pat Heywood, Dermot Kelly, Jake Kavanagh, Rogers and Starr.* Dir & Pro: Stanley Donen. Screenplay: Charles Dyer. (Fox.) Rel: Floating. (Pan & D.) 98 Mins. Cert. X.

Star!
3-hour musical based on the life and career of Gertrude Lawrence and bringing back memories of the 20's and the 30's: with *Julie Andrews* giving a lovely performance in the main role and *Daniel Massey* presenting a brilliantly sustained impersonation of the younger Noël Coward, both as actor (in an extract from "Private Lives" and again in "Red Peppers") and singer. Rest of cast: *Richard Crenna, Michael Craig, Robert Reed, Bruce Forsyth, Beryl Reid, John Collin, Alan Oppenheimer, Richard Karlan, Lynley Laurence, Garrett Lewis, Elizabeth St. Clair, Jenny Agutter, Anthony Eisley, Jock Livingston, J. Pat O'Malley, Harvey Jason, Damian London, Richard Angarola, Matilda Calnan, Lester Matthews, Bernard Fox,*

Murray Matheson, Robin Hughes, Jeannette Landis, Dinah Ann Rogers, Barbara Sandland, Ellen Plasschaert, Ann Hubbell. Dir: Robert Wise. Pro: Saul Chaplin. Written: Wm. Fairchild. (Robt. Wise–Fox.) Rel: Nov. 9. (D.) 174 Mins. Cert. U.

Stiletto
Violent and pretty incredible crime piece based on an early, pre-"Carpetbaggers" Harold Robbins novel in which *Alex Cord* spends his time lushing it up with *Britt Ekland* and *Barbara McNair* or rubbing out a few bad types for a gangster pal. Rest of cast: *Patrick O'Neal, Joseph Wiseman, John Dehner, Tito Vandis, Eduardo Ciannelli, Roy Scheider, Lincoln Kilpatrick.* Dir: Bernard Kowalski. Pro: Norman Rosemont. Screenplay: A. J. Russell. (Avco Embassy.) Rel: June 14. (Colour.) 99 Mins. Cert. X.

Story of a Woman – Storia di una Donna
Torrid little tale of a love affair which begins in Rome, ends when the man's wife turns up, starts again when the girl goes back to Rome with her husband and finally erupts into suicide and deeper understanding between the survivors. Cast: *Robert Stack, Bibi Andersson, James Farentino, Annie Girardot, Frank Sundstrom, Didi Perego, Francesco Mule, Birgitta Valberg, Katherine Riney, Beppe Wolgers, Ingella Rossell, Toivo Pawlo, Elsa Vazzoler, Pippo Starnazza, Gisella Sofio, Marco Raviart, Diana Lante, Anna Liotti.* Dir, Pro. & Written: Leonardo Bercovici. (Universal–Rank.) Rel: Jan. 18. (T.) 83 Mins. Cert. A.

The Strawberry Statement
Smoothly professional film about student unrest in America; the story of one young student dragged into the revolt. The climax is a confrontation between cops and students which drips tear-gas, howls with sirens and each side does their thing with sticks, and stones and broken bones. Cast: *Bruce Davison, Kim Darby, Bud Cort, Murray MacLeod, Tom Foral, Danny Goldman, Kristina Holland, Bob Balatan, Kristen Van Buren, Israel Horovitz, James Kunen, James Coco, Eddia Gale.* Dir: Stuart Hagman. Pro: Irwin Winkler & Robert Chartoff. Screenplay: Israel Horovitz, based on the James Kunen book. (Chartol/Winkler–M-G-M.) Rel: June 14. (Metrocolor.) 110 Mins. Cert. X.

Stuntman
Robert Viharo as the athletic screen dare-devil with few moral scruples, taking crime and women in his stride. *Gina Lollobrigida* is one of the latter. *Marie Dubois* and *Marisa Mell* being others. Rest of cast: *Paul Muller, Jean-Claude Bercq, Giuseppe Lauricella, Claudio Perone, Aldo de Carellis, Carla Antonelli, Benito Boggino, Umi Raho, Marina Lando, Dennis Hall, Sandro Pellegrini, Giuseppe Liuzzi, Maria Pia Nardon, Camilla Moser, Virgilio Conti.* Dir: Marcello Baldi. Pro: Turi Vasile. Screenplay: Marcello Baldi & Sandro Continenza. (Ultra/Marianne–Paramount.) Rel: March 8. (Colour.) 83 Mins. Cert. A.

The Subject is Sex – Un Epais Manteau de Saug
Hot passions along the Mediterranean coast where one crook takes his partner's faithless wife as his mistress.

Cast: *Valerie Lagrange, Paul Guers, Hans Meyer Eric Arnal.* Dir, Pro & Screenplay: Jose Benazeraf. (R.S.E.) Rel: Floating. 83 Mins. Cert. X.

Swan Lake
Film of the Tchaikovsky ballet danced by *Margot Fonteyn, Rudolf Nureyev* and *Members of the Vienna State Opera Ballet*, with the *Vienna Symphony Orchestra.* Dir: Truck Branss. Pro: Robert Maxwell. (United–Assoc.–Warner/Pathe.) Rel: Floating. (E.)

The Switchboard Operator – Ljubavna Slucaj
Untidy but amusing little Yugoslav film which, with excursions into Phallus Worship (lecture), pornography, and criminal investigation, tells the story of a pert and sexy little telephonist who falls in love with a rat-catcher and, when she is pregnant, is murdered by him. Cast: *Eva Ras, Slobodan Aligrudic.* Dir: Dusan Makavejev. (Hunter.) First shown at Cameo-Poly, Aug., 1969. 68 Mins. Cert. X.

Targets
An historically interesting film in that it is the last one to be made by *Boris Karloff* prior to his death: in it he more or less plays himself, an ageing horror film star who wants to retire but is suddenly pitchforked into a terrifying confrontation with a mad gunman killer. Rest of cast: *Tim O'Kelly, Nancy Hsueh, James Brown, Sandy Baron, Arthur Peterson, Mary Jackson, Tanya Morgan, Monty Landis, Paul Condylis, Mark Dennis, Stafford Morgan, Peter Bogdanovich, Daniel Ades, Tim Burns, Warren White, Geraldine Baron, Gary Kent, Ellie Wood Walker, Frank Marshall, Byron Betz, Mike Farrell, Carol Samuels, Jay Daniel, James Morris.* Dir, Pro & Screenplay: Peter Bogdanovich. (Paramount.) Rel: Sept. 28. (Colour.) 76 Minutes. Cert. X.

Taste the Blood of Dracula
Lots of lovely thrills in addition to the Hammer gallery of celluloid Horrors, with the resurrected Count taking his horrible revenge on the three men who have murdered his disciple! Cast: *Christopher Lee, Geoffrey Keen, Gwen Watford, Linda Hayden, Peter Sallis, Anthony Corlan, Isla Blair, John Carson, Martin Jarvis, Ralph Bates, Roy Kinnear, Michael Ripper, Russell Hunter, Shirley Jaffe, Keith Marsh, Peter May, Reginald Barratt, Maddy Smith, Lai Ling, Malaika Martin.* Dir: Peter Sasdy. Pro: Aida Young. Screenplay: John Elder. (Hammer–Warner–Pathe.) Rel: June 7. (T.) 95 Mins. Cert. X.

Tell Them Willie Boy Is Here
About a Redskin youth who, when her father catches him making love to a girl he has been parentally forbidden, shoots dad dead and makes off with the girl into the wilderness – to be subsequently chased and hunted down against some wonderful scenic back-grounds by the white lawmen. And beneath the considerable surface incident are all sorts of significant undertones about racial (and perhaps political!) prejudice and the nature of violence. Cast: *Robert Redford, Katharine Ross, Robert Blake, Susan Clark,*

Barry Sullivan, Charles McGraw, Charles Aidman, John Vernon, Shelly Novack, Ned Romero, John Day, Lee De Broux, George Tyne. Dir & Written: Abraham Polonsky. Pro: P. A. Waxman. (Lang–Waxman–Rank.) Rel: April 26. (Colour.) 98 Mins. Cert. A.

That Cold Day in the Park
Sandy Dennis takes pity on the boy on the cold seat in a wintry Vancouver park and invites him into her flat – and then her life. It all builds up to a highly dramatic and murderous climax. Rest of cast: *Michael Burns* (the boy), *Susanne Benton, John Garfield Jr., Luana Anders.* Dir: Robert Altman. Pro: Donald Factor-Leon Mirell. (Commonwealth United.) Rel: Floating. (Colour.) 105 Mins. Cert. X.

The Ten Thousand Suns – Tízezer Nap
Dignified and gloomy story which distils the history of modern Hungary through the experiences of one peasant farmer and his family, the old man looking back at a hard life enlivened by a few small pleasures. Cast: *Tibor Molnár, Gyöngyi Bürös, János Koltai, János Rajz, Sándor Siménfalvi, Péter Hauman, András Kozák, János Görbe, Anna Nagy, Ida Simenfalvi, Nóra Káldi, László Nyers, István Széles, Mihaly Papp.* Dir. Ferenc Kosa. Screenplay: F. Kosa, Imre Gyongyossi & Sandor Csoori. (Contemporary.) First shown at the Academy. 97 Mins. Cert. A.

The Tender Age – Adolphe on l'Age tendre
Tragic little story of a young moviemaker who falls in love with the beautiful lady who has agreed to play his heroine and so begins a sad romance which ends, inevitably, in tragedy. Cast: *Ulla Jacobsson, Jean-Claude Dauphin, Philippe Noiret, Claude Giraud, Nathalie Nell, Marie-Joseph Facucci, Michel Robert, Jean Riveyre, Jacques Astoux, Maria Mauban, Claude Dauphin.* Dir: Bernard T. Michel. (Planet.) First shown at the Cameo-Poly, Sept., 1969. (E.) 103 Mins. Cert. X.

Therese and Isabelle
Essentially French (though with, apparently, a some-what international parentage) adaptation of Violette Leduc's erotic novel about a lesbian affair between two teen-aged schoolgirls at a French Finishing School. The technical gloss, the superb camerawork, the poetic presentation just about keeps a risqué story this side of pornography. Delicious performances by *Essy Persson* and *Anna Gael* and a magnificent little cameo of a Madame by *Simone Paris.* Rest of cast: *Barbara Laage, Anne Vernon, Maurice Teynac, Remy Longa, Suzanne Marchellier, Nathalie Nort, Darcy Pulliam, Martine Leclerc, Bernadette Stern.* Dir & Pro: Radley Metzger. Screenplay: Jesse Vogel. (Gala.) First shown at Cinecenta and Continentale in Aug., 1969. (Ultrascope.) 111 Mins. Cert. X.

Three in the Attic
Permissive age story about three girls who, when they find the boyfriend is also the boyfriend of the other two, decide to teach him a lesson by trapping him in an attic where they take turns to make love to him and so gradually reduce him to weak desperation. Cast: *Yvette Mimieux, Christopher Jones, Judy Pace, Maggie Thrett, Nan Martin, John Beck, Reva Rose, Eva McVeagh.* Dir & Pro: Richard Wilson. Screenplay: Stephen Yafa. (American International/Anglo–Warner–Pathe.) Rel: Aug. 17. (Colour.) 91 Mins. Cert. X.

Three Into Two Won't Go
Extremely well handled examination of a marriage that is breaking up, with *Rod Steiger* as the electronics salesman who picks up a very modern little Miss (*Judy Geeson*) and then finds he can't get rid of her when she arrives and takes up residence in his house, where his wife (*Claire Bloom*) befriends her. And in the end, rejected by both wife and mistress, the man, destroyed, leaves. Rest of cast: *Peggy Ashcroft, Paul Rogers, Lynn Farleigh, Elizabeth Spriggs.* Dir: Peter Hall. Pro: Julian Blaustein. Screenplay: Edna O'Brien, based on the novel by *Andrea Newman.* (Universal–Rank.) Rel: Sept. 14. (Colour.) 94 Mins. Cert. X.

Tiger By the Tail
Christopher George on his way home towards a war hero's reception drops off for a good time in Mexico and in a fracas that occurs starts his subsequent deep involvement in a dastardly plot which brings about the murder of his brother and, almost, his own disgrace and ruin. Rest of cast: *Tippi Hedren, Dean Jagger, Charo, Lloyd Bochner, John Dehner, Glenda Farrell, Alan Hale, Skip Homeier, R. G. Armstrong, Dennis Patrick, Martin Ashe, Frank Babich, Marilyn Devin, Ray Martell, Burt Mustin, Fernando Pereira, Olga Velez, Della Young, Tricia Young.* Dir: R. G. Springsteen. Pro: Francis D. Lyon. Screenplay: Chas. Wallace. (Commonwealth United.) Rel: March 15. (E.) 99 Mins. Cert. A.

The Tiger and the Pussycat
Vittorio Gassman as the 45-year-old businessman whose shock at reaching grandfatherhood sends him sexily chasing – and being chased by – the young girls: leading him into a great deal of bother. Rest of cast: *Ann-Margret, Eleanor Parker, Caterina Boratto, Eleanora Brown, Antonella Steni, Fiorenzo Fiorentini, Giambattista Salerno, Jacques Herlin, Luigi Vanucci.* Dir: Dino Risi. Pro: Mario Cecchi Gori. Screenplay: Agenore Incrocci & Furio Scarpelli. (Avco–Embassy.) Rel: Nov. 23. (Colour.) 90 Mins. Cert. A.

A Time for Giving
Entitled "Generation" in America, this one takes another look at this terribly topical generation gap, seen through the eyes of an idealistic young couple who refuse to compromise and the girl's father, now a firm member of the establishment but at one time a rebel, too. Cast: *David Janssen, Kim Darby, Carl Reiner, Pete Duel, Andrew Prine, James Coco, Sam Waterston, David Lewis, Don Beddoe, Jack Somack, Lincoln Kilpatrick.* Dir: George Schaefer. Pro: Frederick Brisson. Screenplay: William Goodhart, from his own stage play. (Levine–Avco Embassy.) Rel: June 14. (Colour.) 104 Mins. Cert. A.

A Touch of Love
Realistic story of a young girl who, after her first sexual experience, finds she is pregnant and decides to "go it alone" and not involve the child's father, a television announcer. *Sandy Dennis* as Rosamund, the girl, and *Ian McKellen* as George, the father (who never knows he is!) of the baby. Rest of cast: *Michael Coles, John Standing, Peggy Thorpe-Bates, Kenneth Benda, Deborah Stanford, Roger Hammond, Eleanor Bron, Margaret Tyzack, Maurice Denham, Rachel Kempson.* Dir: Waris Hussein. Pro: Max J. Rosenberg & Milton Subotsky. Screenplay: Margaret Drabble. (British Lion.) Rel: Oct. 19. (E.) 107 Mins. Cert. A.

The Touchables
Rather way-out, unimpressive story about four dolly girls who capture a pop star and take him to their pleasure "dome" with the idea of having their fun with him! Then gangsters get in on the plot and . . . well! Cast: *Judy Huxtable, Esther Anderson, Marilyn Rickard, Kathy Simmonds, David Anthony, Ricki Starr, James Villiers, John Ronane, Harry Baird, Michael Chow, Joan Bakewell, William Dexter, Roy Davies, Danny Lynch, Bruno Elrington, Steve Veidor, Peter Gordeno, Simon Williams, Bryan Walsh.* Dir: Robt. Freeman. Pro: John Bryan. Screenplay: Ian La Frenais. (Bryan–Fox.) Rel: Nov. 16. (D.) 94 Mins. Cert. X.

Topaz
Alfred Hitchcock's international espionage thriller based on the Leon Uris novel: a two-part story about a French agent in America with easy access to Cuba who obliges his American agent pal by going to the island to uncover the facts of the Russian rockets there. Uncovered himself, with his lovely agent-mistress murdered (beautiful *Karin Dor*) he escapes with the secrets. A little less tense, the second part details his adventures when, recalled to Paris by an irritated French government he uncovers there the Russian spies in very high places. Smooth, conventional, supremely workmanlike thriller movie, with little touches of typical Hitch humour and as typical touches to shock. Nicely acted. Rest of cast: *Frederick Stafford, Dany Robin, John Vernon, Michel Piccoli, Philippe Noiret, Claude Jade, Michel Subor, Roscoe Lee Browne, Per-Axel Arosenius, John Forsythe.* Dir: Alfred Hitchcock. Pro: Herbert Coleman. Screenplay: Samuel Taylor. (Universal.) Rel: Jan. 11. (T.) 125 Mins. Cert. A.

The Trouble With Girls
Elvis Presley movie, with a mixture of songs, suspected murder and comedy seen against a background of a strange and peculiarly American family, circa the 20s. Rest of cast: *Marlyn Mason, Nicole Jaffe, Sheree North, Edward Andrews, John Carradine, Anissa Jones, Vincent Price, Joyce Van Patten, Pepe Brown, Dabney Coleman, Bill Zuckert, Pitt Herbert, Anthony Teague, Med Flory, Robert Nichols, Helene Winston, Kevin O'Neal, Frank Welker, John Rubinstein, Chuck Briles, Patsy Garrett, Linda Sue Risk, Charles P. Thompson, Leonard Rumery, William M. Paris, Kathleen Rainey, Hal James Pederson, Mike Wagner, Brett Parker, Duke Snider,*

Pacific Palisade, High School Madrigals. Dir: Peter Tewksbury. Pro: Lester Welch. Screenplay: Arnold & Lois Peyser. (M-G-M.) Rel: Dec. 21. (Metrocolor & Pan.) 79 Mins. Cert. U.

True Grit
Big *John Wayne* giving the performance of his lifetime, as a one-eyed, whisky-swilling, deadly lawman (who always does his best to bring in his men very dead), who is persuaded by an equally determined, very much younger female character to track down the man who murdered her "paw". The humour that pervades the whole film detracts from the cold brutality of the killings; delicious dialogue; glorious backgrounds (of autumn trees against the high snows), plenty of excitement. A really outstanding Western. *Kim Darby* as the girl, *Glen Campbell* as the ex-Texas Ranger who makes up the pursuing trio. Rest of cast: *Jeremy Slate, Robert Duvall, Dennis Hopper, Alfred Ryder, Strother Martin, Jeff Corey, Ron Soble, John Fielder, James Westerfield, John Doucette, Donald Woods, Edith Atwater, Carlos Rivas, Isabel Boniface, H. W. Gim, John Pickard, Elizabeth Harrower, Ken Renard, Jay Ripley, Kenneth Becker.* Dir: Henry Hathaway. Pro: Hal B. Wallis. Screenplay: Marguerite Roberts, from the Charles Portis novel. (Paramount.) Rel: Dec. 28. (T.) 128 Mins. Cert. U.

Twinky
A rather unfortunate story about the romance and marriage of a 16-year-old London schoolgirl to a very much older American writer, and the way it doesn't work out. Cast: *Charles Bronson, Susan George, Trevor Howard, Michael Craig, Honor Blackman, Lionel Jeffries, Elspeth March, Eric Chitty, Cathy Jose, Leslie Schofield, Derek Steen, Robert Morley, Jack Hawkins, Gordon Waller, Jimmy Tarbuck, Norman Vaughan, Orson Bean, Reg Lever, Tony Arpino, Eric Barker, John Rae, John Wright.* Dir: Richard Donner. Pro: Clive Sharp. Screenplay: Norman Thaddeus Vane. (John Heyman–Rank.) Rel: Feb. 16. (T.) 98 Mins. Cert. A.

The Undefeated
A story, based on history, about a couple of groups which at the end of the American Civil War drifted towards Mexico rather than live in what they felt was a conquered land, only to become mixed-up in the struggle between the French Emperor Maximilian and the man determined to topple him from Mexico's uneasy throne, Juarez. Cast: *John Wayne, Rock Hudson, Tony Aguilar, Roman Gabriel, Marian McCargo, Lee Meriwether, Merlin Olsen, Melissa Newman, Bruce Cabot, Michael Vincent, Ben Johnson, Edward Faulkner, Harry Carey, Jr., Paul Fix, Royal Dano, Richard Mulligan, Carlos Rivas, John Agar, Guy Raymond, Don Collier, Big John Hamilton, Dub Taylor, Henry Beckman, Victor Junco, Robert Donner, Pedro Armendariz, Jr., James Dobson, Rudy Diaz, Richard Angarola, James McEachin, Gregg Palmer, Juan Garcia, Kiel Martin, Bob Gravage.* Dir: Andrew V. McLaglen. Pro: R. L. Jacks. Screenplay: James Lee Barrett. (Fox.) Rel: Oct. 12. (D & Pan.) 118 Mins. Cert. U.

The Undertaker
Short, half-hour comedy about Messrs. Rigor and Mortis, whose calamitous day turns out to be a dead loss in the end! Cast: *Bernard Cribbins, Wilfrid Brambell, Clive Dunn, Spike Milligan.* Dir: Brian Cummins. Pro: Peter L. Andrews & Malcolm B. Hayworth. (Paramount.) Rel: May 24. 29 Mins. Cert. U.

Under the Table You Must Go
All-but one hour interest film about the varied entertainment now offered in the pubs; in addition to good drinking, good beer and lots of atmosphere. (Butcher's.) Rel: Floating. (E.) 52 Mins. Cert. U.

The Valley of Gwangi
The finding of a small eohippus, an extinct kind of horse, leads to the discovery of a Lost World in the Mexican Forbidden Valley: and when one of the creatures, Gwangi, is brought back to be exhibited, it almost starts a national panic when it breaks out and goes on the rampage! Cast: *James Franciscus, Gila Golan, Richard Carlson, Laurence Naismith, Freda Jackson, Gustavo Rojo, Dennis Kilbane, Mario de Barros, Curtis Arden.* Dir: James O'Connolly. Pro: Chas. H. Schneer. Screenplay: Wm. E. Bast. (Warner-Pathe.) Rel: Nov. 23. (T & Dynamation.) 95 Mins. Cert. A.

The Virgin Soldiers
Quite amusing story about a group of innocent young soldiers during their training period in Singapore (circa 1950); learning about sex and, latterly, survival. Cast: *Lynn Redgrave, Hywel Bennett, Nigel Davenport, Nigel Patrick, Rachel Kempson, Jack Shepherd, Michael Gwynn, Tsai Chin, Christopher Timothy, Don Hawkins, Geoffrey Hughes, Roy Holder, Riggs O'Hara, Gregory Phillips, Wayne Sleep, Peter Kelly, Mark Nicholl, Alan Shatsman, Jonty Miller, Jolyon Jackley, Robert Bridges, James Cosmo, Graham Crowden, Dudley Jones, Mathew Guinness, Narajan Singh, "Hallelujah".* Dir: John Dexter. Pro: Leslie Gilliat & Ned Sherrin. Screenplay: John Hopkins, from the novel by Leslie Thomas. (Carl Foreman–Columbia.) Rel: Nov. 2. 96 Mins. Cert. X.

The Voyeur
Danish-made adaptation of the Siv Holmes novel "I, A Woman 2" and in fact a continuation of the story of sex-hungry Siv, who, now married, finds her kinky husband is only interested in showing her nude photos around his friends or watching them make passes at her. So Siv ups and goes back to her loose-living life while her late partner sinks ever deeper into perversity. Cast: *Gio Petre, Lars Lunoe, Hjordis Petterson, Bertel Lauring, Klaus Pagh.* Dir: Mac Ahlberg. Pro & Screenplay: Peer Guldbrandsen. First shown at the Cineclub 24, Nov., 1969. (A/S Nordisk Films/Cinecenta.) 95 Mins. No cert.

Wages of Sin – Valerie
Happy-ending story of 20-year-old Valerie, who, running away from her convent, tries hippyism, modelling and prostitution before finding the love of her life. Cast: *Daniele Ouimet, Guy Godin, Michel Paje, Yvan Ducharme, Claude Prefontaine, Andree Flamand, Kim Wilcox, Pierre Paquette, Hugo Gelinas, Henri Norbert, Clemence Desrochers.* Dir: Denis Heroux. Pro: Julien Parnelle. Screenplay: Michel Paje. (Richard Schulman.) Rel: Floating. 95 Mins. Cert. X.

Walk the Hot Streets – Heisses Pflaster Köln
German-made gangster thriller with *Richard Munch* as the obstinately determined municipal prosecutor, battling with brain and sometimes brawn against the gang that have taken over the city. Rest of cast: *Beate Hasenau, Hebert Fux, Klaramaria Skala, Arthur Brause, Doris Kunstmann.* Dir: Ernst Hoftbauer. (S.F. Film Distributors.) Rel: Floating. 90 Mins. Cert. X.

Weird Weirdo – Le Grand Ceremonial
A very odd little French film about a young man who lives with his ma in a love-hate relationship: he sending off each day a rubber doll in a trunk, on journeys he'd like to make himself. Then he meets a kleptomaniac girl who embraces him in a sado-masochistic relationship before cleansing him and teaching him to be happy and gentle! Cast: *Michel Tureau, Marcella Saint-Amant, Ginette Leclerc, Fernando Arrabal, Jean-Daniel Erhmann.* Dir: Pierre-Alain Jolivet (who wrote the screenplay with Serge Ganzi; based on the Fernando Arrabal play). Pro: André Cotton. (Antony Balch.) First shown at Times Cinema in April, 1970. (E.) 100 Mins. Cert. X.

Whatever Happened to Aunt Alice?
Robert Aldrich, the man who made "Whatever Happened to Baby Jane?" and "Hush, Hush, Sweet Charlotte" comes up with this one to make it a trio; all about the battle between widow *Geraldine Page* as the woman who buries the bodies at the bottom of the garden, and *Ruth Gordon* as a friend of one of the late lamented who suspects foul crime. Rest of cast: *Rosemary Forsyth, Robert Fuller, Mildred Dunnock, Joan Huntington, Peter Brandon.* Dir: Lee H. Katzin. Pro: Robert Aldrich. Screenplay: Theodore Apstein. (C.I.R.O.) Rel: Oct. 5. (Colour.) 101 Mins. Cert. X.

Where Eagles Dare
Very large, very long, very exciting war "escape" thriller with unflappable, quick-witted ace agent *Richard Burton*, cool American killer *Clint Eastwood*, pretty assistant *Mary Ure* and their group of dubious supporters, breaking into and then eventually holo-causting out of the "impregnable" and "inaccessible" Schloss Adler, the fortress perched on the peak of one of the South German Alps. With its cable car struggles, its wholesale murder and mayhem (of the Germans and their spies), it adds up to an incredibly holding – and incredible – spectacular for those with a head for heights and a stomach for killings of all kinds. Rest of cast: *Patrick Wymark, Michael Hordern, Donald Houston, Peter Barkworth, William Squire, Robert Beatty, Brook Williams, Neil McCarthy, Vincent Ball, Anton Diffring, Ferdy Mayne, Derren Nesbitt, Victor Beaumont, Ingrid Pitt.* Dir: Brian G. Hutton. Pro:

Elliott Kastner. Screenplay: Alistair MacLean. (M-G-M.) Rel: Jan. 4. (Pan & Metrocolor.) 155 Mins. Cert. A.

Where It's At
Story about a Las Vegas gambling baron, all materialistic, and his more socially conscious and idealistic son and their conflict. Cast: *David Janssen, Robert Drivas, Rosemary Forsyth, Brenda Vaccaro, Don Rickles, Warrene Ott, Edy Williams, Vince Howard*. Dir & Screenplay: Garson Kanin. Pro: Frank Ross. (U.A.) Rel: Nov. 28. (Colour.) 106 Mins. Cert.

Where's Jack?
One in a mini-cycle of films set in bawdy noisy 18th-century London, this one neatly white-washes famous highwayman Jack Sheppard, presenting him as being more or less forced into the business by crooked crook-catcher Jonathan Wild, a duel which ends with Jack's hanging becoming a public holiday. Cast: *Tommy Steele, Stanley Baker, Fiona Lewis, Alan Badel, Dudley Foster, Noel Purcell, William Marlowe, Sue Lloyd, Harold Kasket, Cardew Robinson, Esmond Knight, Eddie Byrne, John Hallam, Leon Lissek, Jack Woolgar, George Woodbridge, Roy Evans, Michael Elphick, Howard Goorney, Yole Marinelli, Carolyn Montague, Carla Challoner, Caroline Munro, Rona Newton-John, Cecil Nash*. Dir: James Clavell. Pro: Stanley Baker. Screenplay: Rafe and David Newhouse. (Oakhurst–Paramount.) Rel: July 20. (Colour.) 119 Mins. Cert. U.

The Wild Bunch
Bloody but good Western set along the Texas border in 1914, where *William Holden* and his gang fail in their plot to rob the railroad and begin to realise that the time for their sort of crime is past, but carry out one more daring hold-up for a Mexican bandit general against whom they eventually march in one great, unequal, bloody battle. Rest of cast: *Ernest Borgnine, Robert Ryan, Edmond O'Brien, Warren Oates, Jaime Sanchez, Ben Johnson, Emilio Fernandez, Strother Martin, L. Q. Jones, Albert Dekker, Bo Hopkins, Bud Taylor, Jorge Russek, Alfonso Arau, Chano Urueta, Sonia Amelio, Aurora Clavel, Elsa Cardenas*. Dir: Sam Peckinpah. Pro: Phil Feldman. Screenplay: Walon Green & Sam Peckinpah. (Phil Feldman–Warner/Seven Arts.) Rel: Feb. 22. (T & Pan 70 mm.) 139 Mins. Cert. X.

Winnie the Pooh and the Blustery Day
The second of Walt Disney's long–short Pooh episodes based on the A. A. Milne stories with *Sebastian Cabot* narrating and *Sterling Holloway* supplying the voice for the tubby little bear. Other voices: *Paul Winchell* (Tigger), *John Fiedler* (Piglet), *Jon Walmsley* (Robin), *Ralph Wright* (Eeyore), *Howard Morris* (Gopher),

Hal Smith (Owl), *J. C. Matthews* (Rabbit), *Barbara Luddy* (Kanga), *Clint Howard* (Little Roo). Dir: Wolfgang Reitherman. (Walt Disney.) Rel: Oct. 19. (T.) 25 Mins. Cert. U.

Winning
Paul Newman as the racing driver who finds life more difficult than driving; a story of a marriage which nearly goes sour but is saved by the stepson's admiration for his new and exciting dad. And the background to this is jazzed-up car racing culminating in the famous Indianapolis meeting. Rest of cast: *Joanne Woodward, Richard Thomas, Jr., Robert Wagner, David Sheiner, Clu Gulager, Barry Ford, Bob Quarry, Eileen Wesson*. Dir: James Goldstone. Pro: John Foreman. Screenplay: Howard Rodman. (Universal/Newman–Foreman–Rank.) Rel: May 24. (T & Pan.) 123 Mins. Cert. A.

Women in Love
Extremely faithful to the original screen transcription by Ken Russell of the famous D. H. Lawrence novel about two very diverse men friends, a glum young coalmine owner and gay artist pal and the sisters they love: the first driving the mineowner to a tragic, suicidal end in the Swiss snows and the second making the artist just the kind of wife he needs. With a nude (male) wrestling sequence and pretty explicit love-making to reflect Lawrence's sensuality and basic distrust of women. Cast: *Alan Bates, Oliver Reed, Glenda Jackson, Jennie Linden, Eleanor Bron, Alan Webb, Vladek Sheybal, Catherine Wilmer, Sarah Nicholls, Sharon Gurney, Christopher Gable, Michael Gough, Norma Shebbeare, Nike Arrighi, James Laurenson, Michael Graham Cox, Richard Heffer, Michael Garratt*. Dir: Ken Russell. Pro & Screenplay: Larry Kramer. (Kramer/Rosen–U.A.) Rel: May 3. (E.) 130 Mins. Cert. X.

World of Fashion – Mini-Midi (Hier, Aujourd'hui, Demain)
Short interest feature (23 Mins.) with *Genevieve Gilles*, who, while sitting on the beach at Deauville reading a fashion magazine, day-dreams her way back through the past and pictures herself in a succession of odd, amusing and stunning fashion set-ups! With a final glance ahead at the possibilities for the 1980s. Dir: Robert Freeman. (du Siecle–Fox.) Rel: Sept. 21. 23 Mins. Cert. U. (Included in last year, "Review" as a Floating Release.)

You Don't Need Pajamas at Rosie's
Wes Stern, Rick Kelman and *Wink Roberts* as the three American boys who at 16 begin to wonder about and want to try sex: and the way one of them during his innocent holiday at Buffalo sends back to his friends such glowingly fabricated tales about a nearby brothel

that, to his embarrassment, they arrive with the idea of sharing the action. Rest of cast: *Jacqueline Bisset, Gerard Parkes, Sharon Acker, Cosette Lee, Vincent Marino, Eric Lane, Murray Westgate, Leslie Yeo, Guy Sanvido, William Barringer*. Dir: James Neilson. Pro: Roger Smith, Allan Carr. Screenplay: Jo Heims & Roger Smith. (Mirisch–U.A.) Rel: Nov. 23. (D.) 90 Mins. Cert. X.

Young Billy Young
A great deal of action and gunfighting as *Robert Walker* (younger gunman) and pal *Robert Mitchum* (older, revenge-seeking gunfighter) go after *John Anderson* (another gunfighter) but tangle with the latter's hired-gun son (*David Carradine*). They all get together for a nice climactic battle before *Mitchum* abducts *Angie Dickinson* – with the best of intentions. Rest of cast: *Jack Kelly, Paul Fix, Willis Bouchey, Parley Baer, Bob Anderson, Rodolfo Acosta, Deana Martin*. Dir & Screenplay: Burt Kennedy. Pro: Max Youngstein. (Talbot/Youngstein–U.A.) Rel: Sept. 7. (D.) 89 Mins. Cert. A.

Z
Brilliant French film: a story of political murder in Greece, based – one imagines – on fact; terribly holding as the magistrate in charge of the case becomes aware of the enormity and the ramifications of the crime. Cast: *Yves Montand, Irene Papas, Jean-Louis Trintignant, Jacques Perrin, François Perier, Charles Denner, Bernard Fresson, Jean Bouise, Jean-Pierre Miquel, Renato Salvatori, Marcel Bozzufi, Julien Guiomar, Pierre Dux, Guy Mairesse, Georges Geret, Magali Noel, Clotilde Joano, Maurice Baquet, Jean Daste, Gerard Darrieu*. Dir: Costa-Gavras. Pro: Jacques Perrin. Screenplay: Jorge Semprun & Costa-Gavras. (Reggane Film–Franco/Algerian Co-Production–Warner–Pathe.) Rel: Floating. (T.) 125 Mins. Cert. A.

Zabriskie Point
Antonioni's first American film; a visual magnificence, reflecting his obsession with colour and background, but otherwise thin and self-indulgent, and well below the standard set in his Italian movies. A fragment of a story about a young drop-out who steals an airplane, takes it to Death Valley, makes love to a girl he picks up there and then takes it back, to be killed as he lands. With a blatantly interpolated erotic sequence about a love-in. Cast: *Mark Frechette, Daria Halprin* (both non-professionals) and *Rod Taylor*. Dir: Michelangelo Antonioni, from a screenplay for which he shares credit with Sam Shepard, Fred Gardner, Tonio Guerra, Clare Peploe. Pro: Carlo Ponti. (Ponti–M-G-M.) Rel: April 12. (Pan & Colour.) 110 Mins. Cert. X.

INDEX

Numerals in italic represent pictorial mentions

Index

COLUMBIA PICTURES Presents

A DINO DE LAURENTIIS PRODUCTION:

ROD STEIGER · CHRISTOPHER PLUMMER

'WATERLOO'

ORSON WELLES as LOUIS XVIII

co-starring JACK HAWKINS · VIRGINIA McKENNA · DAN O'HERLIHY

Screenplay by H.A.L.CRAIG Produced by DINO DE LAURENTIIS   Directed by SERGEI BONDARCHUK
An ITALO-RUSSIAN CO-PRODUCTION: DINO DE LAURENTIIS CINEMATOGRAFICA S.p.a.ROME   and MOSFILM, MOSCOW. TECHNICOLOR®/ PANAVISION®

Books for cinema enthusiasts

YOSELOFF BOOKS

Distributed by

W. H. ALLEN

CLOWN PRINCES AND COURT JESTERS
K. C. Lahue & Samuel Gill

A pictorial history of the golden era of the silent comedy.   70s

DE MILLE: THE MAN AND HIS PICTURES·
Gabe Essoe & Raymond Lee

A pictorial biography, including stills from all his major films.   70s

THE FILMS OF JAMES STEWART
A. F. McClure, K. D. Jones, & A. E. Twomey

A brief biography, a summary of all his films, and a superb collection of stills.   70s

GLORIA SWANSON
Raymond Kee & Richard Hudson

A pictorial tribute to one of the screen's all-time favourite leading ladies.   70s

SEVENTY YEARS OF CINEMA
Peter Cowie

All the high points in the development of the movies since 1895. Profusely illustrated.   105s

Behind the scenes

Scratch an Actor
Sheilah Graham

The famous Hollywood columnist tells you things you never knew about the personalities of the film world.
Illustrated 42s

The Studio
John Gregory Dunne

The funny, appalling, and informative true story of one year in the life of Twentieth Century Fox.
36s

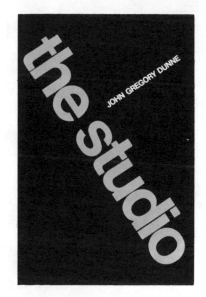

W. H. Allen

Biographies of the great stars

Norma Jean
Fred Guiles
42s

Garbo
Norma Zierold
30s

Julie Andrews
Robert Windeler
35s

Spencer Tracy
Larry Swindell
42s